KILL YOUR MORTGAGE *and* SORT YOUR RETIREMENT

The go-to guide for getting ahead

Hannah McQueen

ALLEN&UNWIN
SYDNEY · MELBOURNE · AUCKLAND · LONDON

First published in 2015

Allen & Unwin
Level 3, 228 Queen Street
Auckland 1010, New Zealand
Phone: (64 9) 377 3800

83 Alexander Street
Crows Nest NSW 2065, Australia
Phone: (61 2) 8425 0100
Email: info@allenandunwin.co.nz
Web: www.allenandunwin.co.nz

A catalogue record for this book is available
from the National Library of New Zealand

ISBN 978 1 877505 51 5

Set in 11.5/16 pt Sabon by Post Pre-press Group, Australia
Printed and bound in Australia by Pegasus Media & Logistics

27 26 25 24 23 22 21 20

MIX
Paper from
responsible sources
FSC® C008194
www.fsc.org

The paper in this book is FSC® certified.
FSC® promotes environmentally responsible,
socially beneficial and economically viable
management of the world's forests.

To Cameron and Madison

Contents

Introduction		1
A note from the author		5
PART ONE: MONEY AND YOU		**11**
1.	What is your financial life stage?	13
2.	Assessing where you are at	23
3.	Budgeting—creating a cash surplus	32
4.	The fritter factor	47
5.	Credit cards—don't trust them	52
6.	Going backwards? What you need to do	58
7.	Negotiating a pay rise	75
8.	Money, relationships and being happy	87
9.	The property ladder	92
PART TWO: KILL YOUR MORTGAGE		**113**
10.	Making a start	115
11.	Putting the plan into action	122

12.	Building up—the next phase	133
13.	The magic of compound interest	138
14.	Buying your first home	143
15.	Getting your first mortgage	149
16.	Kill your mortgage!	166

PART THREE: WEALTH CREATION 179

17.	Wealth-creation options	181
18.	Leverage	186
19.	Why invest in property?	191
20.	Owning your own business	219
21.	Buying a business	225
22.	Starting a business	235
23.	Other investments	242

PART FOUR: RETIREMENT 255

24.	Retirement planning	257
25.	Will the government help me?	264
26.	What's your number?	269
27.	It's time for action	284

PART FIVE: OTHER FACTORS 291

28. Helping your children—a hand up,
not a hand out 293

29. Relationship property 305

30. Trusts 311

31. Death—what happens when you die? 315

Conclusion 318

Special offer 320

Acknowledgements 321

Appendix I—The 10-step programme 323

Appendix II—Financial compatibility
questionnaire 327

Appendix III—Financial assessment
template 332

Introduction

To get ahead it is often said you need to spend less than you earn, invest wisely and start early. These rules applied to our grandparents, and they still apply to us.

Don't be distracted by how simple this sounds, though. It is simple, yes—it's just not easy. And heaven forbid you should have started your run late, be a shopper or have gone through a divorce or some financial setback that forces you to start again!

Despite many teachings to the contrary, we are not all starting from an equal financial footing. Some of us are financially favoured, others are financially challenged. Many of us are starting on the back foot, and as a result will need to punch above our weight.

Financial success is not a rite of passage. Financial success favours the brave and those who have a well-thought-out plan. Irrespective of where you are starting from, you must diagnose your situation accurately, understand your psychology of spending, learn how to budget effectively and save for a property, and navigate the many financial roadblocks life will throw at you. If you have a mortgage, you must learn how to attack it, to kill it.

Do not be naïve enough to think the bank is your friend. Do not be silly enough to think that a celebrity endorsing an investment makes it a good one. You must learn the art of financial warfare.

Paying off your mortgage is a strategic step towards financial success, but this in isolation will not achieve a comfortable retirement. You need to understand how much time you have and the investment constraints you must work within. What is good for the goose is not always good for the gander. Keep your head, understand your options and move forward. Being the underdog simply means you have to take a less traditional route to get to the end. As the saying goes, you have to learn the rules of the game, and then you have to play better than anyone else.

Many a book and movie has been written about ordinary people facing opponents or ideas bigger than themselves. We aptly call it a *David and Goliath situation*. In fact, the phrase 'David and Goliath' has become entrenched in our dialect as a metaphor for coming up against something seemingly insurmountable. For a lot of baby boomers staring down the barrel of retirement, it can feel as if you are up against a powerful opponent—time, and the lack of it—and the consciousness that you may be leaving or have left your run too late.

But whether time is on your side or not is irrelevant. Anyone approaching retirement has a financial place to be and a deadline to get there by. Some of you will be ready to push forward and take more purposeful steps on an already long-thought-out journey, but many of you will be starting off on the back foot, the financial underdog.

This book has been written to help people across the spectrum of retirement readiness. The question is, do you give up before you start? Or do you own the fact you are the financial underdog and use this realisation as the catalyst to sort out your money priorities? My hope is that after reading this book you will realise that being the underdog is not a reason not to try.

It just means you have to take a less traditional route to the destination, as you have a wider space of ground to cover in a shorter amount of time.

I want you to appreciate the opportunities that are in front of you but you may have previously failed to see. I want you to understand that money is not bigger than you, retirement is not bigger than you, but, if we are going to sort this out, I need you to be brave. I will not lie: getting ahead financially can be tricky, especially if you are genetically programmed to shop (as I am), but it is not impossible. In fact, depending on where you are starting from, it may be a lot easier than you realise. This book will teach you the theory, it will show you the reality of your choices, and hopefully it will motivate you to confront yourself and take the required action to achieve a better financial outcome. Your psychology may initially work against you, but as you start to understand your natural tendencies and shortcomings you can set about developing the plan that will work for you.

Many financial books assume you are already in control of your finances. For the vast majority this is simply not the case. This book will start at the beginning, showing you how to diagnose your starting point in order to better determine the route you need to take to a comfortable retirement. It will build on this diagnosis and show examples of how you can change your money personality and how you can do better than the Joneses. It openly discusses money and relationships, including sensitive themes such as surviving financial infidelity and the financial warning signs of new partners. Poor negotiation skills may mean you are not paid what you are worth, and lack of confidence can mean you seldom tackle this head-on. This book also discusses how best you can teach your children what they need to know to get ahead in the disastrous economy we are going to leave behind. Most importantly, this book breaks down the jargon and throws away what you have been taught about saving for your financial success and retirement.

I have a company called enableMe. We call ourselves Financial Personal Trainers. We are a team of chartered accountants and financial advisors working with our clients to get them ahead faster. We are not aligned to any particular investment product or bank. We provide impartial, expert and astute advice. We work with our clients at the coalface, understanding the nuances of each situation and determining the best plan of attack to bridge the gap between where our clients are going to end up if they change nothing and where they need to be in order to achieve their financial goals.

My team and I have worked with over 4000 clients, and in this time have come to realise that anyone can get ahead when the sun is shining and life is rosy, but it is a whole lot harder to make progress when you are hit with your financial Mack truck. As Warren Buffett so eloquently phrased it, it is not until the tide goes out that you find out who is swimming naked. Lack of knowledge, lack of confidence and lack of action means we sabotage our own efforts to get ahead, to make progress, to kill our mortgage and save for retirement.

This book tells you all you need to know to dramatically change your financial landscape and propel yourself to the financial conclusion you deserve. So buckle up, people; it's time that retirement met its match.

We succeed only as we identify in life, or in war, or in anything else, a single overriding objective, and make all other considerations bend to that one objective.
—Dwight D. Eisenhower

A note from the author

I am a chartered accountant with a master's degree in tax, yet I love to shop. I am married to a Scotsman. He is tight with everything apart from the Xbox games he buys. I have two children, which makes me worry about the financial mess they are going to inherit—not from me, but from the wider economy. I am nervous that the Global Financial Crisis (GFC) has seen some of the largest economies in the world start printing money, and no one seems to care. I worry that in trying to protect the market we have failed it. I am disappointed that we do not tax foreigners who invest in our country. I believe to be financially responsible is to be socially responsible. Most importantly, when it comes to your own finances, I believe that your past behaviour need not be a reflection of what you are capable of achieving.

After I graduated from the University of Auckland in 1998, I worked at KPMG for a time. My husband and I had a combined salary of $32,000 and we thought we were doing just fine. Fast forward a few years and we were earning much more than our graduate incomes, yet failed to have any great sense of progress. Sure we were earning good money, but we felt that we had to keep earning to this level in order to maintain our lifestyle. In fact, despite earning almost 10 times the level of our graduate income, we were not 10 times happier and our wealth wasn't 10 times higher. We were caught on a treadmill of our own making that required us to run faster and harder to simply hold our line.

I didn't think that we were outrageous with our spending. Sure, we enjoyed buying coffees, and I tended to buy my lunch instead of packing it, but we were not particularly outlandish. We didn't have really expensive hobbies, although as our incomes increased I found it easier to spend money without much thought. The harder I worked, the more I felt justified in any spending decision. I enjoyed holidays—I still enjoy holidays—and I have always loved clothes. I felt we worked hard and I wanted us both to be able to enjoy the fruits of our labours. At the time, though, I didn't have a reason to question my spending behaviour. We never argued about money—neither of us seemed to care enough, as there was always money when we needed it to do what we wanted to do.

Reality began to catch up with me when we wanted to buy our first property. The property cost $350,000 and we needed a mortgage of $300,000. We had to save our deposit and the bank was prepared to accept our deposit, being around 15% of the purchase price.

When it came to raising the mortgage, we did what everyone does: we played the banks off against each other to get the best interest rate. We did get a good rate, but the interest saving achieved from the discounted rate was comparably low. Sure, it would save us $20,000 over the life of our mortgage, and of course we preferred having this money in our pocket as opposed to the bank's. However, the $20,000 we were going to save was small fry when compared to the $490,000 in interest that we were going to pay to the bank over the next 30 years.

For some reason, I became fixated on how I could lower this interest cost. I kind of understood that compound interest was making it so high, but I didn't *really* understand how compound interest worked, nor did I have an appreciation of how to reduce it. In its simplest form, I recognised that the longer I had the mortgage the more money I would pay to the bank in interest. On a conceptual level it was clear that to save myself interest I would have to repay the loan faster. Agreed. But I did not want to compromise my lifestyle to achieve this outcome. I felt I worked hard and I wanted to enjoy what I earned. Equally, I acknowledged that the concepts of repaying my mortgage faster and living a life I enjoyed were not necessarily mutually exclusive; however, it would require a precise point of balance if I was to achieve both.

I wanted to understand how I could optimise the structure of my mortgage in order to repay it as quickly as possible. It was at this point that I reached out to Dr Jamie Sneddon, then a mathematics tutor at the University of Auckland. I met with Sneddon over the coming months, and after a few pages of calculus we found we had written a formula for structuring debt to repay it as fast as one's circumstances allow while also living the lifestyle one enjoys. I call this Mortgage Optimisation, and I have since patented this formula.

This formula makes one key assumption: that you will have money left over at the end of each week, month, year that can be used to repay your debt faster. This seemed reasonable. However, when trying to apply the formula to my personal situation, I soon realised that, despite earning the most we had ever earned, we had no money left at the end of the month. We were living pay-day to pay-day. We were living well—but there was absolutely no money left over. So, even though I had a powerful formula for debt reduction, it was of no value until I found out where my money was going and why I was not in control of it.

And this is where it got interesting. Being an accountant, I helped clients to manage their money. I could write a budget— I would even colour-code it (which only an accountant would find exciting)—but writing a budget for myself and sticking to it were two completely different things. When I spoke to my friends about it, they acknowledged that, as their incomes increased, they cared less and less about their finances because there was always enough money to do what they wanted to do. While it was reassuring to not be alone in my financial conundrum, it was equally disturbing to realise your money personality or psychology of spending can be more of a driver of your financial outcome than your income level.

Personally, I was and continue to be a shopper. Telling me to go without something is more likely to cause me to want it more. Telling me to spend less than I earn if I want a shot at getting ahead doesn't motivate me. Asking me to spend less than I earn in the hope of future rewards does nothing to excite or encourage me to even try. Because I work hard I tend to think I should be able to spend what I want, when I want and how I want.

This was my predicament. I questioned whether being a shopper, not a saver, meant that I was destined to financial mediocrity.

I may be a shopper, but I am also fairly stubborn. I did not accept that because I was predisposed towards enjoying my lifestyle it meant I wouldn't get ahead. I just needed to understand how to achieve both a lifestyle I enjoyed and financial progress.

For me, I needed a good reason to try and a process to follow. I needed a clear diagnosis of where I was starting from, what I wanted to achieve and whether I was on track to achieve it. I needed a methodology to follow, a way to identify how much money I frittered away.

I respond well to impartial and intelligent advice. I respond better to results. I learned that, as soon as you start out, life inevitably throws curveballs and you need to learn how to navigate around these.

Slowly but surely I determined a way to keep myself on track. I started to understand my financial pressure points and how to overcome them . . . and very quickly momentum started to build. Best of all, I achieved results and sustained them.

When talking to friends and peers it seemed I was not alone. The more people I shared my story with, the more fascinated people became. I talked about money and my experience with it openly and honestly, and shared the lessons I had learned with candour. People reacted to this. People got on board with me. I was able to keep testing and fine-tuning the different paths people needed to take depending on their starting point, end goal and time remaining to get there.

Early on, I formed the company enableMe to help people get in control of their finances. Soon we described ourselves as Financial Personal Trainers. We wanted to help Kiwis get ahead faster, by providing a constructive solution for people who want to become financially successful, whether they are shoppers or savers, with a mortgage or without, on track to retirement or too scared to even think about getting old! Everyone can get ahead faster. If I can do it, surely anyone can.

Money is an emotional topic. Our relationship with money can be a sensitive area. It is intrinsically linked to your self-worth and self-esteem, yet the tools for getting ahead too often deal with the science of finance, not the behaviours behind it.

When clients work with enableMe, they work to a plan, with a clear framework, support, accountability and results. We have worked with thousands of clients throughout New Zealand and the world (including Dubai, the UK, Europe, the US and Australia). Since 2007, our company has grown to have seven branches throughout New Zealand. We expect to have 12 offices by 2018 and a presence in Australia.

In my role as CEO of this company, I have been exposed to many varied and interesting client situations. Some clients are just starting out, others want to retire, many are somewhere in between. Some couples are financially compatible with each other; many aren't. Everyone has obstacles and it is usually these obstacles that upset their momentum. What I have determined is that, no matter where you are starting from, we are all capable of getting ahead faster. The question is, are you ready to start?

Getting ahead is not easy, but it can be done. Making financial progress would be infinitely easier if we didn't have the continual knockbacks that life throws at us—but that *is* life, so the plan we develop needs to be fluid enough that we can absorb the aftershock of these setbacks and still push forward, instead of pretending knockbacks don't happen. In this book I will share with you my experiences with and tips for overcoming the many challenges to making financial progress.

Remember, no matter what financial life stage you are at, to get ahead you must have a cash surplus. This is rule number one.

Part One

Money and You

Chapter 1

What is your financial life stage?

It is commonly assumed that the more money you earn the easier it is to get ahead financially. This assumption, like many things connected to money, is fundamentally wrong. The more money you earn the easier it is to go nowhere in particular, because you are no longer concerned with money. Instead, the security of a higher income has given you permission to disengage from your finances.

Many books have been written about creating wealth and becoming financially free. In my opinion, both phrases are so overused they have become irksome. While the concepts within these books are sound (to some degree), they tend to gloss over the reason why most of us will never, and can never, achieve financial success: our financial behaviour and the fact we tend to live in a money fog.

Getting ahead while living on a budget is simple: spend less than you earn. *Simple*. In reality, most of us don't do this particularly well, and as a result fail to achieve even the simplest of financial outcomes. Interestingly, if we could just master the basics of money management, many wealth-creation techniques would not be required.

For many of us, money is a complex subject and is linked to our self-worth and self-esteem. It plays a critical but often unspoken role in relationships, and is connected to our general wellbeing. Yet many of us fail to grasp the basics of money management, preferring instead to do nothing—maybe because it all seems too hard. If this sounds familiar, this book is for you: for the discerning person who realises that to be financially responsible is to be socially responsible, and to be in control of your money means you have choices, options and confidence in your future, even though you may not be quite sure how to get there.

Being financially competent takes planning, and planning takes time. Read this book to equip yourself with the tools you need to take control of your finances, and then take action. Do not rely on intuition. Do not assume that just because the rules are simple they are easy to apply. Take charge of your money and take charge of your life.

If you choose to stick your head in the sand, watch out for the incoming tide.

When providing advice, many financial experts assume you are already in control of your money. For many of us, this is simply not the case. If you are serious about losing weight, you hop on the scales. Equally, if you are serious about making financial progress, you need to hop on the financial scales.

To get ahead, you need a plan. Not a budget; a plan. A budget is static; a plan is fluid. A plan can be tailored to the nuances of any situation, recognising opportunities and obstacles and, most importantly, changing as life changes.

The first step in creating a financial plan is to take a high-resolution snapshot of your current situation. You need to determine where you measure up, what your financial body mass index (BMI) is and identify some of the wider issues affecting your financial health. I will not lie: getting to know the financial you can be a confronting process, one you might be scared to attempt—but, as I tell my clients, if we are going to get ahead as quickly as possible we need to understand where you are at now, what you are up against, what tools you have in your arsenal (some you might not even realise you have, or don't yet know how to use properly) and what you want to achieve.

It's a necessary but possibly uncomfortable first step—much like the moment you hop on the bathroom scales after a holiday. You may already know that you are financially overweight or fiscally unfit. What you do not know, though, is your financial BMI, which is a detailed analysis of where you are starting from.

To create a financial plan, and before you can diagnose your financial aptitude, you need to address the four facets below.

- What is your financial life stage?
- What is your cash position on a day-to-day basis?
- What is your psychology of spending?
- How much time do you have?

YOUR FINANCIAL LIFE STAGE

The number of life stages differs depending on whether you are a devotee of Shakespeare, who thought seven, or psychologist Erik Erikson, who thought eight. Financially speaking, though, we all fit into three generic life stages, depending on your financial position. You will either be 'Starting Out', 'Building Up' or 'Sitting Back'. There is a traditional route to take when working through each of these stages, although life tends to wreak havoc with financial progress along the way.

Despite each person's situation being unique in some facets, within each stage patterns arise relating to income levels, family dynamics, spending priorities, curveballs and areas of financial concern. While this might give you some comfort—in the sense that you may be experiencing similar problems to other people at the same life stage as you—this is of little benefit, as the average person is also making financial mistakes.

My objective when working with my clients is to move through each financial stage as quickly as possible, while they live a life they enjoy. If they are not living a life they enjoy the plan is unsustainable, resulting in financial binging, general frustration or worsening of relationship dynamics. All these things lead to financial backsliding. Most financial plans do not have tolerance for slippage.

It is not a case of going hard out. Clarity and consistency are the two key components of progress, supported by sustainability. If the plan is too tight, you will not be able to stick with in and will fall off the wagon.

STAGE 1: STARTING OUT—BUILDING A FINANCIAL FOUNDATION

Those in the Starting Out phase are usually in their mid to late 20s or early 30s. At this age, you don't have much in the way of net worth, but you do have time—and some would argue this is a more precious commodity. The sooner you start working on a plan, the better off you will be.

While traditionally most people at this stage are young, in recent times more mature people are finding themselves still in, or catapulted back to, their financial beginnings after a divorce or relationship breakdown or after experiencing a financial Mack truck event.

If you are Starting Out, your net worth will be less than $80,000 (lower if you live outside Auckland). The only exception to this is if you already own a property and have less than $80,000 equity in it. (Property ownership moves you into the next financial stage, Building Up.) Keeping it simple, your net worth or net wealth is the total value of your saleable assets

Financial Life Stage	Traditional Life Events	Financial Events
Starting Out (1)	Enter workforce Get married / live with a partner	Develop financial habits Purchase car Some savings
Building Up (2)	Start a family Career advancement Divorce Career change Inheritance	Purchase home Upgrade home Accumulation of wealth (savings, KiwiSaver, investment property, business, shares) Pay off mortgage
Sitting Back (3)	Retirement Grandchildren Death of spouse	Greater tax sensitivity Liquidating assets (KiwiSaver, downsizing home) Preserving wealth Estate planning

(excluding the value of your vehicle and furniture) after deducting everything you owe (see Appendix III for an example of a Net Worth Statement, or Statement of Financial Position). Or, even more simply, if you cashed everything up today and repaid all debts in full what would you have left?

When you are Starting Out, you are developing your financial habits and starting to become familiar with your natural tendencies around money (your money personality). If you are re-entering the Starting Out phase due to a relationship breakdown or financial catastrophe then you will need time to put yourself back together, both financially and mentally. Much like first-time Starting Outers, it is during this time of readjustment that you will need to create better financial habits to ensure you can still achieve financial success and a comfortable retirement, despite your setback and shortened timeframe. The difference for a second-time Starting Outer is that your income should be a lot higher than when you were first in this stage, making it easier to move up faster. If your income is *not* higher, then you will have to focus on increasing your cash surplus despite income constraints.

Because income tends to be at its lowest when you enter the workforce, when you are Starting Out you face the task of learning how to manage spending and saving within the constraints of your income level. Developing sound financial habits is critical, although often ignored. This is the time when you need to focus on the following things.

- Understand your psychology of spending (see page 25).
- Learn how to prepare a household budget (see Chapter 3).
- Don't borrow unless it is for things that provide long-term value (like an education that will result in a job).
- Avoid the use of credit cards.
- Save 15% of what you earn.
- Join KiwiSaver.
- Set some savings goals (like saving for a car or a deposit for a property).
- Make sure you have adequate insurance.
- Take advantage of employee benefit plans at work.

For those under 30, you should aim to be in this phase for no more than five years. For those over 30, you should be here for no more than three years. If you don't have a plan to move through this stage to the next then you will need an experienced financial advisor to help you. Doing nothing is actually doing something—you have made a decision to do nothing. Burying your head in the sand is a waste of energy. Get help. Move forward.

> Use the worksheets in Appendix III to calculate your annual cash surplus, then divide $80,000 by this number to determine how long it will take you to get out of this stage. Can you move on within the recommended timeframe or what will you need to do to move forward faster?

To achieve your financial goals, you will need a clear strategy to reach the prescribed net-worth threshold and/or property ownership within the specified number of years (see Chapter 3). Your strategy will depend on whether you have taken the traditional route of spending less than you earn, investing wisely and starting early, or if you are on the more common leave-it-till-the-last-minute path, but all strategies start with creating a cash surplus and making it as big as possible.

Note: When I work with my clients, we reduce the target for stage completion from five years to two, and often just 12 months. If you are likely to take longer than the maximum five-year duration then you need to rethink your strategy or speak with an experienced financial advisor. Time is not your friend when you are trying to propel yourself forward; only action and progress are.

STAGE 2: BUILDING UP—YOUR PRIME EARNING YEARS

This stage begins once you have purchased a property or your net worth exceeds $80,000 (note: this represents a 20% deposit on a $400,000 property. If you live in Auckland, you will need closer to $100,000). You are likely to have around 20% equity in your property. This is often a time when your income is rising as well as your expenses. You are likely to start a family and want to upgrade your home. Nicer homes, nicer cars and raising children can easily consume your increasing income. In fact, the more money you earn the harder it often is to get ahead.

This is also the time when the financial decisions you make will have the greatest impact on the financial lifestyle you will enjoy during retirement. By now, you should have accumulated some savings and developed the expertise to make sound choices.

Plan ahead for your big-ticket costs. Children's secondary and tertiary expenses often grind family budgets to a halt.

During this stage, it is important to:

- maximise your cash surplus through budgeting (see Chapter 3)
- have a clear strategy to kill your mortgage—ideally by the age of 50 (See Chapter 16)
- take full advantage of employer-offered retirement plans and KiwiSaver. Contribute enough to earn the maximum contribution from your employer. If you are self-employed, contribute the minimum amount to earn the government tax credit
- determine how much you will need in order to retire (see Chapter 26)
- determine if you are likely to reach your retirement number within your timeframe (see Chapter 26)
- depending on how much risk you can take in financial matters (due to the number of years you have before retirement), develop a financial plan to reduce the shortfall and provide a measure of progress (see Chapter 11)
- invest wisely. Do your homework
- measure your progress towards your retirement plan annually
- adjust your wants as needed
- be sure your insurance requirements have kept pace with your needs. Having adequate personal insurances (life,

income and trauma) to protect your family in case of
your untimely death or serious illness is critical
- prepare an estate plan to ensure that your custodial,
  financial and medical wishes are carried out (see Chapter 31).

Ideally, the above points would be actioned in a timely manner to
ensure you are on track for retirement during most of your adult
life. In reality, however, this doesn't happen.

Kiwis especially seem to take a relaxed view of their lack of
retirement savings, and often do not take their head out of the
sand until they are staring down the barrel of a questionable or
nonexistent retirement and only have a limited number of years
left to work and save. Although your late 40s and early 50s are
traditionally the years of the highest income-earning potential,
it is not until earnings start to wane that many people become
aware of the limited number of years they have left to work.
Not surprisingly, every year we have an influx of 50-somethings
visiting our offices, burdened with mortgages but with no real
plan for how to have them repaid by retirement and no savings
to combat the financial hole they will most certainly fall into.

In this situation, the time left on the working-age clock determines what options you have available and whether there is any
room for further delay or inertia. Clearly the longer you delay planning for your retirement the more urgent your situation becomes,
which in turn necessitates the need for a clear strategy and action.

The great thing about mature clients is that they are highly
motivated to change their situation and are committed to taking
action. These attributes can help them to achieve staggering
results which surprise even themselves—and also lead to the
three most common pieces of feedback I receive.

1. 'I am sleeping so much better.'
2. 'I wish I did this 10 years ago.'
3. 'I can't believe you got away with saying that to my spouse.'

STAGE 3: SITTING BACK—ARRIVING AT RETIREMENT

This is the destination at which you have 'arrived'. You have a mortgage-free home and sufficient money in the bank to fund your retirement. Because of this, your retirement years are supposed to be the most enjoyable and fulfilling times of your life. You have worked hard, have followed your plan and have enough money squirrelled away to live a lifestyle you enjoy. If children and grandchildren are part of your life, having the financial ability to help them can be rewarding.

Having a cash surplus is the key to moving through the life stages as quickly as possible. Maximising your cash surplus requires you to understand your psychology of spending and is the building block for determining the structure of your budget.

Chapter 2

Assessing where you are at

Before you can work out where you need to go, and how you are going to get there, you need to know where you are at now.

WHAT IS YOUR CASH POSITION ON A DAY-TO-DAY BASIS?

The idea of doing a budget can scare people, and while a spending plan is a necessary component of any financial plan you should be able to diagnose your cash position without completing a full budget spreadsheet. Your cash position can be split into one of three categories:

- sinking
- floating
- flying.

Sinking

If you are sinking you are on the back foot and quite probably going backwards on a day-to-day basis. There is insufficient money coming in to cover your living costs and this is resulting in you slowly incurring more debt or using credit cards when life throws you a curveball. You are unable to consistently repay your credit cards in full each month. Your back is up against the wall and, no matter how you try, things always feel tight. The accumulation of debt has a servicing cost (repayment), which in turn puts more pressure on an already stretched cashflow.

Weirdly (in my opinion), some people like to have money in a savings account while they have credit card debt. While this is illogical, they feel the savings account gives them some form of comfort or buffer for a rainy day, despite a similar amount being owed on the credit card.

> **Tip:** Use savings to repay debt, then work on a plan to rebuild your savings balance. It makes more financial sense to use your savings to pay off your credit card, as it will save you more interest than you would earn.

Not surprisingly, people who are sinking do not set out to be in this situation. It usually starts slowly, with being slightly on the back foot. Then a curveball throws you further backwards, and, before you know it, you are picking up momentum in the wrong direction. Many self-employed people or people with commissioned or irregular income sit constantly on the cusp of sinking as their fluctuating income can play havoc with their finances.

Floating

The most common cash category is 'floating'. You are not going backwards, but you are not getting ahead particularly fast either. You may be earning the most money you have ever earned, but you don't feel any better off. You are living a lifestyle you enjoy, and you can repay your credit cards in full each month, but at the same time you are not proactively saving or consciously improving your financial situation. If you receive a pay rise it doesn't make much of a difference, as it seems to be absorbed by your lifestyle. If you were to lose your job tomorrow, you could probably survive for a few weeks with the available cash before using credit or equity in a property.

Flying

Flying means you have no money worries. There is enough cash going around the system to maintain your lifestyle plus you are making regular savings or paying off your mortgage faster.

Once we understand your cash position and life stage, an appreciation of your natural tendencies around money will help to determine the level of detail required in drafting your financial plan.

WHAT IS YOUR MONEY PERSONALITY?

We all have a natural tendency when it comes to money. Whether it is genetic or learned, you will either find it easier to spend money or to save it. This is your money personality, psychology of spending or natural behaviour.

It is not linked to your level of financial literacy, how much you earn or your gender. Financially literate people can have trouble sticking to a budget; in fact, those who manage money as their day job tend to be the worst with money in their personal life. They get it; they just don't *do* it, often because it is the last thing they feel like doing. Don't be fooled. Being rational in normal daily life does not translate to you being rational with your money, and just because you manage money as part of your job doesn't mean that you manage it well in your private life.

Much the same as a builder who never finishes his house, many accountants are shopaholics.

Interestingly, a study published in the *Journal of Consumer Research* in 2008 indicated that around 25% of us are tightwads and 16% are shopaholics, with the masses sitting somewhere in between. (Note: Being a tightwad is not the same as being frugal. Frugal people receive money from savings. A tightwad finds it painful to spend, and spends less than they should on their own wellbeing because of the 'pain of spending' or the anxiety that comes from spending.)

Studies have been conducted using a brain-scanning technique that monitors blood flow to areas in the brain that are activated when performing a task in order to get a sense of what a person feels when they see an item's price tag.

When study subjects looked at a desirable item, such as chocolates, their brains produced a starkly different response than when they viewed the item's price tag. George Loewenstein, the professor of economics and psychology at Carnegie Mellon University in Australia who conducted the study, said researchers would first show the study subject a product. If they liked it, the reward centres of the brain would light up. Then researchers would show the subject the price. In the tightwad subjects, the pain and disgust regions of the brain were activated.

The key reward centre the researchers saw light up was the nucleus accumbens, which plays a key role in pleasurable acts from having sex to hearing music. The specific pain and disgust region involved was the insula, which activates in unpleasant experiences like smelling foul odours or experiencing social exclusion.

These findings suggest that, for a tightwad, the emotional pain or anxiety of actually having to pay for an item works to keep their pleasure-seeking in check. The researchers concluded that the mental anguish is so strong that it overrides rational deliberation; these people don't buy something even when they know they should.

For shopaholics, the opposite is true. The pain of throwing money around does not register in the brain like it does for other people. They experience little to no pain when spending money and thereby part with their money more easily.

Males were three times more likely to be tightwads than females, who showed no bias to either end of the spectrum. The movies might depict females as the shopper with the credit card, but in reality shopaholics are just as often males as females. The use of credit cards can be the financial equaliser, as credit cards weaken impulse control, particularly for those who wouldn't normally be very careful with their money—whether male or female.

If you were to try to categorise your money personality, it would probably fit into one of three broad categories:

- shopper
- plodder
- saver.

Some people can identify their personality without too much prodding. Others show tendencies across the board. To help you quickly identify your money personality, ask yourself the following questions.

- Do I find it easier to save or spend money?
- Do I enjoy spending money?
- Am I rational with my spending?

If you are in a relationship, also ask yourself the following questions.

- Does my partner agree with me around money matters?
- Are we financially compatible?

Your partner's money personality needs to be incorporated into your financial plan. From a financial perspective, no man or woman is an island. The choices of one partner directly affect the other, so it is best to be prepared to deal with this.

Shoppers

Shoppers derive emotional satisfaction from spending money—they like to shop and are usually good at it. Some shop to feel good, some shop because they are feeling good, and yet others shop because they don't have a reason not to. You don't have to be buying big-ticket items. In fact, a lot of shoppers simply make small purchases, but frequently.

'Controlled' or 'bargain' shoppers disguise their tendency from themselves, as they can spend very little on a day-to-day basis, but when they decide to buy something it is usually a big-ticket item.

Subcategories of the shopper include the comfort shopper and the binger. A comfort shopper often spends money as a way of celebration or distraction. If they are happy they spend money, or if they are sad or feeling out of control then they spend money. The extreme comfort shopper does both. The binger can be quite tight on a day-to-day basis, but spend up big when the occasion calls for it. They can budget for a time, then they blow out.

Not everyone is a shopper all the time, but overall shoppers find it easier to spend money than save it.

Plodder

If you do not identify strongly with the traits of the other two personalities it is probable you are a Plodder. Plodders are ambivalent about spending and saving. They take things as they come and have an expectation that if they keep doing what they are currently doing then it should be OK.

Savers

Savers derive more satisfaction from saving than from spending. They are quite happy to go without and have a natural consciousness about money. A saver doesn't have to be industrious, just economical.

Knowing *why* you spend is just as important as knowing *what* you spend when it comes to developing good financial habits.

CALCULATE YOUR FINANCIAL BMI

To determine your starting point and therefore how serious and urgent it is to develop and stick to a plan, work through the Financial BMI Matrix on the opposite page. Answer each of the five questions by circling your response, each number has a value attributed to it, then add up your score. This will give you an idea of where you're at, and where you need to go.

FACE UP TO YOUR DEBTS

When you know you are not in control of your finances, it can be easier, for a short while, to avoid the issue. But the ostrich effect—burying your head in the sand—is one of the biggest threats to a relationship and financial progress. Avoidance of dealing with money issues easily lends itself to anxiety and a feeling of helplessness around money. It feels bigger than you, so you ignore it and in some instances feign indifference.

But money is never bigger than you. With the exception of compulsive debtors, there is no financial problem so big that you have to relinquish control. Don't be the poster child for 'someone else will save me'—the belief that you will be rescued by someone or something, that if you just keep going somehow it will be OK. It won't. Open the unopened bills now and write a list of what you owe.

Financial BMI Matrix

Value	What financial life stage are you at (see page 17)?	What is your cash position on a day-to-day basis (see page 23)?	What is your money personality (see page 25)?	How motivated are you?	How many years until your retirement?
1	Starting Out	Sinking	Shopper	Not very	Less than 10
2	Building Up	Floating	Plodder	Semi	10-15
3	Sitting Back	Flying	Saver	Very	16 or more

Results:

Total: 12-15		Total: 8-12		Total: 7 or less	
Commentary	Tip	Commentary	Tip	Commentary	Tip
Your financial future looks bright. With an overarching retirement plan you should be able to comfortably sit back and enjoy your retirement, possibly even before retirement age.	Your financial future looks favourable. Do not let this lull you into inaction, however. Small, sustainable steps are all that are needed to achieve and maintain financial success.	With a considered financial plan and by taking action you should be able to achieve your financial goal of being mortgage free and having funds available for retirement.	You have some obstacles working against you, but with consistent and purposeful steps towards your financial goals and by keeping your spending in check you should be able to reach a comfortable retirement.	Your situation is tight but with an overhaul of your finances and a willingness to be brave and move forward then you could start to bridge the gap between where you are now and a comfortable retirement.	Getting in control of your finances and creating a plan will be confronting, but ultimately empowering as you take back control. Money is not bigger than you and a comfortable retirement is achievable, but you will need to work hard.

I have had some clients come and see me for the first time with a big bag of stuff. I will assume it is bank statements or the like, but it is actually a wad of unopened bills. My client will sit there opening the bills in front of me, because this is the only time they feel brave enough to confront their reality. At the end of the meeting we have proposed how things will work going forward. We have not started the plan, nor have any of the proposed savings or financial goals been reached, yet these new clients often say, 'I feel so much lighter'.

If you have a stack of unopened bills in front of you, it's OK to be scared. But still open them. Remember, being scared isn't the issue; continuing to do nothing is.

Self-actualisation

Abraham Maslow, who came up with his famous Hierarchy of Needs, claimed that once a person becomes 'self-actualised'—less concerned about the opinions of others and more interested in their own potential—they start to look beyond themselves and don't need as much stuff. I've found it interesting to watch my clients who have become mortgage free. The first thing they do when they get to this stage usually involves giving back to their family or community in some way. It's a joy to watch, as a couple of clients have paid off their parents' mortgages not one week after paying off their own.

Chapter 3

Budgeting—creating a cash surplus

*Tell your money where to go
instead of wondering where it went.*
— C. E. Hoover

Irrespective of income level or age, too many of us can relate to the definition of the new poor: when there is too much month left at the end of your money.

The cornerstone of financial success is having a cash surplus. It is the most neglected of all financial principles. It is not particularly engaging or sexy, but it is the foundation stone to wealth creation. *You must have money left over.*

This leads us to the first question: do you? You will not need to complete a budget or analyse your bank statements to answer this. You do not need to be earning a low income to have no money left. In fact, the higher your income, the more likely you are to be living pay-day to pay-day. Living *well* pay-day to pay-day, but pay-day to pay-day nonetheless.

Having money left over at the end of each week, month or year is critical to achieving any form of financial progress, and this is where most people trip up. However, once you have mastered the ability to create a cash surplus, you can then move on to creating a productive investment with this cash, and that leads to wealth, or a growing of your value.

In New Zealand—whether because of our 'she'll be right' attitude, our lack of financial literacy or our general apathy towards all things unrelated to our national sports teams—it seems we are particularly good at spending money. We pretty much spend everything we earn, irrespective of how much that is. But this doesn't seem to bother us, because property values are increasing faster than we are overspending. We are lulled into a false sense of comfort, which seems to give us permission to care less and less about the speed at which money is leaving our bank accounts.

For those who don't own property, there are always credit cards or loans available to facilitate your overspending or to catch you after you have stepped off your financial ledge. And, weirdly, the speed at which money is spent helps to propel the economy and keep the world going round.

While having a cash surplus doesn't sound particularly sexy, the lack of a surplus will catch up with you—but maybe not in the way you expect. Sure, the obvious end point is that you run out of money, creditors come knocking, debts are called, assets are sold and, at its extreme, you may go bankrupt. In reality, the lack of a cash surplus initially leads to frustration, stress, anxiety, lack of sleep and relationship pressure.

The lack of a cash surplus is directly linked to your personal wellbeing.

Creating a cash surplus can be hard, but planning and controlling how much you consume are key components to wealth building, so you must master this skill. If it doesn't come naturally to you, get help. Finding time to exercise might not come naturally to some people, but just because it doesn't come naturally doesn't mean you shouldn't do it—you just need help, or a different environment to support you to do certain things.

It takes time to plan a budget. A budget is only one component of a financial plan, but if you don't take the time to do the budget first you can't make that plan. Being time-poor is no excuse; if you don't have time to do it, pay someone else to prepare one for you.

Operating a household without a budget is like running a business without a plan, without goals, without direction. If you are spending more than you earn and you can't manage to change this, you need to enlist expert help to kick-start your progress.

WHAT IS A BUDGET?

A budget is an estimation of incomings and outgoings over a period of time. It allows you to think about money in an analytical way and, most importantly, is an effective tool to help you get your finances under control.

The purpose of a budget is not to tell you where your money has gone, but where your money *should* go. It is forward-facing, not backward-facing, and if done right can help you to:

- make informed projections about your financial situation
- enjoy a better quality of life, because it will help you to avert financial disaster
- get in control and allow you to plan for financial changes
- sleep better
- achieve peace of mind
- make your money work for you
- improve your personal relationships.

Despite the many and varied benefits, a lot of us have never set a budget. For the few who have taken the initiative to create a budget, most will attest to the fact that sticking to it is no easy task, with the best-laid plans often ruined by impulsive spending and impetuous decisions.

This chapter talks about how to set a budget that works, while remembering that the best budgets will create a feeling of consciousness around your spending without leaving you feeling deprived.

> If you want to get ahead get organised, as financial opportunity tends to run in organisation's shadow.

Jotting down expenses and making some sweeping assumptions about your financial capability does not create a budget. It might create a table with numbers on it, but this does not in itself make a budget.

A budget must be considered and set—but this is just step one. Assuming you successfully set a budget, you will quickly realise that committing a plan to paper and actually achieving it are two very different things. While setting the budget is important, it is in fact the easy part. Sticking to the budget takes skill, discipline and support. This is step two.

> Achieving a budget, not a particular income level, is what sets the financial athlete apart from the fiscally challenged.

HOW TO SET A BUDGET

Setting a budget requires taking certain steps in a particular order. Each step is as important as every other one.

Step 1: Understand where you have spent money in the past

If you are going to develop a budget, first find out where your money is going so you can catch it before it gets spent. An indicative assessment is easy—if your savings are depleting or you are using debt to live, you are likely to be overspending. But the size and scale of the overspend are what is key. Do not rely on your instincts to determine this, as you will be spending more than you realise, across a number of different costs. Little but frequent (and often forgotten) costs can create the most lasting damage.

You need to *actually look at where your money has gone*. This is called an analysis of spending and a template can be found in Appendix III. However, a summary of your spending to date is not a budget—the purpose of a budget isn't to determine where your money has gone, but where it *should* go. Knowing where your money has been going will help you to understand where it is likely to go if you do not take considered steps to change it.

> **Tip:** Think carefully about the categories you use to classify your expenses. Lots of people over-simplify their budget. Detail your expenses as much as possible to give you a more accurate summary. For example: 'vehicle costs' does not just cover your WOF and petrol. It includes maintenance, insurance, road user chargers, ACC levies, services, tyre replacements, speeding and parking tickets. The devil is in the detail.

Print out your bank statements for the last 12 months. If this is too onerous, then print out your statements for the last three months, provided they are from a typical financial quarter. Extrapolate your quarterly spending into an annual amount. *This amount is what your life is costing you.*

List all income earned by income type, e.g. salary, bonuses, regular overtime, cash jobs, etc. Total all income received. Then subtract your expenses from your total income to ascertain if you are going backwards or have a cash surplus.

If this exercise shows that you do not have enough money coming in to cover all your costs, it will show as a negative number (known as a deficit) and your bank balance will be reducing or your debt increasing. A deficit means that you are going backwards. Some of this shortfall may be made up through creating efficiencies within your budget, capturing the money that is currently getting frittered away (see Chapter 4), reprioritising goals, structuring debt better and getting serious about your financial future.

The second prong to this exercise is that it allows you to *determine what you can actually afford to spend* and how much ground you need to make up when you set the budget.

Your initial budget target is to generate a cash surplus of 10% of what you earn, which can be used to reduce debt or accumulate wealth through investment. This means that you have 90% of your income to allocate to your living costs.

Tip: Write down your expenses by what they are rather than where you purchased them, so you'll be able to figure out later how much you spend in particular categories, e.g. groceries, takeaways, coffees, clothes, etc.

Step 2: Understand your expenses

Most budgets don't work because insufficient emphasis is placed upon the differing types of expense, instead assuming that all costs are linear (that is, always the same) and within your control. But this is not true. While you might be able to annualise costs then divide up how much you need each month, in reality, the timing of those costs is crucial.

Expense types include:

- fixed
- occasional
- non-negotiable
- curveball
- Mack truck.

The type of expense dictates whether you can reduce it or not. Don't bother trying to change things outside of your control; focus only on costs you can manage.

> When you are looking to give yourself a money makeover, focus only on the areas that you can actually change.

You need to plan for both fixed and variable expenses.

Fixed expenses are items like rent and health insurance. The costs are fixed and do not differ depending on how much you consume.

Variable expenses are things like utilities (e.g. power, water) and petrol. Some costs, like groceries, can fall into either category, depending on how much self-control you have. Remember, all necessary costs such as groceries, clothing and power can quickly become unnecessarily expensive if you have champagne tastes. People often get confused about spending on necessities, but the inevitability of a purchase does not justify spending more than you need to. For example, of course you need to buy food, but that doesn't mean that anything and everything you spend on food is justified. The table below shows the range in food costs for a basic, nutritious diet, then a more moderate diet and finally a liberal diet including more convenience and imported foods, out-of-season fruits and vegetables, higher-priced cuts of meat and some speciality foods.

Estimated weekly food costs for 2014 (Auckland)			
	Basic	**Moderate**	**Liberal**
	$	$	$
Man	68	91	109
Woman	58	77	92
Adolescent boy	71	95	114
Adolescent girl	59	78	94
10-year-old	50	66	79
5-year-old	42	56	68
4-year-old	33	44	53
1-year-old	32	43	51

Source: Department of Human Nutrition, University of Otago

You need to plan for *occasional expenses*, whether they are fixed or variable. Budget for expenses that only happen a few times a year such as gifts, birthday parties, doctor's visits or car maintenance. If you have enough room in your budget, you can pay for these as they occur. If you're on a tighter budget, set aside additional savings ahead of time. There is no excuse for going into debt because you 'forgot' that Christmas happens every year. Too often people blame the less regular costs for their financial impotence. Some people try to spread these costs over the year rather than make a single payment, which has some merits, but spreading payments doesn't fix the problem if there are insufficient funds in the first place.

Non-negotiable costs are things that may be frivolous but make you happy, or make your life better. The key is to not confuse your desires with necessary expenditure. Choose the things that are important to you, even if they seem frivolous, and make sure you have money to spend on these things. If it is important to you, then it needs to be in the budget.

The other two types of costs, curveballs and Mack trucks—are a bit harder to manage. *Curveballs* are one-off major costs such as having your car blow up, or needing expensive dental work. Your budget needs to be able to absorb curveballs, so you need to work hard on it to build up a buffer of some savings. It might be tough at the start, but once you've built a buffer things will get easier.

Financial Mack trucks are impossible to plan for: things like relationship breakdowns, serious illness or redundancy, which flatten you financially. These things might push you back to the Starting Out phase.

The seriousness of your situation will determine to what extent you can afford to be generous with yourself. For some, $50 per week to spend on coffees may be all they need to feel OK about sticking to a budget. For others, spending only $5000 on clothes is considered a grim reality, while for others, having $300 to spend on Christmas is considered a luxury.

Assuming you have a cash surplus, you are entitled to some non-negotiables. If you do not have a cash surplus, then all costs are on the table and could be slashed to get a cash surplus.

Everyone has at least three things that are so important to them that they can identify them deal-breakers. Work out what these are for you and look for ways to reduce spending on everything else so as to create a cash surplus. To help you identify areas of spending that you may be able to cut, I have found the most common types of casual wants can be roughly categorised by gender.

- Women tend to like good coffee, a glass of wine now and then, holidays, socialising with friends and buying presents for friends and family.
- Men like buying 'toys', family holidays, alcohol and spending on sports.

Have a think about all the money you spend and distinguish between desires and needs. Remember when you received your first pay check—it went a long way. You were earning less and spending less, but were just as happy (I presume). Some frivolity is needed, but think carefully. If all your desired spending cannot be incorporated into the 90% of your income allocated for spending, recognise that you must let those desires go unsatisfied and move on.

Keep adjusting your budget until you are pretty happy with it. Consider what you really want—nice clothes, a bit of finery, more coffees? Or do you want more substantial assets, the opportunity to work less, to be mortgage free or pay for your children's education? Do you want to have a retirement you can enjoy? The 90% you spend covers the basics, the 10% you save brings the extras.

Step 3: Set the budget

Budget example
See Appendix III for a budget template. Our budget spreadsheet is easily adjustable to accommodate different budgeting needs and styles. On the opposite page is an example.

Monthly budget

Income		Fixed Expenses		Variable Expenses	
Work (after tax)	3000	Rent	1000	Pet costs	100
Cash jobs	100	Groceries	400	Car maintenance/repairs	120
Total	**3100**	Petrol	180	Doctor visit	35
		Health insurance	80	Gifts	25
		Electricity & gas	150	Entertainment (concerts, movies)	100
		Internet	50	Clothing and shoes	200
		Landline	30	Makeup	50
		Mobile phone	60	Miscellaneous	125
		Total	**1950**	**Total**	**755**

Miscellaneous			
Books	25	Total Income	3100
New sheets	40	Total Expenses	2705
Prescription	10	Remaining / Surplus	395
Massage	50		
Total	**125**	Annual surplus	4740

Remember, the purpose of a budget isn't to determine where your money has been going, but where your money *should* go, and to help you to calculate how long it will take you to create a cash surplus.

With my clients I work to an annual target, broken down into quarterly check-ins with weekly targets. With all successful budgets, *consistency is the single most important component*. It is not about starting off hard and fast and ending up with a budget blowout, but about conscious spending and saving. Make small initiatives often. You need goalposts of where you need to be, and by when, to make sure your budget will work. You then track, measure and tune.

Step 4: Tracking your spending

To stick to a budget you need to record your spending, otherwise it becomes a dormant document. So, before you kick-start your new regime, you need to choose the tracking system that will work best for you. You could use:

- a notebook and pen
- a spreadsheet
- financial software (e.g. Microsoft Money).

I prefer the spreadsheet method, but you have to choose what works best for you. Tracking your money this way takes minimal time, and you'll be less likely to forget something.

A lot of my clients hate having to take the time to physically enter each cost or expense and many have asked us to develop our software to allow for bank feeds that pre-populate the spreadsheet without the user having to manually record each transaction. While this created efficiencies and saved our clients time, we found it also resulted in a 20% drop in their ability to sustain their budget, as they were not forced to stay consciously connected to their spending and financial behaviour.

Tip: Do not use automatic bank-statement feeds if you have opted to use financial or online software. Conscious spending is the key to sustaining a budget.

Review your weekly tracking and determine the areas in which you are overspending, or where you could spend less. Continue with weekly check-ins for the 12 weeks. After that first three months, review your position to determine if you have achieved what you had planned to within that timeframe.

Review your budget and tweak it for the next quarter. If you are under-earning, then the solution lies with you (see page 73). Likewise if you are still overspending.

If you have set your budget correctly and, despite trying hard, you are not managing to make progress, there are three likely causes.

1. You have overstated your regular income, or understated your regular costs.
2. You are not financially aligned with your partner.
3. You have been hit by a curveball—something unplanned that has knocked you over or at the very least pushed you into 'survival mode', with financial progress taking a back seat.

The most common cause of struggling to keep to a budget has to do with the *timing* of income and expenses. Some income, despite being fairly certain, should not be counted on in the budget until it is earned. An example of this is bonus income. Even if you are virtually guaranteed this income, unless it is received regularly it cannot be counted on for budgeting purposes. It needs to be removed from the budget along with any discretionary costs that would normally be paid for from this income, such as holidays and presents. Re-work the budget, reducing costs as needed to make sure you stay within the lower income amount.

If your lack of progress stems from misalignment of financial behaviour and goals with your partner, then you are not alone, but you will need to take some serious measures to fix this situation (see Chapter 8).

FRUGAL FATIGUE

A word of warning: if you set a budget that is too harsh, you will probably lose your motivation to follow it and get budget burnout or 'frugal fatigue' (a phrase coined by Paula Rosenblum).

My experience is that people are prepared to make concessions if the cut-back ties through to immediate progress and a measurable result. If they do not see the result quickly, they will give up. This is the predominant reason why clients work with me as their Financial Personal Trainer. They want to get results, they are happy to be told what to do, but ultimately they want to know that they will achieve their financial goals.

One potential pitfall of frugal fatigue is that eventually you simply get tired of being so deliberate with your money. As a result, you might start splurging unnecessarily, with the risk being that, once you start to overspend, you might as well spend up large—much like when you are dieting and open up a packet of lollies promising you will only eat one, only to find your willpower disappears along with the first lolly. You decide you have already fallen off the diet wagon, so you might as well fall off in style.

It's important to recognise fatigue if it begins to affect you. If you feel totally bored with budgeting and sick to death of squeezing pennies, you're at risk of a spending bender. Don't give in to the temptation.

Remember what you are working towards, and if it seems too far away have a review with your Financial Personal Trainer to see if you can get there faster.

Tip: A good measure of progress is if you feel in control and you are seeing actual financial results. Progress takes the form of your debts reducing faster or your savings increasing more speedily.

Chapter 4

The fritter factor

I have found that people tend to fritter away between 10 and 20% of their income. What I mean by 'fritter' is people spending money on things without even realising they're doing it. Or perhaps they do realise, but are unaware of the extent to which they are spending, and that spending is not making them any happier.

To understand what frittered funds are, you need to understand the law of diminishing returns. This law is one of the most famous in all of economics and production theory. The basic definition is that, in a productive process, if you keep adding one more unit of something while holding all other components constant at some point the unit added will produce less. For example, you may say that watering a plant will produce a better flower, and the more you water it the better the flower—to a point. You can continue to water the plant but eventually it will reach a point of optimum water consumption; you could keep watering past this point, but you won't get a better flower. Indeed, you're likely to undo all the good work you did watering it in the first place.

Another example would be an athlete training. There is an optimal level of training and rest for every athlete to enable them to reach their peak performance. Training beyond that point will not produce better results, and can actually have a detrimental effect if they are not refreshed on race day due to excess training.

The same can be said for money and happiness. Money can buy you a warm home, put food on the table, pay for holidays and allow you to be generous with yourself and your friends. It allows you to do things that make you happy. But if you keep spending on a particular thing you will hit a threshold, a point of optimum spend, where your happiness or satisfaction will start to drop off.

For example, I love to buy a coffee from the local café. I love visiting the café, chatting with the barista. I love how they remember my order. The coffee smells great and I thrive on the caffeine hit every morning. Whether the coffee is a necessity or not is irrelevant; it simply makes me happy. It's my little non-negotiable. To some people it would be something they could take or leave, but for me it's staying.

But, if I were to have *two* coffees a day, the experience of the second cup would not be as special as the first. I would still enjoy it, but less so than the first cup. If I were to buy a third, my enjoyment would reduce even further. I would have well and truly hit my saturation point. And some people might be just as happy to make a coffee at work and save themselves the $4.

There is no judgement here over what you spend your money on, but there needs to be some self-imposed gauge as to whether you need to spend to the same level on certain items to be just as happy. Unfortunately the only way to test your threshold of happiness is to spend less and see if you feel it. If you can spend less on a cost and not feel that it affects you differently, then quite clearly that item you had previously spent money on is now a frittered cost.

Around 15% of the money you spend is not making you incrementally happier. This money is what I describe as 'fritter'. That is, you could not spend it and still be just as happy.

The trick to identifying your fritter areas is to know yourself well, and to go through a period of testing. What might be fritter for you might be a non-negotiable for a friend or spouse. Interestingly, what might have been a non-negotiable cost for you previously may become a fritter with time. Budgets must keep evolving as life throws curveballs at you and priorities change.

Fritter is like a virus with few symptoms. It creeps into your spending without consciousness and, before you know it, you are spending more than you realise on things that do not necessarily improve your lifestyle.

The graph below illustrates how fritter works. Money makes you happy to a point, with the more money you spend supposedly making you happier and your life better. But you will reach a point where you could spend more and more on a particular cost that would typically create enjoyment, but it does not make

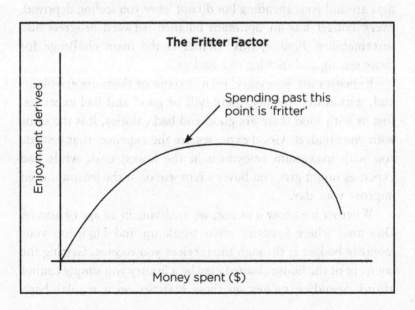

The Fritter Factor

Spending past this point is 'fritter'

Enjoyment derived

Money spent ($)

you any more satisfied. This is the happiness saturation point, or the point at which spending on a non-negotiable and possibly frivolous cost becomes fritter. If you continue to spend freely on this particular cost it may produce less enjoyment, even to the point where it produces dissatisfaction—a point of financial gluttony.

In assessing the extent of your frittering, you must understand what your 'wants' actually cost. Do you want these things because you have always had them, have always wanted them, or because they truly make you happy? If they make you happy, and you are determined that a cost is necessary even if it is frivolous in nature, then you need to ask yourself if you could satisfy the need more cheaply. The answer may be no, but you still have to ask yourself this.

Just because you have always spent money on something does not mean that it makes you happy having it. Some people spend because they do not have a reason *not* to spend.

Remember, the best budgets create a feeling of consciousness around your spending but do not leave you feeling deprived. Every budget has an optimum balance between progress and sustainability. Finding this balance is the main challenge for those setting and sticking to a budget.

Expenses are necessary, even if some of them are frivolous; and, within the frivolity, there will be good and bad expenses. Just as with food there are good and bad calories, it is the same with your budget. Good expenses are the expenses that provide you with maximum enjoyment at the lowest cost, while bad expenses might give you buyer's remorse or at the least not even improve your day.

Whether we know it or not, we are living in an age of luxury. One area where luxuries often sneak up and bludgeon your monthly budget is through the services you receive. Getting the lawn cut or the house cleaned may be a luxury you simply cannot afford. Spending money on these luxuries on a regular basis is one of the quickest ways to reduce your disposable income. Remember, the money you use to pay for these services has been earned and taxed. In spending money on any frittered or unnecessarily expensive cost, you are lengthening the time you have to keep working in order to finance your retirement. Is it worth it?

Budgeting will take sacrifice, and means you need to make better choices. Sometimes these choices hurt. Sometimes it means you don't buy the biggest house on the best street. Sometimes it means you have to settle for a second-hand car instead of a new one.

Budgeting hurts sometimes. Stay on guard though, because it is when it hurts that banks and businesses offer credit cards and interest-free loans to help you justify spending on something you cannot afford, and therefore should not have.

Credit cards offer you up to 60 days of free credit, but in most cases you will pay for this little perk well after the 60 days have ended. You need to understand the history and psychology of credit cards to ensure you no longer fall prey to these little weapons of mass destruction.

Chapter 5

Credit cards—don't trust them

Although the concept of credit has been around for centuries, the idea of a card that could be used to buy products in more than one place was novel when it first appeared in 1950, courtesy of Diners Club. Since their inception, credit cards have become a phenomenon, a way of pushing a spending culture to hedonistic heights. American Express jumped on the credit card bandwagon in 1956, using the phrase 'Don't leave home without it'—an instruction too many have taken to heart!

Some take comfort from the fact that their credit is paid off in full each month. But just because it is paid in full doesn't mean your credit card isn't harming you. Your credit card might be allowing you to spend more without you even realising it, creating wastage, even if you can afford to pay it in full each month. It enables frittering and plays havoc with the shopper.

The reality is that almost 65% of those with credit cards do not pay them off in full each month, and that the average balance of unpaid debts is $6000 [Statistics NZ]. Broadly speaking, if you have to use a credit card to pay your bills because you do not have the cash sitting in the bank, you are going backwards (see Chapter 6).

UNDERSTANDING HOW CREDIT CARDS WORK

Credit cards are a financial product issued by a bank or financial institution which allow you to make purchases or cash advances. They are essentially a line of credit that you can spend up to a preset limit.

The bank charges an annual fee for you to use a credit card. When you use the card, the bank pays the merchant within a day of processing and you are given up to six weeks to come up with the money to pay the bank for the purchase.

Some banks promote that credit cards save you money (which in my opinion is a bit of a stretch). In truth, credit cards can also completely ruin your finances. If you pay off the credit card within the allocated grace period, the purchase hasn't cost you anything. If you don't pay it off, then you are charged interest on your purchase. And this is where it gets both interesting and scary.

A charge card has to be paid in full each month. A credit card doesn't. A credit card allows you to carry a balance indefinitely, as long as you make the minimum monthly payments.

The money you owe is subject to an annual percentage rate or finance charge. While it can vary between cards, it normally ranges from 12 to 24%, with cash advances attracting a higher finance charge (sometimes up to 30%), and without a grace period (that is, you start being charged interest on the money right away).

In conjunction with the annual fee and finance charge, you can also be charged late-payment fees and a higher interest rate if your transactions exceed your credit limit. If you avoid these fees and are able to pay the credit card in full each month, then this means that you have earned enough money to pay your bills—it is not an achievement, as such. (Read Chapter 16 to better under-stand the damage a credit card can inflict when you're trying to repay your mortgage.)

If you cannot afford to pay off the card in full each month, the minimum payment that the bank requires its customers to make is set at 2–5% of the original purchase amount. That means that the lion's share of all minimum payments is simply covering the interest charge (and sometimes not even that), and only a fraction of the payment actually reduces the balance. What is more disturbing is that, each month, if you don't make any more purchases, the minimum payment reduces further—it's like the bank doesn't *want* you to pay off the credit card (I wonder why that is?). The result of this is that, by just paying the minimum payment every month, you could take up to 40 years (*yes, 40 years!*) to pay off the original purchase, with the interest you pay being a lot more than the original purchase price. Not surpris-ingly, banks find their credit card divisions are among the most profitable parts of their business.

UNDERSTANDING THE PSYCHOLOGY OF CREDIT CARDS

It has been said that seeing a credit card logo such as Mastercard or Visa on a website increases the chance of an impulse buy.

In a study comparing cash spending to credit card spending, people valued credit card purchases as equal to 50 cents in the dollar when compared to paying for the same item with cash. Or, put another way, it feels half as expensive, or people are willing to spend twice as much for the same item when paying with a credit card.

People are inadvertently paying more and justifying it due to the points earned or the interest saved on a revolving credit-type mortgage (which I strongly oppose in its traditional definition, and is discussed in Chapter 16). Other studies indicate that using a credit card versus cash causes you to spend 30 cents more in the dollar than using cash.

Studies suggest that less transparent forms of money like credit cards tend to be treated like 'play money' and are hence more easily spent (or parted with). Credit cards allow you to avoid the reality of your spending, and in doing so inadvertently encourage you to keep spending.

What is universally agreed is that you spend more with a credit card than with cash. And the gap between the two payment methods is increasing, with both volumes and the values of credit card payments increasing.

Paying with cash elicits greater psychological pain than other modes of payment. Studies suggest that this is to do with the 'de-coupling' of the actual purchase from the pain of paying for it. In other words, paying cash to someone for a product couples the loss of money with the purchase—you have given something up for something else. By paying with a credit card, consumers don't link the purchase's actual cost with the purchase itself.

I believe greater controls need to be placed around who qualifies for credit cards. Such controls would include the following.

- Beneficiaries should not be allowed credit cards. Preying on the financially vulnerable is socially irresponsible.
- Banks should not be allowed to increase limits without permission.
- Warnings need to be put on credit card statements highlighting the interest that is being charged and calculating how much extra interest you might end up paying.
- Increasing the minimum repayment amount. Currently this sits between 2 and 5% of the original balance. This is too low and allows people to feel that their cashflow is stronger than it really is.
- All credit card statements need to come with a warning that the minimum payment facility should be used only when necessary.

- Ban 'tap and go' cards, because they exacerbate the already dangerous disconnect between purchasers and costs. These cards discourage you from even seeing how much you are spending and remove the approval process (selecting the account and putting in a pin or signing). It keeps spending quick, easy, effortless—and dangerous.
- Prohibit sports teams or celebrities endorsing credit cards or loan companies.

Due to the delayed processing times and application of funds to your account, it is hard to determine where you are at and what you have actually spent at any one time. Interest rates are high, adding a cost to what you have already spent. Even if you pay the card in full each month, the fact you will most likely have overspent offsets any savings or reward points.

If you are unable to pay the minimum payment on your credit card then you are digging yourself a financial hole. Block or cut up the card so you can't spend any more money on it, and work on paying off the balance.

If you are able to use a credit card correctly, paying it off in full each month, and only buying items within your planned spending budget, then it can be a source of flexibility which you can continue to enjoy (subject to some parameters). Read the following tips to ensure you are not paying more for the privilege of a credit card than you need to.

- Always ask for annual fees to be waived. These can range from $20 per annum to $325 per annum.
- If you have more than one credit card, combine the limits on one card and close the others to avoid multiple fees for the same credit limit.

- Check monthly statements to ensure all credit card charges are your own.
- Never give your credit card number over the phone unless you initiate the call. If someone calls you back after making a purchase to ask for your credit card number, tell them you will call them back on the advertised phone number.

Tip: Don't use your credit card for at least three months to get a better idea of what you are capable of when the psychology of credit purchases doesn't apply. You will always spend less. Let this three-month hiatus become the gauge of what you can do without credit. If you insist on using a credit card after three months, ensure you spend in line with your credit card-free levels.

Chapter 6

Going backwards? What you need to do

If you are in a financial hole, you need to stop digging. This sounds sensible, and even simple, but for many it is far from easy.

When you are sinking, you need to take immediate action. There is no room for wastage. Depending on the severity of your financial situation, a hard and fast detox may be just what you need.

As a rule I prefer to avoid changes that are unsustainable, but in some instances this may be necessary. People lose money in many ways—whether they are disconnected from the fact they are spending or their spending is incurring interest costs is irrelevant. We all fritter. We all lose money. To get ahead you have to stop this.

Warren Buffett has been quoted as saying that the first rule of money is never lose money, and rule number two is never forget rule number one. There are many ways that you can save money on living costs, and in most instances you simply need to be more organised. Here are my top tips for saving.

HOW MUCH DOES IT COST IN WORK TIME?

A great way to demotivate yourself from spending is by calculating how much you need to work in order to purchase an item, or how many hours of work have been allocated to an annualised expense category.

Divide the cost of the item by your hourly rate to calculate how many hours you need to work to afford to buy it.

> **Tip:** Divide your annual salary in half and take off the zeros to quickly calculate your hourly rate. For example, if your income is $80,000, then your hourly rate is $40.

USE CASH

Although credit cards are a convenient source of money, if they are not repaid on time they can easily become a drag on your income, eroding your cashflow and costing you extra in interest (see Chapter 5). In addition, credit cards encourage spending—most people are willing to spend more when they use a credit card than when using cash.

Studies have shown that less transparent forms of payment tend to be treated like play money and are therefore more easily used. Cash is viewed as the most transparent form of payment, so use cash where you can. In fact, I require my clients to use cash for their most frequent discretionary costs. People usually overspend on their most regular costs, as they repeatedly spend a little more than they realise.

> **Tip:** Combine what you spend on groceries, take-aways, cafés, restaurants, work lunches and coffees into one amount. Withdraw this amount in cash each week and manage your spending based on the remaining funds.

For practical reasons you may wish to keep one credit card and limit its use to occasional purchases when other methods of payment are not appropriate, for example, internet purchases.

If you have a debt problem, it may be helpful to run your credit card with a positive balance, treating it like a debit or EFTPOS card—ignoring that you can go into credit with the bank, and only spend back to a zero balance.

For example: let's say your credit card has a $1000 limit. You transfer $500 onto this card. If it was a bank account, it would show that you were $500 into positive funds, but could still go into overdraft or credit up to $1000—that you have $1500 in available funds. If you are running your credit card with a positive balance, you will only spend the $500 you put onto it, *and stop spending when you are about to go into your overdraft*, when interest will be charged.

Running your credit card to a zero balance will serve as a mental check on further spending. All other cards should be cut up and thrown away.

WORK-COST REIMBURSEMENT

People often pay for work-related things—taxis or lunches—with their EFTPOS or credit card. Although the money will eventually be reimbursed, this can put unnecessary pressure on your personal finances until it is reimbursed. There is also the risk that you will forget to claim the expense, or not do it in a timely manner.

I recommend you have a separate credit card for these types of situations. You only use it if you are incurring costs for others that you know will be reimbursed later. It keeps things clean and it avoids any costs or delays in reimbursement straining your personal finances.

KEEP BUSINESS AND PERSONAL FINANCES SEPARATE

Many self-employed people run their businesses as an extension of their personal finances, or vice versa. Everything tends to be intertwined, which just means things are a mess. Financial statements are usually manipulated to ensure profit is low, so that the tax they need to pay is low, with little regard for how much money the business is actually earning.

If it is common to be short of money in the business, people may willingly top it up from their personal finances, or not pay themselves a salary. Some business costs are paid from personal accounts or by credit card, and some business owners and self-employed people are more comfortable spending because they believe some costs are tax deductible. Any combination of these points usually ensures that you are not taking from the business what you could and should.

Very few small businesses actually forecast earnings, instead reacting only to provisional tax payments. Forecasting is key. Tracking to a business plan is key. Business strategy is imperative if you are going to grow your business the smartest way.

Another key benefit of keeping everything separate is that it will highlight actual business performance and whether the business in its current state is viable. Not all good ideas translate to good businesses, and not all good operators have a viable product or service.

PAY LESS TAX—LEGITIMATELY

A lot of people believe it is only the self-employed who can find ways to pay less tax but this is not the case. If you are not self-employed there can still be opportunities to claim a tax refund.

For instance, if you pay school or other donations or pay income-protection insurance, you are likely to be entitled to claim these expenses against your pay-as-you-earn (PAYE) income and receive a tax refund, provided you actually complete and submit a tax return. Further, if you have not worked a complete financial year at your current place of employment you may have overpaid your tax, which would also trigger a tax refund.

> **Tip:** Tax returns can be completed and submitted online. Only make the submission if you have calculated a tax refund. If you had tax to pay, don't file the return. Using a tax refund agent does not guarantee a tax refund. They will complete your return and submit it whether there is a refund or not.

If you are self-employed, work with a good accountant to understand what deductions are available to you. Check that your accountant hasn't missed anything. When I review new clients' financial statements, I usually find at least $5000 of tax savings that have been ignored through lazy bookkeeping. Make sure your accountant is picking up on the little areas of tax savings above. These tend to get ignored unless you follow up.

CONSOLIDATE DEBT ONTO YOUR MORTGAGE

As part of our recommended structure, outstanding debts should be consolidated onto your mortgage. Although this means you will owe more on your mortgage, you should pay less interest overall—all your credit card debt and personal loans would now be at mortgage interest rates, which tend to be lower than credit card rates. Importantly, without other payments dragging on your income, you will be able to apply more of your surplus income to paying off your mortgage. However, unless you accelerate your repayments on your new higher mortgage, you run the risk of paying more over the life of the loan.

For example: You have a credit card balance of $10,000 at 20%. This is going to cost you $2000 per year in interest, and you are due to pay it off over two years. (For simplicity's sake, let's say you were going to make a lump sum payment in two years of $14,000 to clear the credit card—the $10,000 debt plus two years' worth of interest.)

If you put this debt on your 25-year mortgage, the interest rate would be lowered to 6%, which would incur $600 in interest every year. But your mortgage is set up to be paid off over 25 years. This means that, unless you channelled that $11,200 into repaying the debt within two years, you would be holding the consolidated loan for longer, with the overall cost being higher.

While debt consolidation can be a good strategy, *it is only effective as long as you do not accrue further debt*. Data from debt consolidation companies estimates that up to 78% of people who consolidate their credit card debt will incur more debt, which will again need to be consolidated. And, as we have seen above, the long-term impact of adding extra costs to your mortgage can actually be more expensive if the overall debt is not paid off faster. This is one of the reasons it is imperative that you measure your performance to make sure the debt is reducing. The interest rate and the length of time you have the debt for will be what determines the overall cost of the debt.

If you have insufficient equity at your existing bank to consolidate your other debts onto the mortgage, then consider refinancing with another bank.

DEBT CONSOLIDATION—NO MORTGAGE

If you do not have a mortgage, it may be worth consolidating your credit card balances to one card with a low interest rate. Some banks allow you to transfer the balance of your credit card and pay no interest for the first six months. However, after six months, the interest rate will increase. Some banks allow you to have a low interest rate for the length of time it takes you to repay the transferred balance.

> If you are transferring your balance, it is important that you use the respite of lower outgoings to repay the debt balance faster.

If you are unable to consolidate your debts, rank all your debts according to interest rate. Pay off the debts in order, paying the debts at the highest rates first.

STRUCTURE YOUR DEBT BETTER

Look at interest rates and different terms—compare banks. Factoring in break costs and possible penalties, should you change the length of your fixed-term loan? Would you be better off refinancing with another bank?

I had one client who was paying 10% at one bank but successfully refinanced with another bank at 7%. Strangely, no break costs applied.

Remember that each bank has slightly different lending criteria. What is a negative for one bank might not be onerous to another.

TACKLE BANK FEES

Ask for all unarranged overdraft capability to be removed from your bank accounts. This way, should you be about to overspend you will be declined. This will prompt you to decide if you do in fact need the item you are trying to buy. If you did decide to go ahead with the purchase, you would have to use an alternate payment method (a credit card or money from a different account) and avoid the $15 or $20 bank fee.

In approximately 50% of these purchases, once having been alerted that the cost would put them into overdraft or that they were about to overspend, most people don't go ahead with the purchase. All they needed was a reminder *before the purchase*. An unarranged overdraft fee tells you that you have overspent *after the fact*—which is useless. Going into overdraft suggests you are going backwards or at the very least you have lazy money management.

Check the bank fees that you are being charged. Don't assume that the bank is calculating these correctly. Studies have suggested that there is a 57% error rate with bank processing and 85% of these errors are in the bank's favour. If the bank makes a mistake, chase them up to correct it and waive unnecessary fees.

I find my clients have around $500 per annum of avoidable fees. The worst I have seen was a client incurring $4000 in avoidable fees. This wasn't because the bank was at fault—it was because my client was both time-poor and lazy.

If you have multiple credit cards, you will be paying multiple fees. Look to combine the available credit between credit cards and apply for one card, increasing its limit accordingly. Cancel all other cards to save in bank fees.

REDUCE YOUR LIVING COSTS

The best way to reduce your expenses is go through them one at a time and look for ways to lower the amount you are spending.

Groceries and food

Food wastage tends to be the biggest cost in everyone's grocery budget. Set a budget, write a menu plan, translate this to a shopping list and take a calculator to the supermarket with you. If you struggle to stick to a tight shopping budget, consider shopping online as it allows you to sort by specials. Online shopping for groceries also eliminates the spur-of-the moment items—usually expensive treats—that get thrown into your trolley as you walk the aisles of the supermarket. With online shopping, you will pay a small extra charge for packing and delivery (if required) but this will be more than likely offset by the money you save by not giving in to temptation and purchasing specials.

Here are some more tips for reducing spending on food.

- Cook and pack your own meals, making enough so you can take leftovers to work the following day.
- Reduce the amount of takeaways you consume.
- Buy produce in season—otherwise you end up paying a higher cost because the food is flown in from the other side of the world.
- Buy non-perishable items in bulk.
- Start a vegetable garden, as it can often pay for itself within the first season of produce—not to mention the satisfaction of preserving your own produce. Focus on vegetables that are easy to grow and are prolific, such as tomatoes, spinach, cabbage, herbs, etc.
- Buy non-brand products where you can. Compare the ingredients between the labelled product versus the

non-branded product and, if the ingredients are the same, opt for the supermarket variety.

- Attend local markets to buy fruit and vegetables.
- Do a weekly meal plan and make a shopping list.
- Buy foods on sale, especially meats.
- Consider buying a coffee pot or machine for home. Spending $1 on a coffee from home still saves you $3 or more compared to buying a similar-tasting coffee from a shop.
- Shop online.
- Never shop hungry. Don't shop in the evenings if you can avoid it.
- Families often run out of bread and milk during the week and frequent their local dairy to top up on necessities. Buy what you need each week at the supermarket and freeze part of it. Write the date frozen on the outside of the package.
- Use store points/vouchers towards grocery purchases.

Travel expenses

- Consider public transport as an alternative to driving to work.
- Consider carpooling— your costs can be shared and you get to use the commuter lanes.
- Sell any unused car or vehicle. So many of my clients seem to have a vehicle or motorbike that isn't being used but is still taking up storage space and requiring annual registration. Flick it.
- Keep the tyres on your car inflated properly. Once a month, stop by a local petrol station that offers to check the air pressure on your tyres. Make sure they are filled to the recommended level. Your petrol usage will improve by 1% for every PSI of air you are able to add.

- When petrol was rationed during World War II, a popular slogan was 'Is this trip necessary?' Ask yourself this every time you get in your car.
- Clean oil and a well-maintained engine can save you money.

Energy bills

- Unplug all electrical devices when not in use, as most electric devices will still use a small amount of electricity (called a phantom charge) even when they are not turned on. Of the total energy used to run home electronics, 40% is consumed when the appliances are turned off.
- Turn off all unused power switches. Your hot water cylinder it is likely to be hotter than it needs to be, and will also lose a lot of heat to the environment. This means you use a lot more energy than you realise to keep the water hot. Install an insulation blanket on your cylinder and drop the temperature to 60 degrees.
- Use a programmable thermostat for heaters.
- Stop the drafts by buying a roll of adhesive foam door sealer and close up the cracks.
- Insulate your property.
- Consider investing in ceiling fans, as they reduce the cost of both heating and cooling by circulating the air more efficiently.
- When you leave the room, turn off the light. If you have children, give one the role of being the family 'energy saver'. Their job is to make sure the family is saving as much electricity as possible.
- Wash your clothes in cold water.

Entertainment

- If you are going to the gym less than once a week, cancel your membership.
- Trim back on your Sky package, or consider going TV-free or basic free-to-air for three months. See if your life falls apart.
- Don't always buy books; visit the library.
- Cancel newspaper and magazine subscriptions.
- Any 'habit' such as excessive drinking or smoking needs to be addressed. If you are ready to kick this habit, your wallet will breathe a sigh of relief, not to mention your body as well.

Insurance

- Shop around for commodity-based insurances (home, contents, car, etc).
- Review your life-insurance policies each year to determine if you can lower the coverage. As you age, your life insurance needs should reduce, because you have fewer years to cover. Further, as you kill your mortgage, your life-insurance needs should decrease because you are improving your situation now, not waiting for an insurance policy to right your wrongs on death.

Communications

- Look at getting a prepaid cell phone if you don't use one all that much.
- If you do use your cell phone a lot, look at the features you are paying for and determine if you can trim these back.
- If you do use a cell phone, do you need a landline at home?

- Use Skype as a free way of communicating with friends and family.
- Cancel call waiting or caller ID on your landline.
- Bundle your communication services.
- Know your data usage and choose a plan that best suits this.

Children

- Look to reduce or eliminate organised children's activities.
- Give your kids jobs to do to fill some of their 'twiddling their thumbs' time.
- Buy second-hand school uniforms and clothes.
- Bake, instead of buying, snacks.

Household costs

- Live small, with just the basics. Think back to what it was like when you were a student or starting out working, when it was OK to just survive rather than having a life full of stuff.
- Eliminate the cleaner, or cut back their frequency from weekly to fortnightly. Better yet, get your kids to do some of the cleaning work in exchange for pocket money.
- If you give to your local church but are struggling to maintain the encouraged levels, speak to the leader of your religious group and explain that you would like to give in time instead of money for a period, while you get your house in order.
- Save water, save money. Invest in a shower-reduction kit. These kits work by reducing the flow of water to the showerhead, meaning you use a little less water, although the change is barely noticeable to the occupant. Better yet, time your showers.

- Repair leaky toilets and faucets.
- Reduce your garden watering to a minimum.
- If you have a pool, keep it covered when it is not in use to reduce evaporation. Invest in a thermal blanket.
- When brushing your teeth, turn off the tap when you are not using it.
- Use the microwave more than the oven where possible, as the cost just to preheat your oven is more than it costs to use the microwave.
- Stop using paper napkins and paper towels. Cloth towels are absorbent and can be used repeatedly. Cloth napkins can be made from old tablecloths and clean better than paper ones do.
- Limit alcohol consumption.

Clothes and grooming

- If you know you spend a chunk of your money on clothes, aim to reduce this spending by 50%. Not surprisingly, spending on clothes is one of the largest cost categories for females. I had one client who spent $60,000 a year on clothes. This is not a worry if you are earning more than a million dollars a year, but if you aren't then that is an extraordinary amount of wastage that would suggest some other issues are in play.

GIFTS TO ASK FOR

It is frustrating that if you want to reduce your daily costs you will initially need to outlay money to help save money in the future. To minimise this initial outlay, consider asking for some of the following as gifts so you don't have to waste your own money on them.

- If you are an avid magazine reader, ask for a magazine subscription.

- If you are a bookworm, ask for an e-reader, so your books cost less.
- If you are a foodie, ask for help setting up a vegetable garden.
- For caffeine addicts, ask for a good-quality coffee machine, so your daily coffee costs you $1 per cup instead of $5.

DO YOUR TAX RETURN

If you have worked for part of year, made a donation, paid school fees or have income-protection insurance, you are likely to be due a tax refund.

> **Tip:** Do it yourself. Tax-refund companies take a cut of what you get back and file the return whether you are due a tax refund or not. What this means is that a lot of unassuming people are hit with a tax bill that they would never have had to pay if the tax return had not been filed.

TAKE ADVANTAGE OF OPPORTUNITIES

Part of managing money when you're broke is increasing your income. For example, you might be able to:
- sell stuff
- get a better-paying job or ask for a pay rise (see Chapter 7)
- get a second job or additional income.

These options aren't available to everyone. But ultimately it's about being resourceful. Look for opportunities to earn more and save more money, then seize those opportunities. Sometimes they might look more like sacrifices in the short term but be brave.

Sell stuff

If you have assets but are income poor, consider selling things you don't need or use in order to liquidate funds and repay debt or create a buffer. For every new thing you buy, try to sell the old one.

> **Tip:** Sell any asset that is not being used but has a holding cost—for example, an unused car.

Get a better-paying job or ask for a pay rise

See Chapter 7 for more on this.

Get a second job or income

Getting a second job sounds intense, but it can be an effective way of propping up your income. Babysitting, mystery shopping, gardening, cleaning and dog walking are all examples of 'extra' income that can be earned without specialist training. I have had some clients pack supermarket shops at night in order to supplement their income. This works for people who have time. If you are time poor, then the easiest way to supplement your income is by getting a boarder or flatmate to share your accommodation costs. This income tends to be tax free.

International schools are often looking for homes for their students, and will pay up to $250 per week per student. Even if you had a student guest for only six months of the school year, this is $5000 of tax-free income.

Tip: You need to have time for a second job, whether it is evenings or weekends. But small amounts of income add up.

I have found that all of my clients are prepared to go through a little bit of pain provided it is going to get them where they want to be and they have a plan for how they are going to get there. Anyone can handle a little discomfort if you know how long it will last. What people can't handle is ongoing pain or inconvenience without any gain.

Come up with a plan. Set small milestones. Seize opportunities. Overall, this will help you to take control. Once you do, you might be surprised at what you can accomplish.

Chapter 7

Negotiating a pay rise

For most of us, the idea of asking for a pay rise is really challenging. Women are especially reluctant and are the first to accept less than their value, often because the fear that 'pushing your case' (in the exact same way a male might) could be perceived as being bossy or demanding.

However, a universal barrier to getting a pay rise is *not knowing how to ask*. It is easy for me to tell my clients to earn more money, but advising them *how* to do this is something I have had to research in order to provide some constructive advice.

Some of my clients, usually female, take the view that you shouldn't have to ask for a pay rise; if your employer values you, they will give you a pay rise without you having to ask.

In some instances this may be the case. But, for the vast majority, this is a naïve view. If the system was going to do right by you, then women wouldn't be paid up to 25% less to do the same jobs as men. Managers are often too busy doing their own work—and ensuring *they* get a raise—to give too much thought to you.

Salary negotiations (like most negotiations) can be difficult, are usually handled poorly and can cause uncertainty and disappointment. Knowing how to ask for a pay rise is a learned skill; and, actually, asking itself is a life skill—and one that less than half of us have. As a poll taken in the UK found, more than half of those surveyed had *never* asked their boss for more money, with the most common reason being fear of damaging their relationship with their employer or becoming the first to go in the event of a restructure.

For many of us, part of managing money well is increasing our income. Just because you feel uncomfortable, don't be afraid to ask for more. Before you ask, though, it is important you look before you leap, by researching the job market and knowing your industry, otherwise you are likely to end up disappointed.

Wanting, asking and getting are three different components of the pay-rise process. Understanding each component will increase your chances of getting what you deserve.

I asked one client when she had had her last pay rise. It was three years ago. I asked where her salary sat in terms of the market average. She confirmed she was towards the top of the band but was demoralised that her manager would not give her a performance review, much less a pay rise, despite her asking repeatedly for a review. Her response was to stop asking and just get on with the job.

This can be a valid short-term plan, but taking this path means your job satisfaction will drop over time, as you will not be able to help feeling undervalued and unappreciated.

I guess it would be natural to start looking for other employment in this situation, but since my client was at the top of her salary band all the other jobs she looked at paid $10,000 less than what she was currently on. Her financial plan didn't allow her to take a pay cut this big—or, more accurately, if she were to take this cut she would need to know how long it would be before she would be back on her current salary. No prospective recruiter could answer this satisfactorily, so again she felt stuck in her current job.

When I started working with her to improve her overall finances, I said she needed to speak to her boss about having a pay review. In fact, this became one of the pieces of homework I assigned her.

To be expected, she felt this was an uphill battle. So together we wrote an email for her to send to her HR department. We spelled out her case as to why she needed and deserved the pay rise. She sent the email and was then called to a meeting.

At the meeting she was able to communicate her case—reiterating the points of the email, which acted as her agenda. She tried hard not to treat the result of the meeting as a foregone conclusion. She felt sick beforehand, during and after the meeting. But she got the pay rise, and it was backdated two years! All she had needed was the confidence to ask.

In my opinion, actually getting a pay rise is of less conse-quence than sticking up for yourself or making the effort to stand up and be heard. The worst that could have happened for my client was that she remained on her current salary. But the exercise of asking for a pay rise was a great means of showing that she thought she did a good job and deserved to be paid more for her work or to be shown the areas her manager wanted her to work on in order to receive a pay rise.

Tip: Not all pay reviews result in a pay rise. Ask your employer what you need to do to get a pay rise. Ask how long it will be before the next review.

In the last few years, there has been a salary freeze in a lot of industries. This has meant that salaries have not kept up with inflation. At a minimum, your pay should be keeping up with inflation. Asking for your pay to be increased each year in line with inflation is not the same as asking for a pay rise, so don't make it a bigger deal than what it is.

For example, if you are on a $70,000 salary then this should be increasing by around $2000 each year to keep you on the same after-inflation income. *Employers should be increasing your pay in line with inflation.* This is a necessary pay increase, and should not be considered a pay rise. A pay rise is when you receive an increase *above the rate of inflation* for your current role.

If a straight pay rise is out of the question, consider asking to take on the extra work and responsibility linked to a pay rise, or ask for a performance-related bonus.

Ask what you can do to move up to the next rung on the ladder. If you feel undervalued, say so—and ask what you can do to increase both your contribution and your remuneration.

THINGS TO REMEMBER

- In most situations, it's easier for your employer to keep you happy than it is to recruit someone else to take your role.
- Know your worth. What is the market paying for your role? Speak to recruiters to get a sense of what the market is offering and look on different job websites. How much would it cost the company to replace you (in both recruitment and training)?
- Make sure you have leverage. Getting a pay rise without leverage is hard to do. The most effective form of leverage is another job offer, that pays more than you are currently getting. (You may be called on this, so make sure the offer is real.)
- Know the difference between the value of the role and *your value,* and don't confuse them. If you are not getting a pay rise it could be because your employer is putting restrictions on the value of the role. Most roles have a ceiling remuneration. Remember, it's easy to believe you

are worth more, especially if you feel like you're giving 150% every day, but you need to be able to demonstrate this objectively by assessing your worth against others in the same industry. Many employers don't give a raise until the employee is doing 20% more work than they did when initially hired.

- Salaries are often dictated by market forces rather than individual abilities.

Not all employers will be in a position to give a pay rise, so find out what else is available. Some things you might ask about include:

- extra training
- education
- professional development
- increased KiwiSaver contribution
- finishing work 30 minutes earlier
- doing your job in four days, but being paid for five
- a bonus scheme, based on you delivering your objectives and then being paid at a later date.

Note: Many managers are paid to keep the salaries of their staff at a certain level.

BUILDING YOUR CASE—THE PREP WORK

A key factor is knowing *when* to ask for a pay rise. This will either be set out in the company manual, and is usually on your job anniversary or at a set time every year If your company doesn't have a manual—or, worse yet, has one but doesn't follow it—then know that budgets are set a couple of months before the start of the next financial year. These budgets typically include funds allocated for increased staff numbers and pay rises for existing staff.

Remember, just because you want a pay rise and you feel like you deserve one doesn't mean that you should or will get one. Asking for a raise is about building a case, not simply making a request. It is up to you to build a case to persuade your employer or manager that you are worth it.

Your case needs to focus on the areas that are important to your employer and demonstrate that you are making their life better by having you.

It is important to realise that your performance is only one of the key factors influencing a pay increase. The performance of the economy, the company as a whole and your overall department will also have a significant influence, and usually a more far-reaching effect than your performance in isolation.

Furthermore, the strength of the talent market is crucial. What are people in your position being paid elsewhere? Is there a shortage of supply, and what would the company need to pay to replace you (in terms of recruitment and training)?

Review your work history and prepare a list of your accomplishments. Arm yourself with evidence, which can include when you had your last pay rise, the length of time you have been with the organisation, above-average performance reviews (where relevant) and salary surveys (contact your industry association). Be sure to use accurate performance measures, not subjective opinions, to prepare a list of your accomplishments. Consider how your input and general performance has improved quality and increased customer satisfaction, raised staff morale and, perhaps most importantly (in your employer's eyes especially), contributed to a growth in profitability.

Pay particular attention to projects you have worked on and problems you have solved. Consider how the business's operation and profits have improved since you started working there. How can you demonstrate that you have done more than you were expected to do, as your employer will argue that you are already paid to do your job well? The most effective measure of anyone's contribution is how it affects the profit, the bottom line.

Think about the following things.

- Do you work overtime to get the job done?
- Do you take the initiative? List the ways you can demonstrate this.
- Have you saved the company time or money?
- Have you empowered your team to be stronger?
- Are you managing more people than you were originally employed to?
- Have you completed or helped to complete a tough project and got positive results from it?
- Have you completed tasks outside your job descriptions, or gone above and beyond the call of duty?

Tip: Print off your job description then list any additional duties you have completed outside of the list.

Decide how much of a pay rise you want. It is important in all negotiations to appear both reasonable and realistic (not greedy). The common tactic of starting high with the view of negotiating down doesn't tend to work well in pay negotiations, as it can be viewed as taking the mickey.

Remember, some of the best pay rises are tools to help you jump ahead professionally, both within the business and on your wider career path. Be open to taking on other things in lieu of money that may be more valuable in the future, for example, shares in the company, a wardrobe allowance, a company car, professional development or external training.

Even if your requested pay rise is reasonable, expect to negotiate further with your boss.

Tip: Always have realistic expectations and put yourself in your boss's shoes. How do you think they would view this salary-increase request?

Before you have a chat with your employer, always make an appointment. Set time aside. This is important, and it deserves to be more than a water-cooler conversation. Your boss may not be expecting this conversation, so ask to speak with them in private and say that you would like to make a meeting to review your role.

Many of my clients get stage fright at this point. If you find this too hard, you might say, 'Can we please meet to discuss my role and ongoing development? I would like your feedback and advice.'

Avoid mentioning anything to do with salary, reviews or pay increases. If prodded say it is a personal matter, or that you want to present a proposition.

Tip: Avoid making the meeting request on a Monday or a Friday. Also avoid having the actual meeting on these days. Most likely your boss will be busy getting ready for the week on Monday, and thinking about the weekend on Friday.

Once you have an agreed appointment, and depending on your relationship with your boss, you could email them your pitch ahead of time to give them a chance to digest it. For some people this takes the awkward part out of the meeting. If you know your boss won't read the email or feel that the in-person version is the best way forward, then be brave and do just that.

HAVING THE MEETING AND MAKING THE PITCH

Once you have done the prep work, it's time to do the asking. It is not until you ask that you will know where you are placed in your employer's perspective, and what you need to do to earn what you want.

In any meeting of negotiation, present yourself well. Stay positive. Be confident, but not arrogant (sometimes this line is easily blurred). Remember, while the meeting is unlikely to be in your office, you are the one who has requested it so in a way you are the host. Run the meeting as follows.

- Start by saying how much you enjoy your job
- Lead into discussion of your achievements
- Tell your boss what percentage increase in pay you would like. Never just say 'I want a raise'. Be specific and demonstrate that you have thought things through. Incorporate market standards or job comparisons. It is up to you to demonstrate that you are worth it
- *Never* mention that your personal situation has changed and therefore you need to be paid more. What happens at home has nothing to do with your reasons for a pay rise, and it is insulting to your employer to lump them with the responsibility of having to pay you more because of this
- *Never* say you are broke. You get a pay rise because you deserve it. Your employer is not a charity

Record the reasons justifying a pay rise in a written document that can be given to your manager to make their job easier if they need to get sign-off from someone higher up the chain.

The meeting can result in one of three responses from your boss.

1. 'No.'

2. 'I need to think about it' or 'I need sign-off from someone higher.'

3. 'Yes.'

No matter what the outcome, thank your boss for taking the time to have the meeting. Follow this up with an email reiterating the findings of the meeting and thanking them again.

HOW TO HANDLE THE MEETING WHEN THE ANSWER IS 'NO'

Never take it personally. If you let the rejection affect your work then your boss will feel justified in their decision. Remember, in reality there is no such thing as 'no'; it is actually a 'not yet'.

It is important to understand the reasons why you are not getting the raise and consider them carefully. Is it because the company cannot afford it, or is there no room in the budget? Discuss non-cash ways the company may be able to reimburse you for your efforts in lieu of a pay rise.

If the answer is no because your employer doesn't think you deserve it, then you need to find out what you can do to achieve a different outcome. Is it about taking on extra responsibilities? Determine how long you will need to take on the extra responsibility before you receive another pay review.

Determine whether the feedback from your employer is fair and right. Are their review points reasonable and the expectation of what needs to be done to get the pay rise achievable? Speak to colleagues and get their feedback.

Tip: At the very least, you should be entitled to a pay rise in line with the CPI (Consumer Price Index), otherwise you are effectively taking a pay cut. Your employer will need to have a very good reason why this cannot be achieved immediately, and this could be a warning about the viability of the business going forward.

If you are instructed to take on more responsibility or duties in order to justify a pay rise, then agree to a time that your pay can be reviewed again to reflect the extra duties entailed. This should be no later than six months away.

Beware if you are given extra duties with no offer of a pay or performance review. To arrange a discussion about an issue like this, write a basic email to your boss to thank them for the increase in responsibility, which is something you welcome. Say that, while you acknowledge this opportunity, you would still like to review your objectives, future development and rewards, along with other opportunities you wish to be offered.

WHAT TO DO IF YOUR BOSS IS NOT THE ONE WHO ACTUALLY SIGNS OFF ON THE RAISE

Unless you are working in a small company, you hold a senior position or your boss is the CEO, it is likely that your immediate boss will not have the jurisdiction to agree on a salary increase on the spot (if at all). In this case it is important that you gain agreement in principle with the case you are presenting. Having prepared a written report will help your boss to communicate the salient points to the higher powers. Make it as easy as possible for them to go into bat for you.

THE VALUE OF YOU VERSUS THE VALUE OF THE ROLE

It is important to recognise the difference between the value of the role and your own value. *The value of a role does not always directly relate to the value of you as a person.* If an employer is unable to give you a pay rise, it may be because the role you fulfil in the company has a salary cap on it. If you find there is a big gap between your expectations of what the role should pay and what you are receiving then it's time to find a role which commands a higher value and corresponding salary.

The best time to negotiate a pay increase is when you are starting a new job. You will have the greatest advantage after you have received the job offer and before you accept the role.

WHAT TO DO WHEN YOUR ROLE HAS A PAY CEILING

If the position you have trained for does not pay enough, and the market agrees with this—that is, no matter where you work there is a salary ceiling on that position—it's time for you to think about your options to earn more money. Some options are:

- take on a boarder
- take on a flatmate
- retrain.

You need to take control of your career trajectory. It is no longer sufficient to sit in a job and not progress financially or professionally.

Chapter 8

Money, relationships and being happy

The role money plays in relationships can make getting ahead a challenge. Not surprisingly, studies have found that starting a relationship with consumer debt has a negative impact on the level of relationship quality. Mismatched money personalities and unaligned financial goals can also play havoc with any relationship, causing arguments, frustration and lack of sleep.

While sleep deprivation can magnify any vexation, arguments around money still tend to be longer and more intense than other types of marital disagreements. Perhaps most disturbingly, research has found that couples who argue about money early in their relationship—regardless of their income or net worth—are at greater risk of divorce.

Financial honesty is hard to come by in couples. A 2011 US study that interviewed 949 adults between the ages of 25 and 55 in committed relationships (married, engaged or de facto) found that 40% prioritised financial honesty higher than honesty about fidelity. This was up from 24% when the same survey had been completed six years earlier. Despite the growing significance of financial fidelity, almost 30% of those surveyed admitted they had withheld information on their own spending or salary from their spouse.

The survey also reiterated the disconnect between beliefs and actions around money. It found that over 90% of those surveyed agreed on the importance of discussing and understanding each other's financial history before the relationship became serious, yet over 25% tended to avoid the topic completely!

Less than half of us discuss our finances openly with our prospective spouse before committing to the relationship. So it is no surprise that, of all the causes of relationship breakdown, the leading one tends to be financial issues. While it is not particularly sexy to discuss money when starting a relationship, if you want to avoid nasty financial surprises and possible financial losses, be prepared to ask the hard questions up front. At the very least, notice if your new partner shies away from conversations about finances early on in the relationship.

Find out if they are a natural shopper or saver, and if they tend to make purchases with cash or credit. Find out if your potential partner has a history of debt, bankruptcy or outstanding financial obligations. Do they save money? What are their financial goals?

A number of my clients cite relationship disagreements as one of the obstacles they face to getting ahead. This in itself need not be a barrier to financial success provided both partners are committed to the same financial goals and are prepared to do something about it. The fact that they are speaking with me and prepared to have some honest and confronting conversations about money, including the role money plays in their relationship, suggests they are ready to do something—otherwise why you put yourself through the pain?

While the statistics are compelling, money does not have to wreck your relationship. The journeys differ, but I know of many challenged relationships where the partners have successfully worked through their issues.

The reason money causes so many relationship fatalities is due to the emotion around it. It mirrors the emotion around being overweight. It is a super-sensitive topic that can cause offence and anger if it's not navigated carefully.

Personally, I think it's better to receive a tough message from someone outside of your intimate relationship if it relates to your own behaviour, so that you don't blame your partner. I think of my personal trainer. I keep a food diary; she reviews it. If I need to improve, she tells me. I take it on board. In fact, I *pay* her tell me what to do, even if I *know* what it is I am supposed to do. I pay her to make me do it and to tell me things I don't want to hear. However, if my husband said the same things, delivered in the same way, I would be likely to be offended and dismissive. In this example, I don't want to be accountable to my partner about my weight and fitness goals. This is not a dynamic I want within my relationship.

Money is the same. People are prepared to do the right thing and are happy to be accountable to something or someone, but it is usually best if it that someone is an expert and independent, someone who can motivate you and keep you on point. Being corrected by your partner, no matter how constructively, is not usually an effective way of growing a relationship.

WHAT MAKES A SHOPPER?

Your attitude to money is formed by your background, experiences and psychological makeup. Your partner will have their own experiences and spending psychology. How do you engage financially? You need to first understand your own personality and then your partner's.

This is especially true if you are a shopper. When I ask what has triggered my clients to be shoppers, the answers vary. Some grew up in a financially dysfunctional family and they are simply mimicking their parents. Others had parents that budgeted well, but they never spoke about money honestly and so the skill of managing it was never passed down. Some have been over-indulged by their parents and partners, so they continue the overspending. Some have had good financial role models and for a while managed themselves to save but, over time, perhaps with excess commitments or time constraints, they replaced good habits with bad. Partners can also lead you astray. Many a good budgeter has been persuaded to loosen their purse strings by a more casual partner. Some just need a compelling reason *not* to spend.

The less obvious reasons for being a shopper can include low self-esteem, avoidance, a need for instant gratification or even self-medicating for depression. Some become shoppers because a component of their life is out of balance.

There is another tranche of shoppers more serious than the rest: the compulsive shopper or compulsive debtor. Although society tends to use the phrase loosely, a compulsive shopper has a serious disorder and shopping is their addiction.

If you are a compulsive shopper, you have a chronic tendency to purchase products far in excess of your needs or resources. Spending money on a particular good or service after making a decision not to, or not wanting to but doing it anyway, are other examples of compulsive spending.

One of the characteristics of a compulsive debtor is 'terminal vagueness', or a systematic avoidance of tracking spending and a reluctance to speak with creditors. This more often than not leads to an exaggeration of account balances.

Co-dependent debtors incur debt to pay for another person's compulsive spending. Not wanting to see their loved one in financial ruin, they step in and clear the slate. This action, although laced with love, enables the same addictive behaviour to continue.

I have only worked with two clients who have had this degree of compulsion. Extreme measures were taken to save them from themselves. One was single, the other married. The marriage didn't last, as the pressure of living with a compulsive debtor is much the same as living with someone with any other disorder, like alcoholism: it is all-consuming, with each day lived without succumbing to their addiction a day fought bravely, but a constant battle nonetheless.

While some researchers have likened compulsive buying to an addiction, the key difference between compulsive buying and other addictions is that it is largely condoned by society. Consumption fuels our economy. Our leaders do not encourage us to go out and take drugs and drink to deal with the stress of modern life, but we are often told to go out and shop.

Instant gratification is a killer. We want what we want, we have to have it now and the media tells us we *deserve* it now. We are becoming a society of short-term hedonists, spending money we don't have on things we don't need. Many of these extra or ad hoc purchases may give us a quick fix, but this is often followed by a much longer-lasting sense of dread or guilt soon after the purchase has been made. Such decisions can in fact lead to reduced happiness. Research has also shown that more materialistic people are less happy and have poorer psychological health and emotional wellbeing.

Tip: If a loved one is in trouble financially, encourage them to get help.

Chapter 9

The property ladder

If you are serious about getting ahead in New Zealand, you need to be on the property ladder. However, owning a property and being on the property ladder are not one and same thing, and this seems to confuse people.

To be on the property ladder, you do need to own a property, but, equally importantly, *the property needs to be increasing in value over time at a rate higher than inflation*. This means that some properties in small towns, low socio-economic or rural areas might not constitute a property investment in the strictest sense of the word. In fact, you would only buy in these areas if a) you needed to be based in that specific area for personal reasons, and b) you couldn't rent the same place for less.

For most of us, the first property we will buy will be our home. If it's in Auckland, it will probably be in an area that is going up in value, so by default you will have taken a step onto the property ladder, even if you are still at the bottom rung.

For you, it might be that living in your own home isn't necessarily the be-all and end-all. In fact, you are just as happy to rent somewhere nice and own a rental property. This tends to make more financial sense, although the average Kiwi struggles with this logic.

A few years ago, you could buy your own home with a 5% deposit and to buy a rental property you needed a 20% deposit. This meant it was usually easier to buy your own home first, because you didn't have to save as much to satisfy the bank and you could get on the ladder quicker. Then the Reserve Bank changed the lending rules, in a bid to slow the property market, and then they changed them again. Bank lending will soon be capped to 80% for all properties, with the exception of new properties (where they may lend more), or existing investment properties in Auckland, where they will lend up to 70% of the property's value. This means that whether you are buying a home or a new investment property outside of Auckland, you will need a 20% deposit. If you are in Auckland, you will need a 20% deposit to buy a home or a 'new' investment property, or a 30% deposit if the property is not new. The main difference between buying a home or an investment property comes down to the level of KiwiSaver you can access, if any.

If you have been a member of KiwiSaver for at least three years, you may be able to withdraw all, or part of your savings to put towards buying your first property. The assumption with this withdrawal, is that you leave the $1,000 kick-start (from when you first joined KiwiSaver) and you will live in the property for at least six months.

With the lower deposit thresholds for home buyers now removed, I encourage first time buyers to consider buying an investment property over a home. The exception to this rule is if you can access your KiwiSaver, and the accessing of KiwiSaver creates a significant difference in your deposit levels, to the point of becoming the difference between you being able to buy the property, or not. In the instance you do access your KiwiSaver, you will have to live in the property for six months, and then consider converting that property into an investment property. Yes this will mean that you will have higher moving costs and may lose the property that you were renting (if renting), but in most instances the ongoing gains of owning an investment property versus a home will far outweigh any of the one-off moving costs. In most cases, continuing to rent, board or live at home and buying a property to rent out (even if it is six months later) is usually the better financial option, provided you buy the right type of property. You will incur the same property costs whether it is a home or a rental property (e.g. rates, insurance, maintenance), but the three key differences between a rental property and a home are:

- the costs of an investment property are tax deductible
- you are less likely to pay more for the property than it's worth, because you are not making an emotional purchase
- you are less likely to over-capitalise on the investment over time, for the same reason.

SHOULD YOU OWN YOUR OWN HOME OR RENT?

It's often said that paying rent is the same as paying someone else's mortgage (i.e. the landlord's), and that you are better off owning the property and paying your own mortgage instead. Like most financial ideas there is some truth in this, but taken in its simplest interpretation it is downright misleading.

The nicer the suburb you live in, you can usually assume that it would be cheaper to rent the property you live in than to own it and pay the mortgage. This is because *property yields* (the rent charged proportionate to the value of the property) tends to reduce as the property's value increases. If you live in a super-expensive part of town, you will pay more rent than in a cheaper part of town, but the rent you pay as a percentage of the property value tends to reduce.

Rent as a proportion of property price is called the 'rental yield' (to work out the rental yield of a property, divide the annual rent received by the property value). As a rule, expensive properties have a low rental yield and cheap properties tend to have a high rental yield. This is the difference between a *cashflow property*, for which you can charge good rent even though the property value is low (see page 96), and a *capital gain property*, which tends to be negatively geared (meaning it produces insufficient income to cover the costs related to it, whether mortgage or running costs, and requires a 'top-up' from the owner in order to cover the outgoings). For the same reason, buying a super-expensive property as an investment doesn't always pay; being the one renting this property does.

I am not saying that you shouldn't own a property. Quite the opposite. For the most part, owning a property (provided it is a good one) makes financial sense. The latest round of government valuations is testament to this, as very few of us could have saved the capital gain that our properties have earned.

Recognising this, why shouldn't you own your own home? The answer is not that you *shouldn't* own your own home, but that you need to recognise that there are *cheaper ways for you to live in a property than being the owner of the property*.

Let me elaborate. The higher a property's value, the lower the rental yield tends to be. What a property can rent for and what it can sell for are two very different things. For example, you can rent a three-bedroom house in Ellerslie, Auckland for $750 per week. This same property is valued at $850,000. A three-bedroom property in Mission Bay is worth $1.2 million and it rents for $900 per week. So, yes, the rent is higher on the Mission Bay property, but only by $150 per week, or 20%, yet the property value is 41% higher. In this example, the rent has not kept pace with the increase in property value.

The Mission Bay landlord is prepared to pay an extra $21,000 per annum in interest costs to buy the more expensive property, and for this extra cost they are going to receive $7800 more rent. However, the increase in rent does not come close to covering the higher interest costs (and other costs) the Mission Bay landlord will face in acquiring a property and mortgage $350,000 more expensive than their Ellerslie counterpart.

(As a side note, there can still be legitimate reasons why someone might buy an investment property in Mission Bay or a similar suburb, where the rents don't keep pace with the property values but where the owner's cash position is so strong they can justify the top-ups. Also, the above example does not take into account the capital gains made when the properties are sold.)

In this example, the financial gain sits squarely with the tenant. Because properties have increased in value, not only do home buyers need a larger deposit, but they also need to borrow more money from the bank, which also means more interest being paid back to the lender. As the tenant living in the Mission Bay property, you are paying $150 per week more than the tenant in Ellerslie, *but your landlord is having to pay $400 per week more to the bank in interest alone*. The saying that your rent is paying off the landlord's mortgage doesn't come *close* to being true in this example. Your rent payment is simply a gesture to the higher interest your landlord is paying to the bank; the landlord is not even chipping away at the mortgage with the rent you are paying.

The underlying assumption with the rent-versus-buy argument is that you could rent for less than the mortgage outgoings would be. And, while this is usually the case, there are examples where it might not be. Certainly if you could own your home and your mortgage payments were less than the rent you would have to pay as a tenant of the same property, then it might make financial sense to own a property, live in it and pay the mortgage.

This type of property is called a *cashflow property*—where the potential rental income outweighs the mortgage costs of the property. Some city apartments or properties in lower socio-economic areas might be an example of this type of investment. Cashflow properties don't tend to experience high capital gains. For the most part it is the capital gains that create the wealth for property investors, so without this you might need to question whether purchasing this type of property is a sensible idea in the first place (again, there can be exceptions to this).

The benefits of being a tenant extend beyond the rent paid. A tenant doesn't need to waste their weekend and wallet on repairs and maintenance; a phone call to the landlord will take care of it. There are no council rates or insurance costs to pay or the threat of higher interest rates to affect you. These extra costs alone can easily amount to $10,000 per annum, sometimes more. Sure, these costs are tax deductible for the landlord, but that simply means that they will get *a portion* of the cost back in tax—about 30%. In the example above, the net cost to the landlord would be $7000 per annum. The tax benefits make the cost lower, *but there is still a cost.*

As an investment-property owner it is imperative that you factor in all costs related to property ownership. This includes the more obvious fixed costs, such as rates, insurance, regular maintenance and accounting, but also needs to factor in the less regular maintenance costs like, new roofs and painting.

As I noted initially, I am not against owning a property, but I am against paying through the nose for a property that you could rent for less. I have many clients who can't afford to buy in the area they want to live in for their kids' schooling. My suggestion to them is to rent in that area, taking advantage of the lower rent yields or the fact that rent hasn't increased nearly as fast as property values have.

This recommendation in isolation might improve their cashflow in the sense that their annual rent cost is likely to be lower than their annual interest cost to own a property in the same area, but improved cashflow doesn't necessarily translate to financial progress. For these clients I also encourage them to own an investment property in a different area, with lower-value properties (and a corresponding lower purchase price and interest cost). Maybe even consider buying two. If they buy right, the rental income will go a long way to covering the mortgage.

Yes, there will be additional costs on top of that and it is still probable the property will require a cash top-up by the landlord. But the top-up, even when added to the rent they are paying elsewhere, would still be lower overall than the cost of buying a property in the more expensive area and not having any further investment portfolio.

Renting your home might not satisfy your hankering for DIY home improvements, but it can make good financial sense. You can still own a property, but make sure it is in a good investment area, where the yields are favourable, to allow you to improve your cashflow, neutralise the impact of skyrocketing property prices and still provide you with capital-gain prospects, but at a lower cost.

HOW TO BUY A PROPERTY

Buying a property, whether it is your home or an investment property, is stressful, and not all properties are created equal. It is too easy to end up with a lemon, so make sure you understand the basic buying process.

1. Before you even start looking for a house, you need to think about how much you would like to spend on a property and how much you can borrow. To find out how much the bank will lend you will need to make a formal application to the bank asking for finance. The bank will assess your personal circumstances and make you an offer of finance. The offer they provide is often called a pre-approval or a conditional commitment from the bank to advance you funds to buy a

specific type of property. Your job is to satisfy all the conditions so you can be comfortable the bank will provide you with the necessary funds to acquire your property.

As a minimum, the bank will want to be comfortable that your income is what you say it is, your deposit exists and that you have good bank-account conduct. They will check your credit rating and review your bank statements, checking for undisclosed debts and the number of unarranged overdrafts. Typically they will request:

    a.   three to six months' worth of bank statements (cheque and savings)

    b.   payslips

    c.   credit card statements

    d.   evidence of your deposit.

2.   There is usually an assumption from the bank that the property will be a standalone property made of appropriate construction materials (not plaster) and be worth what you are prepared to pay for it. The pre-approval will always be

Tip: Many people have lousy bank-account conduct. Without realising it, they are in and out of overdraft, incurring unarranged overdraft fees and various bank penalties. One client I worked with incurred $3000 in unarranged overdraft fees or penalties over the course of a year. She earned good money, but these fees highlighted her lack of care and time when it came to managing her personal finances. Despite satisfying all other bank criteria, her account conduct was so poor that we had to show three months of 'good behaviour' before the bank would provide her with a pre-approval to buy.

subject to a specific property and the way you have acquired the property (e.g. auction or tender), whether it says this specifically on the pre-approval or not. This catches many people out, who innocently look at properties thinking that, because the bank has given them a pre-approval, they are in the market to buy any type of property up to the level agreed on the pre-approval.

However, the pre-approval is generic in nature and applies to standard dwellings bought at arm's length. What this means is that if the property is non-standard in the bank's opinion (e.g. leasehold, plaster, apartment, rural or commercial) the pre-approval may not be valid. To avoid disappointment (and stress), always make sure you advise the bank of the specific types of property you are looking at so they can confirm it meets their standard criteria, to give you confidence that you have the bank's backing.

The pre-approval will also assume that you will pay a fair price for the property and that the price paid indicates its value—that is, that you haven't paid too much for it. If you are not buying through the normal selling process then the bank will likely require a registered valuation to determine the property's true value, and the pre-approval will apply against the lower of the purchase price or the registered valuation. For example, you see a house you like that is being sold at auction. You are prepared to pay $600,000 for it, but the registered valuation for the property is $580,000. You have a 20% deposit ($120,000) and a general pre-approval from the bank for $480,000, so you think you are fine. In this instance, however, the bank will loan you 80% of the $580,000, being the lower of the purchase price and registered valuation, or $464,000. You then have a $16,000 shortfall that you need to come up with before settlement.

Banks will usually require a registered valuation for all properties purchased via tender, auction or private sale. If the valuation is lower than what you are prepared to pay, be mindful that the bank will not lend above the valuation, so you could be out of pocket or not be in a position to buy the property at all.

The pre-approval indicates what the bank believes you are capable of repaying based on their very limited understanding of your finances. In too many instances the level of borrowing the bank is prepared to advance and what you can actually afford to repay are two very different beasts. I have seen clients be offered a loan seven times their combined household income. (For example, their household income was $100,000, but the bank offered them a $700,000 loan.) Because the bank was prepared to give it to them, they were prepared to take it, naïvely thinking that if the bank thought they would be able to repay it then they could.

If you need to save for longer before buying, be OK with this. For every $1000 you save, the bank will lend you a further $4000 (based on them back lending you 80% of the property's value).

3. Find out what you can afford to repay based on a higher interest rate than what is being offered. When I am calculating my clients' tolerance to debt levels, I apply a mortgage rate of 7–8%, depending on how long I believe it will take them to repay their proposed mortgage. If I think it will be repaid in less than 10 years, I am comfortable using a 7% interest rate. If it will take longer than 10 years, I apply an 8% interest rate to build in interest-rate fluctuations over time. When determining what you can pay for a home, also be sure to factor in the legal fees, insurances and due-diligence costs.

4. Find out if you qualify for any kick-start initiatives from the government or lenders. For example, if you are buying your

first home, your combined income is less than $120,000 (for one borrower you can have earned $80,000 or less before tax in the last 12 months) and your first home costs $550,000 in Auckland, $450,000 in other major towns or $350,000 in the rest of NZ, many lenders will require only a 10% deposit (not 20%). Your purchase would fall under the Welcome Home Loan scheme for first home buyers.

Similarly, you could qualify for the KiwiSaver HomeStart grant if you have been contributing to KiwiSaver for at least three years and have income levels below $80,000 (individual) or $120,000 (couple). The two HomeStart grants are $1,000 for each year you have been in KiwiSaver (up to $5,000 per person) and buy an existing home. If you are buying a property as a couple, and have a combined income of less than $120,000, then you could receive $5,000 each (up to $10,000 per dwelling). The HomeStart grant doubles to $2,000 per annum (up to $10,000 per person), if you are buying a new property. The house price caps noted above also apply for the HomeStart grant. The grant and Welcome Home Loan scheme are administered by Housing New Zealand.

5. Make a list of what you want in your property. Specifically identify your non-negotiables. Is it proximity to work and amenities, the number of bedrooms, an internal garage, or the amount of work that needs to be done on it? Understand your deal-breakers and don't bother visiting properties that don't fit your list. Other things to consider are:
    *   school zoning
    *   number of bathrooms
    *   ease of access
    *   proximity to public transport
    *   ongoing maintenance requirements
    *   whether the property is stand-alone or attached to another one

- level of privacy
- child-friendliness—is the section fenced?
- is the legal title cross lease or fee simple?

6. Get a lawyer *before* you make an offer to buy a property. A good lawyer will help you with the process and provide you with specific clauses to protect you through the sale process. As a bare minimum they should review the sale and purchase agreement before you sign it.

7. Do your due diligence. This can be quite an arduous and expensive process, as the checks and reports you should have done for each property you are seriously considering can quickly add up in value. I had a client who went to 10 auctions before they were able to successfully buy a property. Each property they were serious about buying required a builder's report and a review from their solicitor. Because the houses were being auctioned, my client also had to get a registered valuation for each property to determine its value for the bank and therefore confirm how much the bank would be prepared to lend. Each property cost in excess of $1000 in reports alone. But due diligence is just that: the diligent thing to do.

   As part of any due diligence you need to make sure you are aware of any issues relating to the title, the building and the property generally. You need to know that any improvements you want to make are allowed to be done, to what extent the building is in need of repair, what land issues you are inheriting and what a fair value for the property is. Risks can be minimised by doing your homework, or engaging professional assistance.

   As a minimum you will need a title search (done by you or your solicitor), a Land Information Memorandum or LIM (by you or your solicitor), a building inspection (by a qualified builder), a registered valuation (by a registered valuer). Too often the simplest of tools to protect you as a buyer are ignored by the impatient, and often ignorant, purchaser. I have seen smart people buy lemons because they were so sick of looking for properties or missing out at auctions that, when they finally found something that they thought would work, they wanted to secure the deal and put in an unconditional offer without doing their due diligence. Making an unconditional offer can be a good strategy, provided you have worked through the conditions beforehand. Making an unconditional offer before doing any due diligence is stupid.

Doing a title search is the most basic of requirements. Make sure the title of your property is not subject to claims (such as Treaty of Waitangi claims) or unusual cross-lease clauses. Your solicitor will be able to obtain the cross-lease agreement, including covenants and rights of way (easements). Covenants may prevent you from doing some subdivisions or building extensions. Find out what you can and can't do on the property and what issues it may be exposed to. You can do a basic title search at www.terranet.co.nz but your solicitor should be doing this for you anyway.

8. Having a building inspection is a must. Unless you are a qualified builder, it always pays to know about the condition of the house you are buying, as the single largest bills relating to your house will be the ongoing maintenance and improvements over time. As a prudent home owner you need to know what you are likely to encounter and when and how much it is going to cost you, both so you are armed with the knowledge and, most importantly, so you can reflect these issues in the price you offer and in the sale and purchase agreement. A builder's report or survey is an inspection by a qualified builder which attempts to identify property defects,

overdue maintenance, inferior building work, gradual deterioration and other issues. It is distinct from a water-tightness report, although basic leaky issues should be addressed.

A building report doesn't guarantee to find everything that could be wrong with the property, because the builder is limited to a visual inspection and will not normally remove wall linings or floorboards. However, they should make an assessment of the building structure, exterior walls, heating, insulation, doors, windows and ceilings. The inspector should highlight work for which a building permit may still be outstanding, although they won't tend to look at the property records held at council (see point 9 on the next page about getting a LIM).

It is important that your inspector is independent of anyone involved in the sale of the house. Get recommendations from friends about who to use.

Some clients prefer to use friends or family members who are builders to do the inspection for them. This can be a cheap way to get a quick understanding of what you are facing with the property and whether it should be ruled out or is worth pursuing further. If you do decide to go ahead and the rest of your due diligence is satisfactory, I would still encourage you to get an arm's-length building review from someone who can give you insurance that covers you in case something goes wrong.

A building inspection can cost between $300 and $1300, depending on the size, location, age, cladding, access and features of the building. They can take between three and four working days to complete, so always allow a minimum of seven working days as part of your due-diligence process to give your inspector sufficient time to do their job well.

If the builder identifies some issues, this needn't stop you from buying the property, but it does arm you with the facts to make a more realistic revised offer or to push some of the issues back to the vendor to fix before you buy the property. Whether you then re-enter negotiations with the seller to reduce the agreed price or whether the seller agrees to remedy the problems themselves, these negotiations will need to be formalised and included in the sale and purchase agreement.

9. Review the LIM for the property. A LIM is an up-to-date document held by the council on your property. It includes the property's history, where it is and the council's involvement with the property over time.

Much like a builder's inspection, a LIM is very helpful in deciding whether the property is worth purchasing. It details whether building permits have been issued, the property's zoning, any restrictions the property has against it, any history of flooding or subsidence and any resource consents issued for proposed developments in the immediate neighbourhood. The LIM will document if the building or site is historic or has any protected trees, and details land features, as the potential for erosion or the possible presence of hazardous substances.

(Note: Installation of septic tanks and gas bottles may be excluded from the LIM as the council is not obliged to keep this information.)

Once you have the LIM, it pays to go through it with your lawyer. Consider how the LIM's findings will impact your enjoyment and intentional use of the property.

A LIM can take 10 days for the council to create, so if the LIM is not provided to you by the real estate agent ensure you allow 15 days' due diligence from the date of signing the sale and purchase agreement to allow sufficient time to source the LIM and review it with your solicitor. A LIM can cost between $150 and $400, depending on the council.

Tip: Councils are legally obliged to hold information relating to the building prior to 1991. For older properties, some council records may be incomplete. Not surprisingly, councils do not accept responsibility for the accuracy or completeness of these records.

10. Look at the council-held property file. Within these files you will find details on any works undertaken on the property, including building consents and what structures have been permitted. The file will note the drainage plan and the location of stormwater and sewer drains. Always look at the flood plain. Be concerned if it has flooded the area in the past 50 years. Compare the theory of the report with what you see in reality. If the physical structure doesn't match the theoretical council records, then you could be inheriting an unpermitted structure at best, or an illegal structure at worst. The most common unpermitted structures include carports, en suites, garages converted to sleep-outs and outdoor areas that have been concreted when they shouldn't have been.

The reason you need to care about this is because your insurance company may not pay out on an insurance claim if the structure was unpermitted. Worse, you could be required by the council to fix it within a specified timeframe or incur a fine or prosecution. If you come across a property that has unconsented works, or consent is not completed, then do your numbers based on what it would cost to put it back to its legal state. If the numbers still work, and the purchase price is low enough to incorporate any additional costs you may incur, then the deal could still work—but sometimes it is easier to walk away. Depending on whether the works were carried out before or after 1992 will determine what needs to be done to remedy the issue with the council.

11. Find out what the property is worth. The best way to do this is via a registered valuation, or by visiting www.qv.co.nz and talking to your real estate agent about what properties are selling for versus the QVs in that area. If you engage a registered valuer, use one independent of the real estate agent's recommendation. A property valuation report costs between $400 and $800.

12. Complete a sale and purchase agreement with your solicitor. In this agreement you build in a negotiation element, in terms of the conditions you include. If you have not already received a builder's report, reviewed the LIM, satisfied the bank's finance conditions and had your solicitor review the deal, you need to put in a conditional offer. Ideally you would give yourself between 10 and 15 days to work through your conditions.

    This offer is then presented to the vendor and they will either accept it or come back to you with changes. This is the counter-signing process. While the vendor may be OK with the conditions, if the price is too low they are likely to cross out your offer and counter-sign with a higher amount. You then have the opportunity to repeat the process, counter-signing their adjusted purchase price or suggesting a lower one of your own. This process can continue until both parties are happy with the set purchase price. At this point the contract is signed by both parties.

    Then the conditional period begins. You have this time to determine if you are happy with the property. During this time the builder's report is completed, the bank finance is confirmed, the LIM is reviewed and other development considerations (like putting in a granny flat or deck) are checked with the council, to make sure that you are in fact able to do what you want to do. Your solicitor will work through each of these conditions with you. If an issue becomes apparent during this process—for example, the building hasn't had its code of compliance issued for a recent renovation, or there are maintenance issues—this becomes a bargaining tool to get the price down further, or to put the onus on the vendor to fix the problem.

Remember, if you are buying at auction, all offers have to be unconditional, so you must have all your ducks in a row before bidding.

13. Once you are happy that all conditions are satisfied, your solicitor will communicate with the vendor's solicitor, confirming that the sale is now unconditional. You are now legally obliged to settle on the property.

14. Take out house insurance for your new property at this point. If something goes wrong with the property between now and settlement, you could be still obliged to settle.

15. Inspect the property before settling to make sure that all the chattels that you agreed on in the sale and purchase agreement remain. The sale and purchase agreement should list the things you want to be included with the property. These chattels do not form part of the structure of the property, so will be excluded unless you specifically request their inclusion. Common chattels include: dishwasher, curtains, rangehood, alarm. Additional chattels you may request to be included could be: rugs, pot plants, fridge, washing machine, table and chairs. If you are unable to negotiate the price, you may want to sweeten the deal for yourself by adding extra chattels without increasing the price—the attraction to the vendor being that the chattels are one less thing to move.

16. Confirm the structure of your borrowings and the entity in which you will be purchasing the property with your bank.

This is discussed in more detail in Chapter 16. I would initially elect a monthly repayment plan, which means the first mortgage payment will come out one month after you have settled and moved into the property. These extra weeks can be a lifeline if you have already stretched yourself financially.

17. Settle and move in.

18. Kill your mortgage!

WHAT IF YOU DON'T HAVE A DEPOSIT?

If you want a property, you need a deposit. This is a barrier to entry for many first home buyers, because they never seem to be able to save enough fast enough.

Banks typically require a 20% deposit before they look at advancing 80% of the purchase price (refer to the Housing New Zealand website www.hnzc.co.nz for how to qualify for a 10% deposit requirement). For many, saving this deposit is too hard and is taking too long, with property prices racing away, especially in Auckland.

It is hard, but it is not impossible. Remember, the world doesn't owe you any favours, and the universe is not necessarily going to make this easy for you. If you are serious about getting on the property ladder, you need to be prepared to suck it up and start moving forward. Wealth comes to those who not only want it but also do something productive about it. When I work with my clients we try to save enough for a deposit within the first 12 months—but we go hard.

If you want to fast-track your deposit saving, look to adopt some of the tips below.

1. Move in with friends or family to drop your lodging outgoings. If you are paying rent of $400 a week, but you could move in with friends for six months and pay

$100 a week, then do this. *But make sure you bank the difference.* Alternatively, get some flatmates in to reduce your outgoings.

2. Cut back on every cost within your budget. Look to save an additional 15% of your income. Take a rain-check on holidays, expensive hobbies and technology purchases.
3. Tell friends and family that this is your objective and how much you need to save. Find out how long it is going to take you to get there. If you don't think you will be able to achieve the goal within 12 months, enlist someone to help you. When working with my clients I make it clear that we only want them to go without if it will mean they can achieve their goals. Too often people think that if they go without they will naturally achieve their goals, but deprivation and financial success have less of a correlation than people realise. If you want to achieve your financial goals you need a plan that is achievable, with measurable progress.
4. Consider house-sitting as a drastic way of reducing your costs. I had one client who did this for 18 months.
5. Sell some of your assets.
6. Work longer and work harder. Look for a second job. When my husband and I were saving for our first home, we were working four jobs between us.
7. Determine how much you will get from KiwiSaver. Investigate your eligibility for the First Home Subsidy and other benefits available to you.
8. Lower your expectations as to what your first home needs to have, and where it needs to be.
9. Consider buying your first property with a friend or family member to lower your deposit requirements. This comes with risks, but I have seen it done successfully.
10. Borrow from your parents' equity to satisfy the bank requirements. This can create real financial benefits for

all parties, but can also be a nightmare to administer if not done correctly. Chapter 28 discusses this in more detail.

If you are serious about getting onto the property ladder, then your first property may need to be an investment property to allow you to leverage the capital growth from this property to get you into an area you prefer. First step: get on the property ladder. Second step: start to climb the ladder.

As I said above, determine if you could have a deposit saved within 12 months. If not, enlist help. Please note that before I work with my clients, I ask them if they are in fact ready to do what is necessary to get them into a property. If they are ready to take control, then I can help them. If they are not, then I explain to them that engaging my services is a waste of money and time.

If you are ready, then you are prepared to delay your life for 12 months and do what is required to achieve your goals. Only you can determine your level of readiness.

Part Two

KILL YOUR MORTGAGE

Chapter 10

Making a start

*Continuous effort—not strength or intelligence—is
the key to unlocking our potential.*
— Winston Churchill

No matter what your starting point—whether you are sinking, floating or flying—you need to have a plan and to begin sorting out your finances and planning for a comfortable retirement now.

To do this, you must be honest. You must understand what you own and what you owe. You need to know exactly how much you earn and what you spend your money on.

Sorting out your finances takes time. If you are time-poor, get someone else to do it for you, but make sure you are accountable for the results. There are no shortcuts.

In order to plan any journey, including managing your money, you must understand the exact distance that needs to be covered, what terrain you are likely to encounter and what the best vehicle will be to get you to your destination.

FOUR BIG QUESTIONS

When starting out on your financial journey, ask yourself the following four questions.

- Where am I financially?
- What potential do I have?
- Where do I want to be?
- What is standing in my way?

Money troubles and denial typically go hand in hand. Refusing to recognise or acknowledge the true situation often causes people to create serious financial issues for themselves. For example, when your bank statement comes in do you open it or do you throw it in a pile to look at later? Do you even know how much money is in your bank account? When was the last time you deposited money into your bank account, not including your pay? Do you even know how much you are paid? If you can't answer these questions you are either hands-off with your finances or in denial about your financial situation.

If you are going to start making progress towards your financial goals, you need to be honest. Leaving everything to your spouse is not delegation; it is shirking your own responsibility. Successful delegation means you still have a handle on things, you know what is happening and why, and you could step in at any point.

While managing the finances is often left to one partner, if you are not both on the same page your progress will be uneventful—if there is any progress at all. Furthermore, the person who is 'carrying the can' often feels stressed or frustrated at their partner's lack of buy-in, leading to conflict or dissatisfaction in the relationship.

Articulating your personal relationship with money and the role of money in your relationship can be stressful for some people, and I must admit that some clients have even been reduced to tears the first time they meet with me.

WORKING TOGETHER

The first time I meet with a client, we set about diagnosing where they are at financially. Part of this process is to ascertain if they are naturally on track to achieve their financial goals. If they are on track, we then spend time establishing whether they can reach their goals faster by doing certain things differently. If they aren't on track, however, I want to find out what might be standing in their way, and what they could be doing to get a different outcome. For most people this first meeting is a pretty full-on but ultimately rewarding experience.

It is compulsory for both partners in a relationship to be at this first meeting, as I think it is important for people go through this process with their partner—I won't work with them otherwise. This is because, in my experience, a spouse not willing to attend this first meeting is usually a key player in the couple's current financial position. Trying to fix the financial landscape without their engagement is like trying to drive a car with a flat tyre—no matter how much energy is put into steering the vehicle, you will continue to be pulled in the wrong direction.

Strangely, at least 10% of new clients are desperate to attend this first meeting by themselves. I have heard all of the reasons you could possibly imagine and then some, including 'I'm the problem, not my spouse', 'My partner has no idea of where things are at—they don't manage the money' and 'My partner doesn't listen to me anyway'. *If you are in a relationship, both you and your partner have contributed to your financial situation.* Therefore you both need to develop new life skills to correct this situation.

If your partner has no idea where things are at, it is time they stood up and started paying attention. Everyone has a moral and social responsibility to know how they are doing financially. Burying your head in the sand is not good enough.

Having both partners at the first meeting gives them each a new understanding of the other and what makes them tick financially. People often incorrectly assume that the spender in the relationship is responsible for their financial demise or lack of progress, but this is only one determining factor. Often the person who is tight on a day-to-day basis decides that when they do want to buy something they will spend 'whatever is needed' to get what they want. Usually it is the spending on big items that creates a problem—not the occasional little treats.

I once had a man visit for a first meeting without his wife because they had a sick child. This was the first time he had truly confronted the state of his finances and he was embarrassed. He earned more than $400,000 per annum and was in a very high-profile job. I emailed a summary of the meeting to the household's joint email address and he called back within five minutes. He asked me to omit certain details of their financial situation from my original email because he didn't want his wife to know the cold, hard truth of their situation.

My reply was, 'You have successfully managed to get your household finances into a mess without your wife being any the wiser. You have had your turn and it didn't work. If you want to fix this situation, you need to do what I say, and that means everything has to be out on the table, because we all need to be on our game to fix your situation.'

In all honesty, I was just as frustrated with his wife, who had happily buried her head in the sand and taken a hands-off approach to their finances, but that was beside the point. Both spouses need to be on the same page, otherwise they are going to have issues.

I did not resend an amended version of my original email. I did, however, send a follow-up email that said no matter how dire their situation seemed it could be fixed, provided they were prepared to do whatever was necessary. If they were, they could be sure of a positive outcome. (You will be pleased to know that they both came to me and got their situation sorted out.)

Although I can understand why people might hesitate to share all the information with their spouse, especially when it makes them look bad, it is a pretty short-sighted approach. Everything comes out in the wash in the end.

Omitting financial details is not uncommon for many couples. Somewhere between 5 and 10% of my clients find out information about their joint finances at their first meeting with me that they were not previously privy to—possibly because they didn't care to ask. This is consistent with data from the US that has showed that 9% of spouses are prepared to keep silent about aspects of their financial situation because knowing about the issue would worry their partner. (You don't say!) Using a circular logic, 7% of respondents said they'd kept something secret because telling their partner would damage their relationship. One has to ask—if in knowing the truth the relationship might be damaged, doesn't that imply it already is?

WORKING OUT YOUR FINANCIAL POSITION

Whether you know all the details of your current financial position or not is irrelevant before starting this exercise. The objective is to know your position *after* you have completed the exercise. Fill in the worksheets in Appendix III to get a snapshot of your current financial position.

Here is the series of questions I ask new clients to get a snapshot of their financial position.
1. What are your tradable assets?
2. What are your liabilities, including your student loan?
3. Do you have any credit card debt?
4. Do you pay off your credit card in full every month?
5. Are you contributing to KiwiSaver?
   — If so, at what rate?

6. Do you have savings?
   — If so, how much?
   — If not, why not?
7. What does your situation feel like?
   — Do you feel in control of your money?
   — Do you feel that you are getting ahead?
8. If you lost your job tomorrow, what would happen to you?
9. Do you have children?
   — If so, how many and how old are they?
   — If not, do you want children?
10. Do you owe tax?
11. Do you own investment properties?
    — If so, are the properties negatively geared or does the rent received cover the mortgage and rates?
12. Is your employment secure?
    — Have you reached your income potential?
    — Are you likely to receive any pay rises or bonuses?
    — How much do you get paid in the hand (going into your bank account) every week, fortnight or month?
13. Are you self-employed?
    — Do you draw a regular wage?
    — Can you put costs through the business?
    — Do your financial statements show income paid to you?
    — Are you paid cash or with contras?
    — Who manages the money?
    — Do you have to juggle things each week?
14. Do you own your own property in a trust? (See Chapter 30.)
    — If not, why not?
15. Who manages the money in your relationship? (If you are in a relationship.)
    — Why?
    — Are you both engaged with your finances?

16. How many bank accounts do you have and how does money flow between them?
17. Do you find it easier to spend or save?
18. What are your non-negotiable costs? For example:
    — Do you have to go on a family holiday each year?
    — Do you want your kids to have swimming lessons?
    — Do you need to buy a flat white every day?
19. Do you think you fritter away your money?

The answers to these questions help to paint a picture of your current financial situation and what obstacles or attitudes are holding you back. Basically, I need new clients to tell me their stories so I can incorporate everything I notice into a workable financial plan for them.

Once we all know where my clients are, they need to understand how they got to that point. Is it because they have frittered away money, paid more tax than necessary, overused their credit card(s), made poor financial decisions in the past, or simply that they need a good plan to stick to? If they've lacked motivation in the past, what will motivate them now? (See Chapter 2 for more on money personalities, common obstacles and money traps.)

Don't judge your spouse's non-negotiables. It will end in tears.

Understanding the nuances of each unique situation is critical when developing a realistic plan to help individuals and partners to achieve the perfect financial balance. All these questions need to be answered honestly before I even begin to look at numbers such as income versus spending. Before I consider people's actual spending I need to know how it feels for them on a day-to-day basis.

Chapter 11

Putting the plan into action

I spend the first four weeks of my relationship with any new client preparing a financial plan. The plan has to be fluid enough to absorb the effects of life's curveballs and unexpected expenses, but also make it possible to get ahead when windfalls happen. Most of all, the plan has to be achievable if it is going to build momentum.

Most people do not know what they are capable of. Looking at bank statements does not define what you *could* do—it simply tells you what you *have done*. I am reluctant to dictate your potential from your bank statements—which is reassuring for many of my clients, who are embarrassed by the state of their spending.

In developing a plan with my clients, we start with a best guess of what they think they can achieve. We need to get all their ducks lined up so that positive results are evident as soon as the plan is put in place. Basically, in the first four weeks of working together, my clients and I tidy up or restructure everything that has previously been an obstacle so that the odds of success are well and truly tipped in their favour.

In addressing obstacles, the best approach is to work out a budget or spending plan to capture the money that has previously been frittered away, restructure bank accounts so that money cannot be inadvertently spent so easily, cancel credit cards and restructure mortgages or business affairs to minimise tax payments going forward. Every decision from this point on is going to have an impact that can be seen and felt.

After the first four weeks, often after I have restructured a client's mortgage and bank accounts, they are in a position to start testing their budget. They then have to draw a line in the sand and suck it up.

After this first four weeks of preparation, every client is chomping at the bit to get started, but they are also often a little scared of what lies ahead. But we're now at the business end of the equation, where results need to be achieved. We need to establish if the plan is doable.

Within every plan it is important you have enough money to do the things that are important to you, otherwise the plan won't work. Once my client is comfortable that the budget is achievable, I explain how things need to work on a day-to-day basis. This is quite detailed, including how much money the client has to spend on a weekly basis to cover weekly costs, such as groceries, takeaways, coffees and petrol. This money is put into a separate account using a weekly automatic payment. They can manage this money as they see fit. I encourage people to use cash, but it is up to my clients to take responsibility to ensure that this money covers their weekly costs. If the money runs out, it runs out, and they need to wait until the next week before it is topped up again. Bills such as electricity, phone and internet, rates and Sky TV, are paid from a separate account to avoid confusing fixed costs with more discretionary weekly expenses.

For the next 12 weeks we track actual spending on the budget, to establish whether the plan is, in fact, sustainable. Twelve weeks is short enough for anyone to commit to, but also a sufficient length of time in which to see a result. The goal is for the client to reach the end of the 12-week period having an awareness of every dollar they have spent, but not to the point where they feel deprived. If they can achieve this, the budget is working and we can all have confidence that it should continue to work.

It is important that progress is tracked to the dollar. If you should have saved $2000 in the first 12 weeks, then this saving needs to be visible.

Consideration needs to be given to any unforeseen or unusual expenses or changes in the next quarter, and new targets are set. Then we repeat the process of tracking and measuring actual results to forecasted capability after another 12-week period.

If clients are on track after the first 12 weeks but their situation feels too 'tight', tweaks are made to the budget to ease the pressure on spending, because if things are feeling tight there is a likelihood that clients will stray from their plan.

For most people, after the first 12 weeks the results speak for themselves. Sure, the plan may need some refinement, but, if they can see the result of their efforts, money is no longer a misunderstood phenomenon; instead, it's something that is understood and under control. Money makes friends with those who stick to the rules, and laughs at those who do not. If you stick to the rules, you will get the result, guaranteed.

My job from here on is to keep my clients on track, refine the plan, keep emotion removed from the process and, at times, to force the results until the client's confidence grows enough to build momentum. I am accountable to the results as much as the client is because I believe that, once the emotion is removed, the results are sure to follow.

If you are not working with me, to keep motivated you need to ensure you are achieving your targets. Set goals, know what you are capable of, and what is and isn't possible. Don't make things too tight. Allow for treats. Understand the timing of one-off costs and how they are going to affect your cashflow. Some months are going to be tighter than others depending when big bills are paid. Plot this; get your head around it. You will feel in control when your money progress is in line with what you expect.

WHERE DO YOU WANT TO BE?

Your financial destination is not just where you want to be but what you want to achieve along the way. The journey can be broken down into short-, medium- and long-term goals that mark the road to your success.

Along the way to a comfortable retirement you may have other more specific goals. Although each person's path will vary, you must keep checking your progress against your road map to ensure you remain on track overall. In the absence of clearly defined goals, people become strangely loyal to performing daily acts of trivia (distractions that ultimately get you nowhere.)

It is not enough to take steps that may, someday, lead to a goal—each step must in itself be a goal and a step in the right direction. Make every step count so that you can achieve the perfect balance, getting ahead as fast as your circumstances allow.

Setting goals

Because a lot of people are intimidated by money, they fail to set goals for themselves and never change their financial outlook.

When encouraging my clients to set goals, or to think about the things they want to achieve, I ask them to list their goals for the next 12 months, the next two to five years, and beyond. The most common goals I find people have are listed below.

Short term: next 12 months	Medium term: next 2–5 years	Long term: next 10+ years
Feel in control of my finances	Replace my car in X years, spending $X	Be mortgage-free
Develop a plan	Renovate my property, spending $X	Save for retirement
Repay short-term and credit card debt		Complete retirement planning
Pay off my mortgage faster	Take a holiday in X years, spending $X	Buy an investment property
Stop living pay-day to pay-day	Buy an investment property	Buy a holiday home
Remove money worries from my relationship	Protect my wealth	Buy a boat
Live a lifestyle I enjoy	Start a family	Take at least six months off work
Know my longer-term goals are in hand	Pay for a wedding	
Buy a property		
Start a family, and go down to one income		
Refinance		

With each client, we ensure that they achieve their immediate goals over the first 12 months and then refine their plan, where necessary, to achieve their medium- and long-term goals faster. The sooner all your goals are achieved, the sooner you can stop working!

ACKNOWLEDGING OBSTACLES

As part of developing a plan for success, you need to identify obstacles that have prevented you from getting ahead in the past. Your general attitude, lack of time and ambivalence towards money or the role money plays in your relationship are all valid obstacles. Until you are aware of your weaknesses and how they create obstacles for you, you will not be able to overcome them.

Common obstacles I find people face include:

- not knowing your financial capability
- not having a compelling enough reason to try
- frittering money away or spending a little bit more than you realise across a lot of expenses
- not knowing where you are going
- having good intentions, but being unable to sustain the results you want
- being on the back foot so you cannot correct any backwards movement
- disagreeing with your partner about money or having a different approach to money from your partner
- owing too much money
- being behind in payments to the IRD and incurring penalties
- having cashflow problems
- having nothing put aside for a rainy day—no savings.

STRATEGIES FOR SUCCESS

The following simple tricks will help you to keep on track to your financial goals.

- Separate out your weekly costs from all other costs.
- Always use cash or EFTPOS—avoid credit cards or finance options, as they usually attract interest penalties.
- Set a budget.

- Track your spending.
- Tweak your budget to make it sustainable.
- Measure your results.
- Have a budget fluid enough to absorb curveballs and the timing of purchases.
- Celebrate progress!

CASE STUDY 1—HIGH DEBTS, NO PROPERTY

Natalie came to me at the age of 28 with high debts and no property. She was on a salary of $65,000 per annum before tax, and had a $47,000 debt from spending on herself. Natalie thought she had a great relationship with her personal banker because she could call her up and ask for an extension on her credit card or personal loan and it would be available to access within 24 hours.

Natalie struggled to repay her debts, so she consolidated and refinanced with another bank, repeating this process twice. Each time she refinanced for slightly more and kept on spending. Her main vice was clothing—she always looked good, but she was going backwards.

She was given a stark reality check when she finally went to a budget advisor and they told her to declare herself bankrupt. She called me and wanted to know what to do. We met and worked through her spending.

For some people, bankruptcy is a legitimate option, although it is not usually the only option. Natalie *wanted* to repay her debts—she felt strongly about them being her responsibility. She didn't want to hide from the consequences of her actions, but she also didn't have the tools to address the problem.

We listed all her expenses and debts. At a push, we could clear her debts within 18 months if she was prepared to commit to a plan. The plan was tight and required very close monitoring to ensure she was making the best possible progress for her circumstances. It was important for her to see results quickly, otherwise she would lose momentum.

After listing every creditor, we prioritised her debts and estimated how much she could afford to repay each one. She then contacted every creditor, explained her situation and started making repayments. Not once did she default—she was ready and determined to sort things out once and for all. As her debts were repaid in order of priority, she had slightly more money to pay the remaining creditors. Whenever a debt was repaid, she contacted the remaining creditors and advised them she could afford to pay them at a higher rate. She kept this up for six months. She became known as the girl who did what she said she was going to do. Instead of seeing her as a bad debtor, her creditors were viewing her more favourably.

Over the first 12 months her income increased slightly and her contract changed to receive commission payments. She asked me what she should do when she received her first commission payment. I told her to call her creditors and ask what they would accept as a full and final payment of their account. Surprisingly, one of her last creditors, to whom she owed $20,000, accepted $10,000 as full and final repayment of their account!

Just 15 months after meeting and starting to work with me, Natalie was debt free and in control of her financial destiny. Now she is saving for a house.

I initially asked Natalie to commit to a strict budget for 12 weeks, to allow us to get some runs on the board. We slashed her clothing budget during this time and I asked her to make do with her existing wardrobe, or massage other costs down to allow her to spend money on clothes if she needed to. She stuck to the plan, though. She was determined. And when she saw the result after 12 weeks she was motivated to keep going (although I did increase her clothing budget after that, as I didn't want her to fall off the wagon and have a clothing-binge attack!).

CASE STUDY 2—BUYING A HOUSE

Roger and Renee were aged 31 and 29 respectively and living in a de facto relationship when they first came to me. Their combined after-tax income was $95,000 per annum. They had savings of $20,000, and although they used credit cards to pay for their lifestyle the bills were all paid in full each month.

They wanted to buy a house, but their savings were not quite enough to enter the housing market. As a result, they had started spending all their income each month and feeling ambivalent towards money.

Renee was the higher earner of the couple, and she was also the spender. By nature, Roger was a saver. They both wanted to become self-employed, but felt that this was not possible because of the likely financial impact. Roger accepted that, because he earned significantly less than Renee, he didn't have a right to question her spending. He felt disempowered as a result.

They wanted a house, but they did not know what they needed to do to actually get the house they wanted or how long it would take. They were fearful that buying a house would mean their lifestyle would be significantly and detrimentally impacted.

After our first meeting, we identified $30,000 per annum that was being spent that didn't need to be. *Many people spend because they have no reason not to.* Roger and Renee soon learned they could live the lifestyle they enjoyed without that money being frittered away. Over the course of the first six months, they saved a further $15,000 and started looking for a property.

After a couple of months of what seemed like endless searching and attending lots of challenging auctions, they still hadn't managed to buy a property, and again became despondent. They lost their focus and decided a trip to New York was just what they needed, so off they went and spent half their house deposit. They loved their trip but on their return realised they still wanted a house!

After that setback we reset the plan. It is important to accept that what has been done is done, and not to bother focusing on what cannot be undone. Too often couples feel aggrieved by their spouse's financial behaviour and focus on this. I see little point: focus on what you can change, and make up the lost ground as quickly as you can.

Six months later, with a concerted effort and a combined pay rise of $15,000, they were even further ahead than when they had left for New York. They purchased their first home for $320,000. They renovated and refurbished it, but these costs had been factored in right at the beginning so there were no financial surprises. When they announced they were getting married the cost of their wedding was factored into the plan too, including the cost of a honeymoon in Thailand.

Roger is now self-employed. Before this transition, they worked to build sufficient headway on their mortgage to mitigate set-up costs and loss of income while he began to build his business. They optimised their mortgage by restructuring it to allow them to get ahead as fast as possible in their new circumstances while they continued to live a lifestyle they enjoy.

A correctly structured mortgage, coupled with a fluid plan, allows you to access your equity as you need it, but still ensures your long-term picture remains rosy. Remember, *a successful plan stretches you to your full potential and also adjusts to changes in circumstances*. If you are waiting for the perfect time to start a plan, it will never come—financial stability is earned not inherited, and the sooner you make a start the sooner it will be assured. Mortgages and plans must never be static.

An initial snapshot of Roger and Renee's mortgage structure showed they could be mortgage free in six years—assuming they had no children. Five years into this plan, they remain on track to be mortgage free within the next 12 months. No children are on the cards, but a home upgrade is likely, which simply means we will refresh the plan, understand what new mortgage we have to work with and then systematically kill it.

When Roger and Renee finally purchased their first house, their lifestyle did not change; we simply replaced rent with mortgage payments and added in costs specifically related to property ownership. Because they had worked on their spending for some time they knew exactly what they needed to spend to have a lifestyle they liked. Without changing their discretionary spending, we simply channelled the surplus funds into repaying their mortgage faster.

Chapter 12

Building up—the next phase

Once you have mastered the art of creating a cash surplus, by working to a budget, you need to use this money to make more money. Creating a cash surplus is step one and probably the hardest of all the steps. Creating enough surplus to make an investment is step two.

To move from the Starting Out phase to the Building Up phase you need to have at least $80,000 of equity, or own a property in a market where values are increasing. The lion's share of the clients who come to me are at this stage—that is, they have their home and they have their mortgage. Most know that they should be paying their mortgage off faster but they struggle to do this as there seems to be no spare cash around to be used to repay debt faster.

To fix this, they need to learn or re-learn the key skill of the Starting Out phase: they need to master the art of creating a cash surplus, and then how to kill their mortgage. This becomes more challenging the older you get and the more you earn. (I tend to find older people are more set in their ways, while people with higher incomes naturally disengage from thinking about their money.)

The short game hinges on creating a sustainable cash surplus, with the medium-term goal of paying off your mortgage faster and the longer game being retirement. For the most part, you will need to be mortgage free by the time you stop working if you are going to have a shot at a comfortable retirement. But, while mortgage-free status is encouraged for retirement, this in isolation won't solve all your problems, as you can't eat your house when you retire— you are going to need more funds from somewhere.

Creating a cash surplus first, buying a property second, then killing the mortgage are the founding principles of a retirement plan. They are not particularly sexy, but they are critical to lasting progress. It is not until you are on the way to killing your mortgage that you can start to consider other strategies in order to get you to retirement, whether it is saving more, buying an investment property, investing in shares or managed funds, or even starting a business. There are many and varied options for growing wealth. What suits you might feel uncomfortable to another, and what one person's financial situation can allow another's might have no tolerance for. You need to understand your options and keep moving forward.

You need to know if you are going to be mortgage free by retirement. If you are not, or are only just, then it is unlikely you will have much time to physically save for retirement, as all your funds and energy will be going into getting your mortgage paid off.

If this is your reality, you have four options: earn more, work for longer, spend less, or borrow against your property to buy another property. *Those are your options. There is no magic dust.* This is what you have to work with.

INVESTMENTS

If you do have some saved funds, or are able to leverage against your property, looking at investment, from managed funds to shares and even property, as an additional source of income is an option.

A lot of financial advisors hate property. This could be because they can't charge a management fee if you buy property, so they make no money! Or it may be because they simply love shares and managed funds (investments on which they *do* earn a living).

Haters are gonna hate, but the reality is that if you have no monetary savings—and most of us don't and won't—then property is your only investment option. This is because property is unique among investment options. It is recognised by the banks as something they are prepared to lend against. You can take the bank's money and buy a productive investment, and, provided the return outweighs the interest rate you are being charged, you can take advantage of the bank's offering for your own gain. (You can also borrow to buy a business and in some instances shares, but the bank will lend you less and the interest rate will be higher.)

I believe shares and managed funds have their place, but the main disincentive of these types of investments is that *you need money to invest in them*. Many Kiwis do not have the money available to consider these types of investments, simply because they are spending everything they earn. While they might own their own home, it most likely has a mortgage against it and there is no spare cash for investment—and, even if they did have cash, I would suggest it went towards paying off their mortgage in the first instance.

Once you have mastered the creation of a cash surplus and have purchased your property, killing your mortgage is the next critical step to creating more options. Once you have no outgoings to the bank for mortgage repayments, your cash surplus will grow faster and you will then have the funds needed to consider all investment options.

There are some common mistakes people make with leverage (borrowing against their own home for investment), which need to be avoided if they are serious about getting ahead, such as structuring their debt incorrectly. Getting it wrong is an unacceptable outcome when your home is exposed.

Whether in the form of a home, investment property, business or shares, you need to be accumulating assets. I favour investment property, KiwiSaver and businesses (if you have the know-how) over a home, shares and managed funds. I understand the logic behind these investment vehicles and have applied it to my personal situation and those of many clients. It is not to say that shares and managed funds are bad investments; owning your home could also be defined as being an unproductive investment, usually costing you more than it should unless you use the equity in your home to your advantage. But shares are a different beast with a mind of their own. If you are experienced, you can make a solid return, but it takes a lot of knowledge and a tolerance for daily updates and an emotional market dictating the value of your investment.

I personally don't have the stomach for shares, though I will later on discuss the advantages of this form of investment, as well as managed funds (see Chapter 23). Property, by comparison, is a tangible investment that you can readily borrow against, insure and get a tax benefit from. These characteristics distinguish it from shares, and mean that, when coupled with the Kiwi hankering towards owning it, property holds a greater attraction.

Owning a business holds its own risks. A staggering 386,000 Kiwis are self-employed—despite high failure rates for start-up enterprises. Almost 45% of self-employed people are over the age of 55. Becoming self-employed holds more attraction as you get older and can be a viable way of keeping yourself in the work-force, when being an employee may no longer be an option.

KiwiSaver is a great option, but in isolation is unlikely to be sufficient in funding a retirement. Nevertheless, if you can afford to be in it, you should. If you are self-employed—so you are the only person making contributions—it is not so critical, but if you are an employee it's a no-brainer.

Remember, it is not the smartest who get ahead, but the bravest. When you are you are trying to get ahead, you can't play not to lose; you have to play to win. It is imperative that you surround yourself with people you can learn from.

> *Opportunity is missed by most people because it is*
> *dressed in overalls and looks like work.*
> *—Thomas Edison*

Chapter 13

The magic of compound interest

Compound interest really is magical. It's said that Albert Einstein once declared it to be the most powerful force in the universe. It consists of putting money into an account and letting it earn interest from that moment on. The interest you then earn on the interest already earned is called compound interest.

Over the short term, compound interest is not all that exciting. But, over longer time periods, the results are impressive and obvious.

Let's say you put $1000 in the bank at 5% interest per annum. At the end of the year you will have $1050. If you leave the entire amount in the bank for another year at the same rate of interest, you will then have $1103. In the second year, not only did you get interest on the original investment, but *you also got interest on the interest you earned the prior year*. This is when compound interest kicks in.

Compound interest is of relevance to anyone leaving their investment to grow over a long period of time. The $1000 investment mentioned above, when invested for 40 years at 5%, will end up being worth over $7000, without you putting in any more money!

The following compound interest chart shows how the future value of an investment grows most spectacularly in the later years. In this example, half of the future value is earned in the last 10 years.

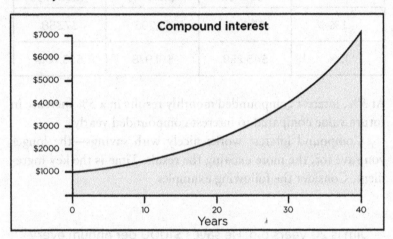

Mortgages follow the same principle, but in reverse. If you commit to the bank's predetermined mortgage length (25 or 30 years), you are not going to start making obvious dents in the loan balance until the last 10 years of the loan.

The longer the term, the more pronounced the effect of interest rates. At first glance it might be tempting to say that the difference between investing at 5% and 6% would not be significant. However, an increase of a single percentage point on an investment can result in a 50% increase in the future value of that investment over a 40-year period.

The frequency with which interest is applied to an investment account can also be important. The more frequently the interest is paid, the better for savings growth. Most compound-interest projections assume that interest is added annually. But there are opportunities to earn interest daily, monthly or quarterly.

The following table, for the value of a $1000 investment after 40 years, compares the effect of compounding interest monthly, quarterly and yearly.

Interest rate	Interest paid yearly	Interest paid quarterly	Interest paid monthly
5%	$7,040	$7,298	$7,358
10%	$45,259	$51,978	$53,700

At 5%, interest compounded monthly results in a 5% increase in future value compared to interest compounded yearly.

Compound interest works nicely with savings—the longer you save for, the more exciting the result. Time is the key ingredient. Consider the following examples.

Jim is 20 years old. He saves $1000 per annum every year for the next 10 years (to accumulate $10,000). He then stops saving, but does not withdraw any money, leaving his savings in the bank account until he turns 65. His savings are earning interest at 5% per annum. The interest earned is added to the savings made each year. When he turns 65, he has $81,834 sitting in his savings account.

Kathy is 35. She also starts saving $1000 per annum. She continues this saving regime until she is 65, so over that 30 year period she has physically saved $30,000. Like Jim, the interest she is earning over time is added to her savings balance and she makes no withdrawals. She is also earning interest at 5%

per annum. When she turns 65, she has saved $74,082.

Kathy has saved $20,000 more than Jim, *but ends up with $7752 less.*

The moral of this story is not to marry someone 15 years younger than you, but instead to get started on sorting out your financial situation sooner rather than later.

Compound interest respects no man or woman, but is dictated by time. Have a look at the following examples below.

Saving $10 per week from the age of 20

Start saving $10 a week when you're 20, and by the time you're the age in the left-hand column you'll have saved the amount in the right-hand column. Look at how the power of compound interest makes your savings grow!

Age	Capital	Interest 2.5%	Total*
25	$2600	$170	$2770
30	$5200	$700	$5900
35	$7800	$1640	$9440
40	$10,400	$3050	$13,450
45	$13,000	$4980	$17,980
50	$15,600	$7510	$23,110
55	$18,200	$10,710	$28,910
60	$20,800	$14,680	$35,480

*Rounded to the nearest $10 [Source: www.sorted.org.nz]

Saving $50 per week from the age of 20

Now look at the same example, but saving $50 a week from the age of 20.

Age	Capital	Interest 2.5%	Total*
25	$13,000	$850	$13,850
30	$26,000	$3500	$29,500
35	$39,000	$8200	$47,200
40	$52,000	$15,250	$67,250
45	$65,000	$24,900	$89,900
50	$78,000	$37,550	$115,550
55	$91,000	$53,550	$144,550
60	$104,000	$73,400	$177,400

*Rounded to the nearest $50 [Source: www.sorted.org.nz]

Chapter 14

Buying your first home

Compound interest is all very well, but greater gains can be made from investing wisely in property. While I am sure that there are some people who like to see their wealth increase on paper, the main purpose of wealth is to allow you to live a lifestyle you enjoy—to live in a home you like, drive the car you want, provide for your family, take holidays when you want to and enjoy yourself during retirement. One of the key ways to prepare for retirement is to have purchased a home and repaid the mortgage well before you stop working.

The reason for this is twofold. If you don't own your own home, you have to pay rent, so you have an outgoing no matter what. Whether you pay rent to someone else or continue to pay off a mortgage, the money is still leaving your bank account. The beauty of being mortgage free before retirement is that the money that was paying off the mortgage no longer leaves your bank account, allowing you to save more while you are still working. You will also spend less in your retirement, so any savings will last longer.

If you're like most first-time home buyers, you've probably

listened to friends and family and looked to the media for advice, much of it encouraging you to buy a home. In New Zealand in particular, people love buying property. It accounts for half of the net wealth of New Zealand households. We have more money locked up in property than in all other asset classes put together, including superannuation, life insurance and shares.

House prices seem to keep increasing—especially in Auckland—yet salaries are not increasing at the same rate. This means it is going to get harder and harder to buy your first home. But as soon as you buy a property you get on the property ladder and start to benefit from the increasing prices.

For some, the idea of buying their first property is intimidating, and the process of home ownership unfamiliar. The more you know about why you should own a home, and what to expect from home ownership, the less frightening the entire process will seem.

There are many benefits to owning property, some financial, some emotional. Although it is important to go into property ownership with your eyes open, there are clear reasons why getting on the property ladder is important.

Property tends to increase in value quicker than savings in the bank do. Furthermore, properties are not easily converted into cash so, while they might increase in value, that does not mean you necessarily have access to this extra money like you would if it were in a savings account. You can increase the value of most properties independent of the property price cycle through small DIY initiatives. Instead of paying rent, you are paying down a mortgage. It is still an outgoing, but at the end of 20 or 30 years you are going to own something for yourself instead of creating profit for your landlord.

Psychologically, pride of ownership is one of the most important forces driving people to want to own their home. The property is yours to treat as you see fit, to express yourself with and to live the lifestyle you want, instead of being curtailed by your landlord. You can change the look and feel of the property according to your taste, without having to ask permission. Home ownership gives you and your family a sense of stability and security. It's making an investment in your future.

WHY YOU NEED TO GET STARTED NOW

The house-price-to-income multiple is an internationally recognised measure of housing affordability. It represents the ratio between median house price and median annual household income, and is otherwise known as the median multiple. The United Nations' World Bank says this ratio is 'possibly the most important summary measure of housing market performance, indicating not only the degree to which housing is affordable by the population, but also the presence of market distortions'.

Based on the World Bank's official research work, it has become accepted that a median multiple of 3.0 or less (that is, median house prices are no more than three times the median annual household income) is a good marker for housing affordability.

The following figures are based on Real Estate Institute of New Zealand (REINZ) median house prices, and the median household income made up of one full-time male median income plus 50% of one female median income, both in the 30–34 age range, and including the Working for Families income support they would receive, based on them having one five-year-old child.

New Zealand house prices have massively increased in comparison to incomes from about 2001. Back in the early 1990s, the ratio was only around 4:1, which slowly increased until 1998 and then it simply took off—peaking at just under 8:1 at the height of the housing mania in late 2007. It's now a whopping 9:1 in some areas, or nearly 10:1 in Auckland Central.

What this says is that, over the past 20 years, house price growth has outstripped wage growth by a factor of 2:1. This is

New Zealand house-price-to-income multiples, as at April 2015

Updated 16 April 2015	Population Mar-15	Median House price Mar-14	Median H'hold Income Mar-15	Median multiple				
				Mar-15	Feb-15	Jan-15	Mar-14	Mar-13
NZ total	4,560,000	$475,000	$82,050	5.79	5.25	5.21	5.44	5.11
Whangarei	80,500	$295,000	$79,485	3.71	3.86	3.53	3.84	3.55
Auckland metro	1,486,000	$720,000	$86,008	8.37	7.86	7.70	7.52	6.83
- North Shore	225,800	$853,004	$91,174	9.36	9.05	8.73	8.29	7.55
- West	204,500	$645,522	$84,435	7.65	7.43	7.03	6.61	5.61
- Auckland Central	444,100	$888,367	$88,928	9.99	8.86	8.13	8.48	7.73
- South	368,500	$536,038	$80,167	6.69	7.42	6.88	6.82	6.12
Hamilton	145,600	$350,000	$79,993	4.38	4.41	4.45	4.76	4.45
Tauranga	115,700	$432,000	$78,129	5.53	4.74	4.96	5.04	4.62
Rotorua	68,900	$262,550	$79,760	3.29	3.01	3.21	2.86	3.34
Gisborne	46,600	$225,000	$72,070	3.12	3.03	3.34	3.06	3.46
Hastings	75,500	$291,500	$73,629	3.96	4.42	4.60	4.41	4.22
Napier	57,600	$287,500	$73,402	3.92	3.83	3.54	4.00	4.29

New Plymouth	73,800	$360,000	$75,147	**4.79**	4.97	5.17	4.65	4.55
Wanganui	43,500	$150,500	$71,628	**2.10**	2.10	2.31	2.60	2.06
Palmerston North	82,100	$301,500	$79,763	**3.78**	3.67	3.69	3.89	3.66
Wellington metro	487,700	$421,000	$88,699	**4.75**	4.63	4.50	4.58	4.65
- Kapiti Coast District	48,900	$365,000	$77,612	**4.70**	4.72	4.80	5.00	4.48
- Porirua City	52,700	$439,000	$84,929	**5.17**	4.59	4.93	4.94	5.21
- Upper Hutt City	41,500	$334,000	$86,260	**3.87**	4.20	4.17	3.67	3.86
- Lower Hutt City	103,000	$370,000	$87,147	**4.25**	4.37	4.25	4.32	4.37
- Wairarapa	40,800	$226,000	$63,217	**3.57**	3.96	4.13	4.01	4.30
- Wellington City	200,100	$553,107	$98,678	**5.61**	5.17	4.99	5.25	5.46
Nelson	46,200	$383,000	$74,901	**5.11**	4.91	4.78	4.93	4.81
Christchurch	367,700	$459,798	$81,057	**5.67**	5.51	5.36	5.44	5.02
Timaru	44,700	$285,000	$75,729	**3.76**	3.90	3.73	3.82	3.57
Dunedin	126,000	$280,000	$69,924	**4.00**	4.03	3.83	4.05	3.93
Queenstown-Lakes	28,700	$640,000	$75,292	**8.50**	7.56	7.09	8.91	7.52
Invercargill	53,000	$186,000	$72,924	**2.55**	2.88	2.88	2.43	2.92

Source: www.interest.co.nz

one of the reasons why it is seen as important to own property—it only gets harder to climb onto the property ladder the longer you wait.

On one hand, I think it is unsustainable for property values to stay as high as they are, but until the cost of building a home and net migration reduce, and the supply increases, I cannot see how it will correct itself, in the Auckland market especially. That said, *never pay more than what a property is worth*, and if possible negotiate a discount up front so you can make an immediate equity gain.

Chapter 15

Getting your first mortgage

If you're considering purchasing a home in the near future you need to be up to speed on getting a mortgage, from the pre-approval process through to how to use the mortgage to your advantage once you have bought your first home.

For many people, getting a mortgage is easier than they think. Banks tend to chomp at the bit to lend money to people to buy a house. They are usually guilty of offering you more money that you can comfortably afford to repay. However, since the GFC, bank lending has tightened, which means banks are less likely to lend you money unless you have a deposit saved. This seems logical, but in the lead-up to the GFC banks were handing out money to people who never should have qualified for a mortgage, which no doubt contributed to the problem.

In most instances, as a first home buyer, you will need to have saved around 20% of the property value. You can access the 20% deposit through your own savings, KiwiSaver, a gift from your parents or equity in your parents' property (or a combination of all of the above). Where this money comes from doesn't seem to make too much difference. Provided you have a good savings history and a high enough income to pass the bank's servicing test (that is, the bank is confident that you can make the repayments), the rest is pretty easy.

The bank lends you the money and you pay it back over a period of time, usually 25–30 years. You pay interest at a nominated rate on the money provided. Each month, part of your monthly payment is applied to the principal balance of your loan, which reduces your debt.

With a table or amortised mortgage, the principal portion of your principal-plus-interest payment increases slightly every month. It is lowest on your first payment and highest on your last payment. On average, every $100,000 of principal will reduce in the first year of a table or amortised mortgage by about $500. The rest of your repayments will simply cover the interest payable on the loan. Because the loan balance is reducing by such a small amount each year, the balance remains higher for longer. A table mortgage drip-feeds the reduction in mortgage balance to allow the bank to charge more interest for longer.

Therefore, it is important to reduce your mortgage as fast as possible by making payments in addition to your standard mortgage payments, in order to reduce your overall interest costs.

To get a mortgage you need to have the following things.

- A saved deposit of at least 20% of the property value. Some banks will lower this to 10% if you look like a superior customer with a reasonable explanation as to why you don't have the required 20%.
- Good account conduct—such as not going into unarranged overdraft (see page 99).
- A good credit rating—such as no unpaid fines. This is crucial. Check with a company such as Veda Advantage Ltd (www.veda.co.nz) to see if there is anything unusual showing on your credit history. If you have any unpaid fines, pay them.

- Solid and consistent employment. It is usually harder for the self-employed to get a mortgage, unless they have been in business for a few years and their financial statements show a strong and reliable profit.
- The ability to pay the mortgage based on the bank's calculators, which often use a higher interest rate than the current rates on offer to try to build in contingency for interest-rate fluctuations over time.
- It can help if you already bank with the bank you are seeking a mortgage from, but this is no longer a priority, as customer loyalty counts for little nowadays.

HOW MUCH CAN YOU AFFORD TO BORROW?

Banks are usually happy to lend you money as long as they are confident that you can afford the repayments. However, they determine your ability to repay using their own calculators. These calculators allocate predetermined living costs, and disregard what your actual living costs might be. They build margins into the interest rates to exaggerate interest repayments. They tend to discount some income streams like rent, or disregard other legitimate income types, such as child support. This can mean that, even if by your calculations you can afford to borrow a certain amount, the bank might say no. Conversely, the bank's calculations might indicate that you can service a higher mortgage than your lifestyle really allows. That said, in theory it is in the bank's interests that you are able to pay your mortgage, so you would expect that they will lend you only what they believe you can afford to repay (or for what they can insure their loans for).

Housing expense debt-to-income ratio

Debt-to-income ratios give lenders a quick rule of thumb to determine how much they can loan. However, because house prices have increased faster than incomes, the debt-to-income ratio that is now accepted is considerably higher than 20 years ago.

For example, the bank might say they want your housing expenses to be less than 40% of your gross monthly income. So, if you earn $6000 per month gross—before taxes—and your bank wants your debt-to-income ratio to be below 40%, the calculation of the upper limit of your monthly mortgage payments will be:

$$6000 \times 0.4 = 2400$$

In other words, your bank wants you to spend no more than $2400 per month on mortgage payments (paying interest only and not factoring in principal repayments).

To work out how much this allows you to borrow, you need to annualise the monthly interest charge and then divide it by the average interest rate:

$$\$2400 \times 12 = \$28,800$$

$$\$28,800 \div 7\% = \$411,000*$$

(*rounded to the nearest $100)

Therefore, $411,000 is the maximum your lender will let you borrow.

SHOULD I FIX OR FLOAT?

When you take out a mortgage, you usually have the option of fixing the interest rate or letting it float. Typically, a fixed rate will be lower than the floating rate, although that is not always the case.

With a fixed-interest loan, the interest rate you pay is fixed for a period from six months to five years (some banks will allow you to fix it for up to 10 years, but this is not common). At the end of the term, a fixed-interest loan should automatically move to the floating rate, with your monthly repayments changing to reflect the new rate. Be careful on this point, though. When the floating rate is lower than the fixed rate, not all banks automatically reduce your repayments to reflect the lower payment, instead requiring you to sign off on the new repayment amount. Unsurprisingly, though, if the floating rate is higher than the fixed rate you have been paying, they will automatically increase your repayments to reflect this.

It is possible with some banks to negotiate a new fixed-interest loan up to six weeks prior to the expiry of the existing fixed term without incurring any break costs or penalties.

The key benefits to fixing your loan are that you know exactly what your monthly or fortnightly repayments will be, making it easier to budget for. *Do not underestimate the power of certainty.* Certainty covers a multitude of budgeting sins. Having a fixed term means the repayment amount does not change during the period of your fixed term, irrespective of what is happening in the global economy or changes to our domestic interest rates. Normally, if market interest rates are rising, you can lock in lower rates for longer periods. Furthermore, as I mentioned above, fixed rates tend to be lower than the floating rate (normally by 1–1.5%).

The main disadvantage of a fixed rate is that you cannot easily repay the principal faster than you are scheduled to without incurring penalties, or the amount you can repay is pre-set by the bank. What's more, if you were to pay it back at a higher rate, you won't be able to easily access in an emergency any funds voluntarily applied to the mortgage. That said, most New Zealanders do not have surplus funds to invest in their mortgage anyway, so the idea of not being able to pay the loan back faster is no real disadvantage.

Floating rates, on the other hand, are variable and can change regularly, often without warning. Banks can increase or decrease rates at their discretion, although this is usually dictated by wider market changes. Interest-rate changes affect your repayments, meaning that your repayment amount will increase if rates are increasing, and decrease if rates reduce. Where fluctuations are not foreseen, or no buffer exists in your budget to cover these movements, the ramifications can be huge.

The key benefit of floating rates is that, if you are one of the few people in a position to repay your mortgage faster than your current mortgage repayments dictate, you are able to repay the loan at your discretion without incurring any penalties from the bank.

It is also possible to split your loan between fixed and floating rates. This lets you make extra repayments without charge on the floating-rate portion while you get lower rates on the fixed portion. This might seem like a good idea, but most people are not in a position to make extra mortgage repayments, so there is no point in having a floating mortgage or exposing themselves to a higher interest rate for the sake of being able to repay the loan without penalty.

HOW LONG SHOULD THE TERM BE?

I believe you should maximise the length of your mortgage term, then find a way to voluntarily repay it faster as funds are available to you (see Chapter 16). Taking out a 30-year mortgage at a fixed interest rate is generally the safest and best bet, especially if you expect to live in your house for more than five years.

The exception to this rule is if you are over 50. If this is the case, the length of your mortgage term should be connected to the time until you plan to retire. This means if you are 50 your mortgage should be for no more than 15 years, to ensure that you are on track for repayment by retirement.

What surprises me is the banks' reluctance to force this issue. I have seen 60-year-olds be given a 20-year mortgage. It's unlikely that they are going to continue to work until they are 80, so it lulls them into a false sense of comfort, translating the bank's loose mortgage criteria as an endorsement of a purchase. *The two are not related.* Just because the bank has given you money doesn't mean you can afford to repay it in the time you have left to work.

How long you fix your loan for will depend on your situation, what interest rates are doing generally and what your goals are. If you intend to stay in your house for the next few years, and interest rates are increasing, it makes sense to lock in a lower interest rate for as long as you can afford. Prior to the GFC, the average interest rate over 10 years was 8%, so if you can afford it there is an argument for fixing for as long as possible, provided the rate you are fixing at is below this long-term average.

However, if you intend to sell your home in 18 months, there is little sense in fixing for longer than this, as you may be exposed to break costs or penalties when you eventually sell the house and repay the mortgage.

When determining the average interest rate to apply, use the following assumption.

Time mortgage fixed for	Interest rate to use
Up to 5 years	The current advertised rate (if you are fixed for three years, use the three-year rate, etc.)
5-10 years	7%
10 plus years	8%

HOW FREQUENTLY SHOULD I MAKE PAYMENTS?

You have the option of paying your mortgage weekly, fortnightly or monthly. In general, people should match their payment frequency with their income frequency. So, if you are paid weekly, pay your mortgage off weekly. If you are paid fortnightly, set up your mortgage payments to be made fortnightly, and so on.

Some people believe a secret saving can be made by making payments weekly or fortnightly versus monthly. Yes, you can pay off your mortgage faster if you make payments fortnightly rather than monthly. This is due to the fact that you pay more back to the bank each year by paying fortnightly than monthly (there are 12 months in each year, but 26 fortnights). It stands to reason that, if you pay the mortgage back faster, you will be mortgage free sooner. The extra fortnightly payments do reduce your debt a bit faster, although saving to pay that extra fortnightly payment can be stressful.

When working with clients, I place little importance on the frequency of payment, instead focusing on channelling all surplus money into paying off the principal faster.

SHOULD I BREAK MY MORTGAGE?

Interest rates are nice and low at the moment, but the only people who benefit are those on a floating interest rate. If you are unlucky enough to still be fixed on a high interest rate when current rates are low, it can be tempting to break your existing contract and take out a new mortgage at today's rate. While it is possible to do this, there is often a cost or penalty incurred for breaking the contract early.

Break costs are designed to act as a deterrent to you breaking your loan early. They aim to neutralise any gain that you might make if you changed from one interest rate to a lower one. The penalty is prepaid to offset any future reductions in interest charged for the remaining term of the initial contract, and is calculated using a fixed formula described in very small print in your mortgage documents. The calculated fee is based on the size of the mortgage being broken and how far the comparative interest rates have fallen since the loan was first fixed, combined with how many months remain until the fixed-interest period was supposed to end.

Although it sounds complicated, the fee roughly equates to $1000 per $100,000 borrowed for every 1% fall in rates, and for every year of its remaining fixed-rate term. So, if interest rates fall by 3%, a customer with a $200,000 mortgage on a five-year fixed rate with two years still to go will face a penalty fee of around $18,000—ouch!

However, there is one notable exception to this rule. If you are going to break your contract and pay the penalty, you can still make a financial gain if you are able to contract at a lower rate than that used in the penalty calculation. This can be achieved if you fix for a different term. So, instead of fixing for five years (on which the break cost was first calculated), you fix for a shorter period, like three years if the three-year interest rate is lower than the five-year interest rate. In calculating the penalty, the bank will compare your fixed-rate term with today's rate for the *original fixed-rate period*.

For example, if you have a $400,000 mortgage and have fixed your interest rate for five years at 8%, and you are three years into the contract, the calculations, assuming today's five-year rate is 6%, might look like this:

The difference in the five-year interest rate = 2%

There are two years left to run on the
$400,000 loan

$400,000 × 0.02 × two years = $16,000

Interest charged per year on $400,000 loan:

8% = $32,000

6% = $24,000

Annual difference = $8000

So, based on the calculations above, if you were to break your mortgage you would pay $16,000 in break costs. However, each year for the next two years, you would pay $8000 less in interest costs, so over time you are actually no worse off.

However, nowhere in your bank documents does it say that you have to re-fix your mortgage for the same term if you break your original contract. So if rates were looking favourable on a one-, two- or three-year term you might consider changing the interest term, to save more over the next two years.

For example, say the rate for a three-year term was only 5%. The penalty for breaking your contract remains $16,000. But, if your new mortgage is fixed at 5% for three years, your interest charge would be $20,000 per annum (compared to the $32,000 it was originally, at 8%). So you will save $12,000 a year over the next two years. Overall, you would gain from breaking your original mortgage. Yes, it will cost you $16,000 initially, but you will save $24,000 in interest costs over the next two years, putting you $6000 in the black overall.

> Remember, although the bank uses the equivalent fixed-term rate to calculate the break cost, you are not obliged to re-fix for the same term at the lower rate. Financial gains can be made if you re-fix at a lower rate than was used to calculate the penalty, or if you go to a floating rate that is less than the rate you were fixed on. You can also break your mortgage

and keep it on the floating rate, and wait out further reductions in the official cash rate (OCR), before refixing. This will cap the break cost but allow your interest savings to be higher again.

Generally, banks do not charge break costs if you are breaking a contract to go onto a higher rate by comparison. But this may also be a way to make savings. For example, if you were fixed for five years at 7% and today's five-year rate was 8% per cent, but the two-year rate was 5%, you could break your contract and not be charged a penalty (as the bank will compare the same-term fixed rate), and then fix for two years at 5%, making a saving. Remember that if you are going to break your mortgage you will be required to pay the break cost up front, with either cash or by increasing your mortgage balance by the amount of the break cost. The interest saving is earned over time, so there is a delay in the benefit that will be derived.

NO ONE IS IMMUNE TO HIGH INTEREST RATES

At some point during your mortgage, interest rates are going to be high and you are going to struggle to keep up with the payments. Those unlucky enough to have had a mortgage in the late 1980s will remember the crippling interest rates in excess of 20%. If you are unlucky enough to have your mortgage due or your fixed-rate loan expire when the market is offering high rates, you might not have the option of floating your mortgage and waiting out the high rates for lower average rates to emerge.

I am not necessarily suggesting rates will go as high as 20%, but in the years preceding the GFC fixed rates were in excess of 10% and floating rates hit 12%. Many people could not afford the option of floating their mortgages and exposing themselves to higher rates, especially when the word on the street was that the floating rates were not likely to come down any time soon. So they had no option but to fix so as to gain what little respite they could from the slightly lower fixed interest rates.

The impact of this decision is still affecting some people. I have clients who were fixed for five years at a rate in excess of 8.75%, because this was the only rate they could afford. They didn't have the option of breaking their loans to enjoy the floating rates and lower repayments, as they did not have enough equity to pay the break cost. So, while the rest of us have been enjoying historically low interest rates, they have had to ride out the storm of unfortunate timing.

You need to build your budget around the scenario of higher interest rates so you have room to move when the storm comes.

REFINANCING YOUR MORTGAGE

There are times when you can get a better mortgage deal at a different bank. Perhaps it's because mortgage rates differ between banks, the equity in your property has increased, or your type of property is recognised more favourably at a different bank. Whatever the reason, you can make clear, tangible and persuasive financial gains when refinancing for the right reasons.

It makes sense to refinance your mortgage if your bank is not assisting you—for example, if interest rates are lower at a different bank and the cost of penalties to change banks is less than the future interest saving, or if your bank is not prepared to consolidate debt and as a result you are paying a higher average interest rate. Note, too, that some banks offer special interest-rate discounts to those working in certain industries (such as government employees) or organisations, or conversely might increase interest rates if you have low equity.

I know a lot of people do not like their bank, but most banks are the same. It is worth shopping around from time to time, but don't expect that you are going to get radically improved service by going to another bank—this is seldom the case.

> **Tip:** Check with your HR department to find out if your employer has a special relationship with a bank which you might be able to capitalise on.

MORTGAGES TO AVOID

Mortgage offset and revolving-credit mortgages are two valid ways of repaying your mortgage faster. In reality though, without clarity around your debt-repayment progress, these types of mortgage strategically encourage any tendency you have to over-spend, which ironically derails any promised savings. They do have benefits, but until you learn to master their disadvantages you will be lured by a promise that is less likely to be realised.

Revolving-credit mortgages

Revolving-credit—or *revolting*-credit, as I like to call them—mortgages are a license for disguised overspending and an increase in your mortgage balance over time. A revolving-credit mortgage is like a giant overdraft that charges interest at the standard floating rate. Banks encourage you to put all your money into the revolving-credit account, then put living costs each month onto your credit card. You pay off the credit card in full each cycle, therefore paying no interest on these purchases. The money you would normally be spending on bills sits in your revolving-credit account until it pays off the credit card at the end of the month, minimising the amount of interest you have to pay on your debt. The banks will argue that technically you have saved interest, and this argument is technically true.

But let's dig down a bit. If your average annual living costs (excluding mortgage payments) are $60,000 per annum, that means that $5000 of costs are being charged to a credit card each month, without incurring interest, for up to 60 days. This is a saving of $25 per month. In reality—and the reality is more important than the technicality—you are more likely to spend $25 per month more than you realise by the simple fact that you are using your credit card all the time and have no real transparency on your spending.

Most people who have a revolving-credit mortgage do not pay it off within the expected timeframe. Most inadvertently spend more money than they would have otherwise, and lack the transparency to record their progress. The balance on a revolving-credit account, when used in the traditional fashion, tends to fluctuate, which makes measuring your progress nigh on impossible. (The easiest way to gauge progress is to look at your balance today, and the balance exactly 12 months ago. The difference between the two is how much progress—or lack thereof—you have made.)

I have many issues with revolving credit, the biggie being that you can be going backwards, eating into your credit balance and technically sinking financially, but it all seems so painless. It encourages you to be removed from your behaviour, and this is what we need to circumvent.

For a revolving-credit mortgage to work successfully, you need clarity. Using a credit card for any spending, but especially on day-to-day living provides no transparency of behaviour or ease of measurement. Living off your credit card is a recipe for disaster irrespective of whether you can afford to repay it in full each month or not. *Repayment of your credit card is not the trick to success.* The trick is your mortgage balance reducing over time, and reducing as fast as it possibly can.

Most of us shouldn't use this type of mortgage as we do not have the discipline to use it to our advantage. Furthermore, this type of mortgage uses a floating rate, which tends to be higher than a fixed rate. It means people are exposing themselves to a higher interest rate in exchange for the ability to repay debt faster, but in most instances they aren't actually doing this because they don't have any money left over after they've paid off their credit cards. They're unable to tap into the advantages this type of credit should offer, so the only one who wins is the bank.

However, if you can overcome the negatives of this structure through implementing a clear framework and evidence of faster debt repayment, then it does bring some undisputed advantages.

Its biggest advantage is your ability to re-access any funds you have put against it. For example, if you had a cash surplus of $20,000 you could transfer this against your overdraft balance and be able to access it again the next day if you needed to. With a traditional fixed-term mortgage, if you wanted to make a $20,000 lump-sum payment, you might be faced with break costs. Furthermore, if you needed to re-access the funds the next day because of some emergency, you would typically have to complete another mortgage application to verify to the bank that you were still a good credit risk. This can prove challenging if your curveball event was being made redundant from your job.

Obviously this flexibility can work against you if you are not operating within a clear financial framework. However, if you are disciplined, it can allow you to throw everything you have at your mortgage, knowing that if you have a major curveball experience, you can easily re-access the funds. (See more on page 171 about using a revolving-credit mortgage to your advantage.)

Banks tend to give you an umbrella for a sunny day. Structure your affairs so you are not reliant on the bank.

Offset mortgages

Offset mortgages allow you to reduce the balance on which interest is charged by deducting the value of your savings or term deposits from the gross mortgage loan amount. For example, if you had a $400,000 mortgage and $100,000 sitting in a savings account, the savings balance would be offset against the mortgage to reduce the balance to $300,000, with interest being charged on the reduced balance. No interest is earned on the savings as a result of this.

Banks claim that the key advantages of mortgage offset accounts are:

- you could save thousands on your interest payments and reduce the length of your home loan
- your accounts stay separate, giving you the flexibility to access and manage your money to suit your needs
- immediate family can help you pay off your home faster by giving up the interest they would earn on their savings to offset your mortgage interest payments.

These benefits do exist. But what is not discussed is the overall risk this product brings, and the likelihood that the disadvantages will outweigh the advantages if you blindly follow the bank's guidelines.

A mortgage offset situation means you will pay less interest on your mortgage; no one is disputing this. However, the direct benefit of paying less interest should be an increased cash surplus, because your outgoings are reduced. This can also be true, *but, unless this increased cash surplus translates to you paying the principal off faster, the gain is forfeited through a higher amount of frittering.*

Using the example above, not having to pay interest on $100,000 of debt would mean that your cash surplus should be $6000 higher (assuming a 6% interest rate)—or that your mortgage should have reduced by an additional $6000 per annum.

In reality, though, the advantages of this kind of set-up seldom translate to real progress, because any gains are lost in overspending before real progress can be made.

Offset mortgages, like revolving-credit mortgages, can be used to your advantage, but in most instances they result in a false sense of progress, a lack of transparency and a higher overall cost.

Tip: Whenever the bank is promoting a product, you need to ask yourself, *What are they gaining?* It is our behaviour around money that disables us; the banks know this, and use it to their advantage (and our disadvantage). Making record profits every year must come at ever-increasing costs to their customers.

Chapter 16

Kill your mortgage!

To kill your mortgage, you need a gun loaded with a cash surplus. You then take the cash surplus and aim it at the mortgage—square in the head—and you shoot, continuously, until the entire debt is repaid.

When my husband and I purchased our first property for $350,000, we needed a mortgage of $300,000. The interest rate was 8%, so we were going to be paying back just under three times what we had borrowed over the 30 years of the mortgage—including $490,000 in interest.

We knew we needed to get on the property ladder, and although the mortgage payments were slightly higher than our rent at the time I could see the merit in owning property. I also understood that I couldn't own property without the bank's investment, but $490,000 seemed a lot to pay for the privilege of being loaned the money.

Each year your repayments will pay off more and more of the principal, but initially the slow rate of principal reduction can be demoralising. This is emphasised by the annual letter from the bank confirming how much you have paid over the previous 12 months, and how little your mortgage has reduced. For example, after the first 12 months of our mortgage we had repaid $26,000 to the bank, yet the principal had only reduced by $2300. Talk about depressing!

I always assumed that in year 15—the halfway point in the life of our mortgage—our monthly repayments would be evenly split between paying interest and paying off the principal. But this was not the case. *For a 30-year mortgage, you do not start paying more principal than interest until year 24.* Using this example, you would pay the bank $565,000 over the first 24 years of your mortgage, but your principal balance would only reduce by $138,000.

I wanted to pay my mortgage off faster, but I did not want to commit to a shorter term, as I couldn't guarantee that I would be able to afford the increased repayments, and nor did I want my mortgage dictating the lifestyle I wanted to live. I still wanted to take a holiday and replace my car. I also knew I wanted a family at some point. The prospect of going down to one income for a time definitely meant we couldn't afford fixed higher repayments. I wanted flexibility but I wasn't sure how to get this; flexibility typically comes at a higher—floating—interest rate.

THE POWER OF CALCULUS

How much flexibility did I need? How fast could I repay my debt?

Dr Jamie Sneddon, a calculus tutor at the University of Auckland, helped me to understand the maths behind how banks structure debt, and how I needed to structure my mortgage to repay it as fast as my situation would allow, while living a lifestyle I could enjoy. With this tool I was able to strike the perfect balance.

Jamie and I (mainly him, to be fair) used algebra and calculus to determine the exact amount of debt each person should have floating and fixed to ensure the fastest repayment of debt and the corresponding maximum interest saving. The formula takes into account things like the nuances of a client's situation, the current interest rates, one-off costs and the amount of cash surplus to determine the 'how' of debt repayment.

This now-patented formula, which is eight pages long, makes one key assumption: *that you have money left over at the end of the week, month or year after paying any one-off costs—for example, holidays or car replacements—and that these surplus funds can be channelled into repaying debt faster.*

At the time I didn't have a cash surplus—credit cards were my buffer for random, one-off costs and there were times when I couldn't repay my credit card in full. As it turned out, my husband and I were frittering away close to $20,000 every year, and spending more as our incomes increased. I don't know exactly where all the money went but I do own a lot of shoes!

Once we had a general idea of where the money was going we found $20,000 we could save—and therefore channel into our mortgage—without affecting our happiness and lifestyle, and without a pay rise above the rate of inflation. We found that we could be mortgage free in nine years and save $368,000 in interest costs. (In actual fact, we repaid our mortgage even faster than that because of pay rises and the fact that we picked up momentum.)

The graph below shows our initial mortgage balance of $300,000 and the speed at which it was reducing. Sticking to the bank repayments (standard bank repayments line on the graph), you can see we would have been mortgage free in 30 years. Channelling our new-found surplus of $20,000 per annum into our mortgage repayment, we were able to reduce the term to just nine years.

Repaying your mortgage as fast as your lifestyle allows is usually the best strategy to grow wealth because the average guaranteed risk-free return on repaying your mortgage is 7% after tax and inflation, using a 10-year average interest rate. This is the equivalent of a 12% gross return.

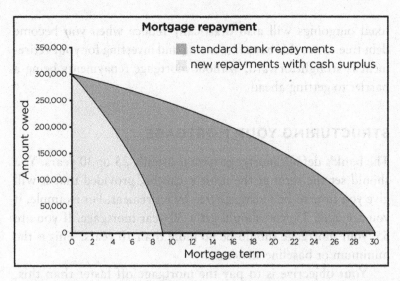

I am often asked if it makes more sense to repay debt or to save. It usually comes down to the numbers for return versus risk. For example, if you had a guaranteed risk-free return on an investment or term deposit of 10% gross—7% after tax (excluding inflation)—then saving would be a valid substitute to repaying debt. However, it is unlikely such an investment exists—with the exception of KiwiSaver—and if it did it would be unlikely that the return would be no-risk and guaranteed. So taking this into account debt repayment is always the preferred choice.

The key, though, is *not to force money towards your mortgage*. Instead, live a lifestyle you enjoy, capture the money left over and channel any surplus towards the mortgage. If you do it correctly you will not feel like you are on a budget. If it feels effortless, and you are seeing results, then it becomes sustainable. If you do not have a sustainable cash surplus, then all your energy needs to be channelled into fixing this first.

In the example above, not only would you be debt free in a minimum of nine years, but you would also have saved a lot of money that would otherwise have been paid to the bank. Your fixed outgoings will also drastically reduce when you become debt free. Once this happens, saving and investing for your retirement is straightforward, without mortgage repayments being a barrier to getting ahead.

STRUCTURING YOUR MORTGAGE

The bank's default mortgage term is usually 25 or 30 years. You should set the term at the most it can be, provided that it will give you time to be mortgage free by retirement. For example, if you are aged 35, you should get a 30-year mortgage. If you are 55, your mortgage should be no more than 10 years. This is the minimum or baseline structure.

Your objective is to pay the mortgage off faster than this, but you want this to be at your discretion, not the bank's. The problem with locking in a shortened term with the bank is that you are obliged to make the (higher) repayments consistently, and should you fail or default on a payment—even with legitimate reasons—you will have to pay default fees, get poor account conduct on your record (which could work against you if you want to refinance) and, worse, you could be deemed to have broken your mortgage agreement, which might incur a break fee.

Even if I believe a client could be mortgage free within a five-year period, the journey is seldom smooth. In fact, if I was to drill down on their five-year target, it would have ups and downs each month and each quarter—which might all come out in the wash and not compromise the five-year objective, but does highlight the difficulty in guaranteeing a smooth repayment.

A client's operational cashflow (normal living costs) plus their one-off costs affect their ability to repay debt and the rate of debt repayment. When determining how to structure a client's mortgage, I break it down into 12 monthly chunks. Within each chunk I set quarterly and monthly goals. The objective is for the client to repay the chunk of debt as quickly as possible while still living to their financial plan and maintaining the lifestyle they want. I tend to place a chunk of their debt on a revolving-credit mortgage, a chunk fixed for one year, another for two years and so on up to three or sometimes five years.

I use a revolving-credit facility because it provides flexibility (which is great), a floating interest rate (which tends to be a bit higher than a fixed rate—not so good), the ability to repay debt without penalty (good), but a whole lot of temptation (not so good). I want to take the good from this type of mortgage, but ring-fence the bad. The easiest way to do this is to use it as an account against which you can measure your overall progress by repaying the overdraft, but you can't have EFTPOS or credit card access to this account.

HOW LONG WILL IT TAKE TO KILL YOUR MORTGAGE?

When I work with my clients, I determine what their financial capability is with regards to mortgage repayment. I then break this down to quarterly and annual mortgage-repayment goals. I then measure their progress against the set goals, keeping them accountable to their goals and capability. I have illustrated four clients' scenarios in the following pages.

Example 1

A married couple, both in their mid-40s. They had a mortgage of $375,000 that had not significantly reduced in five years despite their incomes increasing; in fact, their mortgage had increased through mortgage top-ups. These clients were sick of making no progress, despite having a combined income of just over $120,000. The husband had just been promoted at work and had received a $20,000 pay rise that they were scared was going to be frittered away unless they took some constructive steps to do things differently. They described themselves as spenders and had previously been going backwards, but they never really felt like they were sinking because they had access to credit cards and, if times got too challenging, they would top up their mortgage to right all wrongs. Their non-negotiables were upgrading their car and going on a family holiday to Europe in two years.

My initial projections suggested they could be mortgage free in nine years, saving around $388,000 in interest. This assumed that their projected cash surplus of around $29,000 was real—and we could capture it before they inadvertently spent it.

These clients are currently nine months into their first year and $500 ahead of schedule. They are excited to be making the progress on the graph below real.

Each year their progress will be more dramatic, as the interest they were once being charged on the principal that has now been repaid will increase their cash surplus and allow them to pay off even more debt the next year, and so forth. For example, if they paid off $100,000, they would save $6000 in interest costs each

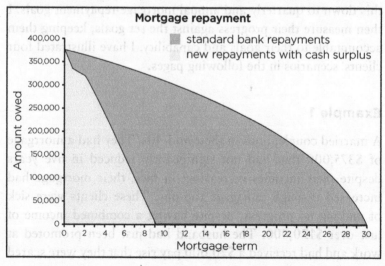

year. Without having to pay out this money, their surplus will be $6000 higher, allowing them to pay off even more principal the following year.

All things running smoothly, they should be mortgage free by their early 50s, therefore allowing them 15 years of saving for retirement without having a mortgage to pay off. Initial analysis suggests that they should be able to save in excess of $550,000 in the 11 years between being mortgage free and retiring. On the assumption that they can reduce their lifestyle costs by around $5,000 per annum in retirement, they could fund their lifestyle until age 89.

Example 2

A self-employed couple in their mid forties with a higher mortgage and higher disposable income than the couple in Example 1. They had a mortgage of $550,000 and a combined income exceeding $200,000, with a strong cash position. Their businesses were very profitable but they spent this money 'living the dream'. In fact, they frittered away $80,000 per annum!

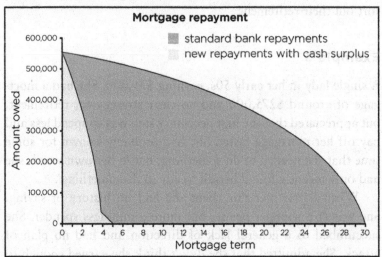

They seemed to be more focused on putting as many personal costs through their business as possible to increase the tax deductions than they were on determining if the expenses were necessary in the first place. This meant that they frittered away money both personally and in the business. There was no clarity around what they were capable of, what they needed to do and, perhaps most importantly, whether the result would be compelling enough to get them to try.

If they were ready to work to a tighter framework and be accountable for their spending, I believed we could structure their debt better, save more in tax and, most importantly, capture the money that was being frittered. The combination of these forces showed their mortgage could be paid off in a little over four years.

These clients are now three years into their programme. They have recently become mortgage free—15 months ahead of schedule.

The power of clarity, transparency and accountability came into play for them to fast-track their success. But their plan doesn't stop there. The next stage is using the next 15 years to sort out their retirement.

Example 3

A single lady in her early 50s, earning $75,000. She had a mortgage of around $275,000 and no clear strategy for retirement, but appreciated that the first necessary step was to spend less and pay off her mortgage faster. She had probably known for some time that she needed to do something, but in her own words she had only recently found herself 'ready to do something'.

When I first met this client she had no history of saving. She wasn't a shopper per se, but more a mindless spender. She succumbed to a general lack of direction and had no plan of attack. She admitted that she didn't think she earned enough to

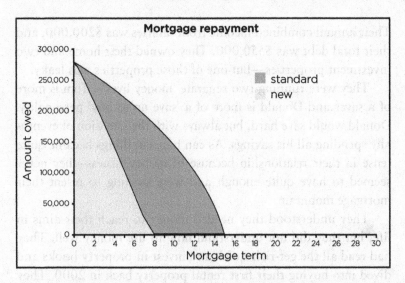

make any real inroads on her mortgage, which was strange—she earned plenty, but she just spent it all.

I calculated that her mortgage could be repaid in seven years, instead of 15. This was going to save her $88,000 in interest. Most importantly, though, it gave her eight extra years to save for her retirement without mortgage payments.

This client is now 18 months into her plan and $2500 ahead of schedule. This progress was made by an unexpected pay rise and a delay in replacing her car.

Crucially, we now know that she can stick to the plan to make this level of mortgage repayment work—which means we will be able to run retirement strategies alongside her mortgage-repayment goals. (For many of my clients, who are either motivated or have left their retirement run late, we often run parallel strategies.)

Example 4

Tom and Donald were both 43 years old when they first came to me. Tom was a company director and Donald was a teacher.

Their annual combined income from salaries was $200,000, and their total debt was $550,000. They owned their home and two investment properties—but one of those properties was leaky.

They were running two separate 'money lives'—Tom is more of a saver and Donald is more of a 'save up to buy' personality. Donald would save hard, but always with the intention of eventually spending all his savings. As can happen, things became quite tense in their relationship because of money issues—they never seemed to have quite enough and were starting to resent their mortgage mountain.

They understood they needed money to reach their aims in life, but they did not understand how to use money well. They had read all the get-rich-quick and invest-in-property books and dived into buying their first rental property back in 2000. They felt they were doing the right thing—according to the books, at least—but there was just never enough money to get on top of the large mortgage, household costs and credit card bills. Even though they were experiencing high levels of financial stress, they bought their own home in 2006, but found they still could not get ahead. They were asset rich, but they were paying interest only on all their mortgages and felt the assets weren't really theirs—they were owned by the bank.

They received a reality check in 2009 when they discovered the first rental property they had bought was a leaky building. The repair bill could have been as much as $150,000 and would need to be paid over the next five years. Who would lend them that money? How could they afford to pay interest on an even larger mortgage?

They had also just lost some savings in a collapsed finance company, so their money issues were causing them more stress than ever. This is when they called me. I worked through a plan and discussed the implications with them.

Essentially, they were spending too much on their day-to-day costs, while not doing everything they could to minimise their tax liability, and they had no cohesion in their finances or financial goals. They had been frittering away a lot of money—over $40,000 per annum.

Initially they had $550,000 of debt that was going to take them at least 30 years to repay. (I say 'at least 30 years', as the mortgages were interest only, which suggests they were never going to be paid off.) They felt that they were struggling to keep up with their current mortgage repayments, so the likelihood of paying off their mortgage faster was not viable until there was money left over.

My first projections suggested they could repay all their debt in less than eight years, even after factoring in holidays and car replacements. A key part of optimising their financial position involved the following steps.

- They would have only one credit card and pay off the full amount owing whenever it was due.
- They would only ever use cash, not credit—in their case, they chose to use EFTPOS—for petrol, groceries and meals out.

After 18 months, they had cleared their hire-purchase debt, cleared their credit card debt and paid $155,000 principal off their mortgage. Most of the accelerated mortgage repayments were the result of new savings they had accrued by sticking to their new budget programme, coupled with a slightly improved tax position. Money was now left over at the end of the week and that surplus, although quite small to start with, consistently built over the course of time and was systematically applied to the mortgage.

Together they have changed the way they use and manage their money. Not only are their finances in better shape, but they now also have a family trust, decent wills, affordable life insurance and a day-to-day budget, plus their bills are all budgeted for and paid automatically each month.

And it gets even better. In the past five years they have enjoyed many overseas trips—one to California, one to Europe and too many to count to Hawaii—all budgeted and paid for as they went. They still can't quite believe how they did this with so little money stress! And their leaky home is now being fixed.

Most importantly, they are ahead of their scheduled progress, which means they are on track to repay the mortgage 18 months sooner than the eight years initially projected. It is one thing to project an outcome—it is quite another to monitor progress and be accountable to achieving the projection. I still meet with them every 12 weeks to refine their plan, make allowances for new expenses and keep them motivated and on track.

They were initially nervous about giving up their freedom to spend money how and when they wanted. Now that they have learned how to create a budget and stick to it, they have also discovered that the key to killing a mortgage is to fast-track how you pay off the principal. The interest rate is a cost for having the mortgage but, to be honest, the actual interest rate you are paying is not that important. It is more important how quickly you can pay off the principal.

Tom and Donald are no longer afraid of money or of budgeting. They still love to spend but they factor this into their plan, so there is no guilt attached. Money is no longer a key issue in their relationship and they no longer run separate money lives. They actually work better together as a couple now with a set budget and defined money goals.

Reducing debt as fast as possible is the most beneficial and effective way to reduce stress. Above all, it allows you more choice about how you live your life. It is not so hard to change your behaviour when you follow the right process and see results quickly.

Part Three

WEALTH CREATION

Chapter 17

Wealth-creation options

Before you can start to determine what retirement planning options you have available, you need to answer one key question: *Are you on track to kill your mortgage before you retire?*

If yes, will you then have time to save for retirement?

If yes again, then you will be able to entertain a wider range of investment options, from property to managed funds.

If you are not on track to kill your mortgage by retirement, you need to determine whether you could earn more money, either by negotiating a pay rise, developing a business or taking on extra work—or, if none of these options are viable, you *must* spend less. If spending less is not possible because your budget is already at austerity levels, you need to consider whether you can downsize your home, or if you can leverage off (borrow against) the equity in your property to buy another property. Those are your only options. Many people need to do all three.

If you are on track to be mortgage free, but you fail to save or do not save enough, then the same three options apply to you. The majority of Kiwis will not have sufficient savings to fund their retirement, which means they can only earn more, spend less and leverage against their property.

While I discuss all investment options in the following pages, the lion's share of the more traditional investments (shares, managed funds, etc.) are not appropriate while you are still trying to kill your mortgage.

LEVELS OF RISK

There is no such thing as no risk when it comes to putting your money to some use or investing it. It is said that investing at a conservative term-deposit rate is the safest form of wealth creation or investment. This is because it is assumed the financial institution—usually a bank—has sufficient income to pay back your deposit if asked. Generally that is the case, but not all banks are created equal, as evidenced by the recent Global Financial Crisis.

Setting the GFC to one side, the inherent disadvantage of putting your money in the bank is that the returns are low. This makes sense, because there is less risk.

For many people, returns from the bank are not enough to meet their financial goals, so they set about looking at other investments. *The key to investing wisely is understanding what you are investing in.* Because New Zealanders have one of the lowest levels of financial literacy in the developed world, we are attracted to what we understand and know will work.

Property ticks this box. Looking back over time, we can see that the typical family home with a reasonable section has consistently increased in value in most cases. We also like the fact that a house and section is a physical asset. It is appealing that even if the market crashes you will still own the asset—provided you keep paying the mortgage.

The same cannot be said for investment in businesses and financial institutions, as many people learned the hard way after the GFC—many businesses and banks were not around for people to collect their money.

What's more, you can insure a house. So even when natural disasters strike, such as the Christchurch earthquakes, you have ring-fenced and protected your wealth against natural disaster. Although, as we've learned from the earthquakes, even with insurance you're not always guaranteed a quick or easy pay-out!

Not all properties increase in value at the same rate. Some properties that do not possess any land—for example, apartments or leasehold buildings—may not increase in value at all. But, in general, for your typical family home in a good area near good schools you can expect an increase in value over time. This increase is greater than any gain you could have earned if you had invested the money in a bank, yet it is not perceived as being significantly more risky.

Low-risk options such as term deposits can be a great way to *store* wealth but are not usually recommended as a way to *grow* wealth. In fact I cannot recall one person who has become rich by leaving their money in the bank. Money left in a bank will actually decrease in value over time, not increase. Unless the interest rate exceeds the inflation rate, the capital is dropping in value.

If you are serious about getting ahead, then you need to engage a two-pronged attack: first, create a cash surplus, then make an investment.

WHAT ARE THE OPTIONS?

Investment options
- KiwiSaver
- Savings
- Property investment
- Business

- Shares
- Managed funds

The two most popular wealth-creation options in New Zealand are owning an investment property or building a business. Not all of the options on the previous page will be right for you, but it is important that you understand how whichever tactic you choose to grow your wealth works. You must understand the risks and be comfortable that you have taken all necessary steps to mitigate your financial exposure.

As a rule, in my opinion, Kiwis are useless at taking ownership of their financial position and decisions. We are happy to take a laissez-faire approach to our finances. Many of those lucky enough to have money to invest are too easily persuaded to invest in a product endorsed by a famous or friendly face, without looking more closely at what they are actually betting on. In some instances, an investment might look worthwhile on the surface, but scratch a little deeper and you will see that the risks involved are so high its success is little more than a gamble. And we wonder why finance companies collapse and people get burnt.

You need to understand the principles of building wealth if you want to build and keep it. The first principle is that wealth seldom comes to those who adopt a get-rich-quick mentality. For those who get wealth quickly, it can leave them just as quickly. I continue to work with two first-division Lotto winners who each received over $1 million of income, yet within five years had little to show for it. Of the people who come into money, whether through Lotto, a payout or an inheritance, 80% will have lost most of it within five years. Easy come, easy go.

The next principle is that you need to have a cash surplus. And the third is if you need a tax rebate to make an investment work financially then you probably can't afford it.

A good investment in my view has two components: income (in excess of inflation) and capital growth. Capital growth is fundamental to increasing wealth. You could invest in any of the wealth-creation options listed on the previous page, but, unless you understand your risks, there is a good chance you could lose money.

I appreciate the liquidity of cash, but I don't like the fact that it doesn't grow. I like the ease of share transactions, but I don't have the stomach for the market's volatility—I hate that you can lose everything you have invested because a company fails and in some instances the commentators never saw it coming (as in the GFC or the 1987 stock-market crash). It's often said that being a successful investor is not about getting it right first time, but merely about minimising the number of mistakes you make. The best way to avoid these mistakes is by being armed with the right information. If you invest successfully, you'll also successfully increase your cash surplus.

Chapter 18
Leverage

Leverage is best described as buying an asset using borrowed funds in the belief that the income from the asset (the asset's appreciation) will be more than the cost of the borrowing. Almost always there will be a risk that the borrowed funds will be larger than the income earned, or that the value of the asset will fall.

Basically, leverage is using the bank's money to buy another asset. Banks see standard residential property as a fairly safe investment. As a rule, they are prepared to lend or 'gear' up to 80% of the value of a property. Yes, you have to pay for this loan—or your rental income is supposed to pay for it—but, as the asset increases in value, you are the one who enjoys the spoils, with comparatively little money invested. Property is seen as more secure than shares, with banks willing to lend three times more against property than shares.

The leverage available in property investment is one of the reasons it is my preferred medium for wealth creation. You can leverage shares, but not to the same extent as property. The interest rate you pay to leverage shares tends to be higher than the interest rate on property, and the term (or length of the loan) is much shorter than the 30 years you can get on property. The share market is more volatile than the property market, going up and down daily. This volatility means the bank can more readily demand you to suddenly put more equity into the shares to keep the debt level in check (relative to the value of the assets). For most residential property deals, even if the property does drop in value it is unlikely you will even be on the bank's radar, provided you keep a low profile and keep paying the mortgage.

Negative gearing means the amount of rent you are receiving is insufficient to cover the mortgage payments. But the lovely thing about negative gearing is that the government is prepared to pay you for it. The Inland Review Department (IRD) will give up to 33% of the shortfall back to you by way of a tax refund. While the tax benefits in isolation should never be the reason for taking on an investment, they are a nice little cherry on top.

If the government was serious about taking the heat out of the property market, they would remove the tax benefits for property investors, or place a higher tax on people who own land but aren't developing it.

LEVERAGE IN ACTION

Let me illustrate leverage working for you. Let's say you are buying an investment property for $350,000. In the three scenarios below, you have different levels of deposit, meaning the amount of money you borrow from the bank varies.

Deposit	Bank borrowing	Purchase price
$350,000 (no gearing)	Nil	$350,000
$175,000 (50%)	$175,000 (50%)	$350,000
$70,000 (20%)	$280,000 (80%)	$350,000

Putting the cashflow of the property to one side, let's assume the property goes up in value 6% every year. In the space of 10 years the property will be worth around $600,000, irrespective of the level of money you invested initially. But the equity that you will have gained will be drastically more if you used leveraged funds.

A property purchased outright with no funding gives you a return on your investment of 79% over 10 years. This is a solid return on the money you have invested.

But if you decided to borrow 50% of the purchase price from the bank, using $175,000 of your own money and borrowing the rest, this would mean your initial equity in the property would have been lower, as the bank would have owned $175,000 or half of its value. But the bank's ownership is limited to the funds borrowed, so the return on your investment is actually higher, at 158%.

What's more, if you had used 80% gearing you would only have had to put in $70,000 of your own equity up front, which when coupled with leverage would have given you a 395% return on your initial investment.

This effect is magnified over time, as shown by the chart on the following page.

Tip: The property market doesn't move in a straight, upward line, but in cycles. At the start of a cycle, interest rates can be high, and affordability and credit is tight. Towards the end of the cycle, credit frees up, interest rates are lowered and it is easier to get loans.

While the property market is seen as less volatile than shares, the value of property can drop at some points in the cycle. If this happens and you are heavily leveraged, then you may be required to put more equity into the deal to appease the bank. I have seen this happen with big developments or with investors who have more than $1,000,000 of lending at one bank.

Year		0.06	Debt				Funds Invested		
	350,000			0	175,000	280,000	350,000	175,000	70,000
			0%	0%	50%	20%	6%	12%	30%
							Return on investment		
1	350,000	21,000	371,000	371,000	196,000	91,000	6%	12%	30%
2	371,000	22,260	393,260	393,260	218,260	113,260	12%	25%	62%
3	393,260	23,596	416,856	416,856	241,856	136,856	19%	38%	96%
4	416,856	25,011	441,867	441,867	266,867	161,867	26%	52%	131%
5	441,867	26,512	468,379	468,379	293,379	188,379	34%	68%	169%
6	468,379	28,103	496,482	496,482	321,482	216,482	42%	84%	209%
7	496,482	29,789	526,271	526,271	351,271	246,271	50%	101%	252%
8	526,271	31,576	557,847	557,847	382,847	277,847	59%	119%	297%
9	557,847	33,471	591,318	591,318	416,318	311,318	69%	138%	345%
10	591,318	35,479	626,797	626,797	451,797	346,797	79%	158%	395%
11	626,797	37,608	664,404	664,404	489,404	384,404	90%	180%	449%
12	664,404	39,864	704,269	704,269	529,269	424,269	101%	202%	506%
13	704,269	42,256	746,525	746,525	571,525	466,525	113%	227%	566%
14	746,525	44,791	791,316	791,316	616,316	511,316	126%	252%	630%
15	791,316	47,479	838,795	838,795	663,795	558,795	140%	279%	698%
16	838,795	50,328	889,123	889,123	714,123	609,123	154%	308%	770%

> To minimise your exposure to property-cycle drops and the resulting need to find money that doesn't readily exist, consider limiting your debt to $1,000,000 at any one bank.

WHAT IF YOU DON'T HAVE THE CASH DEPOSIT FOR AN INVESTMENT PROPERTY?

Cash is not really needed, provided you have equity in your home that the bank is prepared to recognise. For example, if your home is worth $600,000 and you have a $350,000 mortgage, you have $250,000 equity. The bank will usually be prepared to lend you up to 80% of your home's value. This means that it would lend you $480,000 as a total mortgage, or $130,000 more than your current mortgage. So, while you have $250,000 equity in your property, you actually have another $130,000 of *productive equity*—or equity that can work for you, and that you can invest.

You could use that $130,000 to buy a tiny property in a small town, owning the investment outright, or you could use this equity as a deposit on a higher-value investment property. Using the power of leverage, this $130,000 would constitute a 20% deposit, with the bank willing to lend you another $520,000 to allow you to buy an investment property up to the value of $650,000. If you are using equity in your home as the deposit for an investment property the banks will always prefer to cross secure the properties. To avoid this, increase the mortgage on your home up to a level so that you can take the needed 20–30% deposit for the investment property. Then with this deposit, obtain a preapproval from another bank. Doing it this way limits the exposure of your home to the deposit portion.

Chapter 19

Why invest in property?

Reserve Bank analysis concludes that the highest yielding asset class in New Zealand (after farms), is residential property, when compared to other investment mediums. In fact, if you add rent received to the capital gains earned, residential property is bearing down on, and at times outperforming equities (shares), usually with a lower level of risk. This is not to say that equities are not a viable investment alternative, they can be. But there remains a pull towards residential property, and its appeal is not unique to NZ. In fact, of the world's millionaires, 80% have made their money from property. For most of us, though, being wealthy isn't the goal, but merely being able to retire at 65.

In New Zealand, just over one-third of properties are owned as an investment (with Housing New Zealand being the biggest landlord). But most ordinary people don't go near the property market because they don't understand it, find property investment confusing or are scared off by media headlines. They don't understand the rules of the game, so they choose to do nothing.

In my view, understanding the rules of property is a lot easier than understanding the rules of shares. In New Zealand, property has some unique characteristics which differentiate it from other wealth-creation vehicles. These benefits, if exploited, can dramatically increase your wealth over time. Like most investments, property can produce an income (rent), and it will grow in value over time (usually). But the two characteristics that distinguish it from other asset classes, are the options to leverage your asset and the ability to insure it.

Not all properties are created equal, and not all properties make a good investment. Also, being able to ride out a property cycle, no matter how long, is a critical component to successful property investment.

UNDERSTANDING THE PROPERTY MARKET

Before you invest in property you need to understand the philosophy of the rental market, how it works and why residential property can be a good investment. You need to recognise the signs of a lemon and understand the factors that directly influence the property market.

The key drivers of property prices are:
- population growth
- interest rates
- new housing consents
- global factors
- rental growth
- affordability.

The fundamental assumption with real estate is that, the longer you hang onto a property, the more it'll be worth. To that end, property is about two things: the rate of return, and time. Property is supposed to go up in value over time and, if you take a long-range view, this is usually the case. But what you need to appreciate is that the value of property does not increase in the same increments year after year. The gains are not linear—it goes up and down, and sometimes it even stays still. Any property investor needs to know this, and to ensure they can hold the property through the bad times in order to realise its capital-gain potential.

But what drives property values, and how come some properties are increasing in value at a faster rate than others?

Property prices are driven by the basic economic notion of supply and demand. If there is a limited supply, then prices increase. If there is an excess supply, prices technically fall, although many simply hold onto their properties to stave off making a loss on sale. Conceptually this makes sense, but you also need to understand what drives the supply and demand.

Demand is ultimately driven by the number of people needing a house to live in. This is driven by net migration, internal migration (between cities) and organic population growth. Net migration is the difference between people coming to New Zealand for a long period of time (immigrants) and people leaving. We are currently experiencing a net annual migration in excess of 40,000—the highest on record in New Zealand. This equates to a new person arriving every minute. While migration has peaked, it is likely to remain strong for some time. And, the more people that arrive, the more properties that are needed. The majority of migrants flock to Auckland, as this is where the job opportunities tend to be. This also fuels internal migration.

In conjunction with net migration, you also have organic population growth which takes into account births, deaths and increasing lifespans. With people living longer and baby boomers aging, it is estimated that soon almost 20% of our population will be over 65.

When considering what areas to invest in, not all locations are created equal. Just because the population is increasing doesn't mean the value of properties in your town will increase. You need to understand where the increased population is going to be based, because it is within this area that the demand will increase, and this might not necessarily flow down to your town. So buying a property in Invercargill, despite it being cheaper than a property in Auckland, might not result in any capital gain because there is limited demand for houses in that area.

Statistics New Zealand prepares calculations on the projected population growth of different council areas up to 2031. Within the regional population projections, it highlights the top three areas for growth proportionate to the current population. The following table shows what these areas were as at October 2012.

	Average annual % growth*	Amount of projected population increase
Auckland	1.5%	595,100
Waikato	0.7%	76,700
Canterbury	0.7%	109,000

* Using medium projections

Therefore, demand for properties is expected to be highest in these areas.

A high demand for properties is a good thing, but this in itself does not make investing in these areas a sure thing; it simply increases the odds in your favour. Personally, I prefer not to invest in smaller areas that have a dependency on one industry or employer, such as a sawmill or meat works. If the industry falters or goes through a bad patch, this directly affects house prices. Jobs are lost and families need to move to find work. This is scary to me. Stick to the big cities is my rule.

Once you have determined the areas likely to have higher demand due to forecasted population growth, you then need to find out how quickly those areas can meet that demand with an increase in supply. That is, how quickly can they access more land to build more houses. Some councils are better at addressing this than others. For instance, the Waikato has plenty of flat land

and seems to add subdivisions in the blink of an eye—compared to Auckland, at least. What this means is that, while Waikato is tipped to have a large proportion of population growth, its ability to meet this demand is higher than Auckland's. Using economic principles, this suggests that property values will not increase to the same extent because the market is able to correct itself more quickly, and meet demand with supply.

The easiest measure of this is the level of new housing consents being granted. When consent numbers are high then the supply is up, which means that property values could stall or not increase as drastically. If consents are low, it means we are under-building or not keeping up with the demand. As you can see in the graph below and the table on the following page, new residential building consents have not kept up with demand in Auckland, resulting in high demand and skyrocketing property values.

Building consents data for new residential buildings in the Auckland region is annual to February 2014
Sales price shows 12-month rolling averages to February 2014.

Source: www.crockers.co.nz

Housing Supply & Demand

Auckland Region

Year to June	2004	2005	2006	2007	2008	2009	2010	2011	2012	2013	2014*
Estimated population	1.326m	1.349m	1.373m	1.396m	1.417m	1.439m	1.462m	1.486m	1.508m	1.529m	1.571m
Annual increase	28,400	22,900	24,100	23,100	20,700	21,800	23,300	24,100	21,600	21,800	42,000
New dwellings required**	9161	7387	7774	7451	6677	7032	7516	7774	6968	7032	13,548
New dwelling consents	12,937	9435	7250	6781	5769	3212	3656	3394	4197	5343	6794
surplus/ deficit	3776	2048	-524	-670	-908	-3820	-3860	-4380	-2771	-1689	-6754
Net migration to Auckland	12,150	6814	7753	8319	6134	8611	8805	6220	5079	5286	25,500
Dwellings required for migrants**	3919	2198	2501	2684	1979	2778	2840	2006	1638	1705	8225

*Year to June 2014 figures are indicative forecasts by interest.co.nz, based on migration and building consent data to April.

**Assumes one new dwelling required for every 3.1 extra people.

Source: Statistics NZ

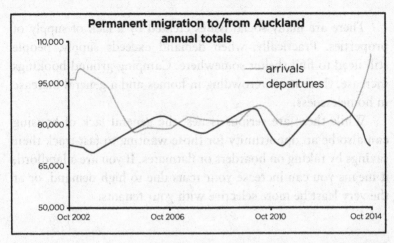

Source: Statistics NZ

The housing minister, Nick Smith, said at a ministry meeting in 2014 that, despite the high growth in the number of new dwellings in Auckland receiving building consents, it will be at least five years before supply meets demand, and this is without addressing the existing shortfall of more than 20,000 homes.

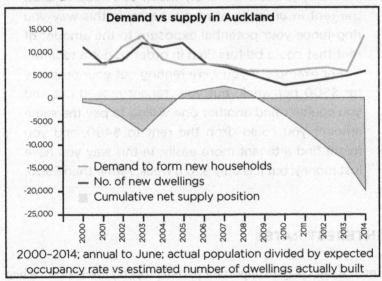

Source: Statistics NZ

There are many social issues created by a lack of supply of properties. Practically, when demand exceeds supply, people still need to find shelter somewhere. Camping-ground bookings increase, there is overcrowding in homes and a general increase in homelessness.

While these are serious issues, the general lack of housing can also be an opportunity for those wanting to fast-track their savings by taking on boarders or flatmates. If you are a landlord, it means you can increase your rents due to high demand, or at the very least be more selective with your tenants.

Tip: One of the great things about residential investment property is the ease with which you can find tenants. If there is a shortage of tenants because the property supply exceeds demand then this doesn't mean that the property will stay vacant indefinitely, but it will likely mean you need to drop the rent in order to attract tenants. In this way you ring-fence your potential exposure to the amount of rent that could be forsaken in order to get a tenant.

For example, if you were renting out your property for $500 per week, but your tenant moved out and you couldn't find another one willing to pay the same amount you could drop the rent to $480, and you might find a tenant more easily. In this way you have lost money, but it is only $20 a week, rather than $500.

INTEREST RATES

Interest rates play an important part in property investment. When they are low they encourage people to borrow, and when they are high they can slow the housing market. Rises in interest rates is one of the biggest threats to investment-property owners, because this can make the cost of holding onto the property too high.

As you probably know, the Reserve Bank is charged with managing inflation. Using monetary policy, the Reserve Bank is able to increase or decrease the supply of money in the economy with changes to the official cash rate (OCR; the interest rate set for bank-to-bank lending) and legislation.

If reducing interest rates does not stimulate the economy then the Reserve Bank's next option is to print money, known as *quantitative easing* or QE (see page 200). When you print money, you devalue the dollar, which is great for exporters but not so good for importers.

Conversely, comparatively good interest rates can attract overseas investors who believe they can get a better return investing their money in a New Zealand bank than they might get back home. This then pushes up the demand for the New Zealand dollar, which in turn slaps exporters in the face, lowers our gross domestic product (GDP) and decreases the supply of money because our exporters are not making as much, which puts downward pressure on inflation. To increase the supply of money, credit needs to be offered and it needs to be at an attractive rate. The Reserve Bank can lower the Official Cash Rate (OCR) so bank lending is cheaper. A lower OCR pushes retail interest rates back down.

I go into this detail here because I consider the mortgage interest rate one of the greatest risks to any property investor. If you can hold a property indefinitely (15–20 years plus), it doesn't matter what the market is doing in the short term because eventually it should right itself. Interest rates are the biggest obstacle to this outcome, as higher mortgage rates may reduce affordability and therefore how long you can hang onto an investment property.

Do I think the Reserve Bank will increase interest rates? Over time it is likely, but I don't expect them to radically increase and nothing dramatic within the next few years. Higher rates, relative to our international trading partners, will likely result in a stronger currency than historical averages, and will further increase the damage to our exporters and possibly grind the economy to a halt. For our interest rates to seriously increase it would have to be due to a major increase in inflationary expectations, which are fuelled by a significant improvement in the global economy. While this is possible and some inflation is definitely more desirable than deflation, it is unlikely for some years.

The first sign of the major economies getting back to a more normal state of affairs will be the increasing of interest rates from virtually zero (or even negative in some cases) and an end to quantitative easing. This will only occur when the authorities are convinced that a sustainable increase in growth is under way.

Why interest rates won't rise any time soon— quantitative easing explained

Governments and central banks around the world like there to be just enough growth in an economy—not so much that it could lead to inflation getting out of control, but not so little that there is stagnation. Their aim is the so-called 'Goldilocks economy'— not too hot, not too cold. In this, the New Zealand Reserve Bank is no different.

One of the main tools central banks use to control growth is raising or lowering interest rates. Lower interest rates encourage people or companies to spend money rather than save. If they are spending more, then more jobs are created and this boosts the economy.

But, when interest rates are almost at zero and government stimulus packages are not viable, then central banks need to adopt different tactics to kick-start economic growth—such as pumping money directly into the economy. This process is known as quantitative easing or QE. The Bank of Japan deployed QE in the 1990s.

The central bank buys assets, usually bonds from investors such as banks or pension funds, with money it has 'printed'—or created electronically these days. It sounds a little uneventful, but it has serious effects which are yet to play out on the world stage.

Spending this 'new' money increases the amount of cash in the financial system, encouraging financial institutions to lend

Quantitative Easing: The Theory

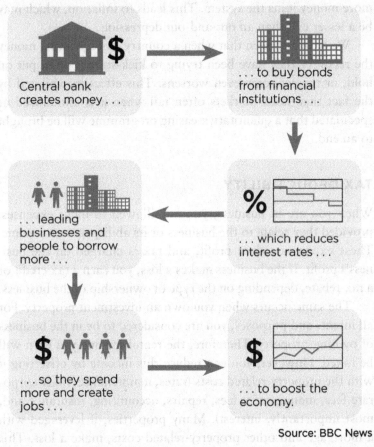

Central bank creates money . . .

. . . to buy bonds from financial institutions . . .

. . . leading businesses and people to borrow more . . .

. . . which reduces interest rates . . .

. . . so they spend more and create jobs . . .

. . . to boost the economy.

Source: BBC News

more to businesses and individuals. This in turn should allow people to invest and spend more, hopefully increasing growth.

While in theory it can work, the long-term effects of QE are yet to be felt. One of the immediate problems is that QE pushes up the market price of government bonds. If a bond price increases, this reduces the return or yield paid out to investors. In other words, investors have to pay more to get the same income. This means that some pension schemes are showing sharp deficits in recent years.

The main fear of QE is the upwards pressure on prices as more money joins the system. This leads to inflation, which may be a lesser evil than an out-and-out depression.

We have also seen that when a country stops printing money the recovery they have been trying to kick-start is often put on hold, or the economy even worsens. This effect is exhibited by the fact that stock markets often fall when it is announced or speculated that a quantitative-easing programme will be brought to an end.

TAX DEDUCTIBILITY

When you are in business, you are allowed to incur expenses, provided they relate to the business or its ability to earn income. These expenses reduce profit, and tax is charged on the business's profit. If the business makes a loss, you earn a tax credit or a tax rebate, depending on the type of ownership of the business.

The same occurs when you own an investment property. For all intents and purposes, you are considered to be in the business of owning property. Therefore, the rental income you earn will be taxed. However, you can reduce this income by offsetting it with the property-related costs (rates, maintenance, body corporate fees, management fees, repairs, accounting, insurance and, most importantly, interest). Many properties, if leveraged with a mortgage and other property-related costs, make a loss. This means you don't have to pay tax on the income because you have not made a profit.

Often when people buy their first home they build up equity through repaying debt in conjunction with capital gain. When they decide to upgrade their property, they consider keeping it and converting it to an investment property. This can make financial sense, although I don't recommend it as a rule—you have to check that the numbers work for you.

Many people assume that the costs of borrowing the extra money to buy a new home can be loaded against the investment property and become tax deductible. *They cannot.* The only way to legitimately push more debt against the investment property is to sell the property to a new entity (either a company or a trust).

For example: a client had paid off her first home (worth $450,000) and then met the love of her life. Together they wanted to buy a family home. She wanted to keep her original property and rent it out.

The family home they wanted to buy was going to cost $700,000. My client's new partner was bringing $250,000 towards the purchase price. This meant that they needed to raise a loan of $450,000. The banks were happy to do this because the couple made excellent borrowers due to their high incomes and strong equity.

My client rented out her original property, receiving $500 per week in rent. But she then had to pay tax on this income because there was no debt against the investment property—all the new borrowing was against the family home.

The only way to push the debt against the investment property was to sell the property to a new entity, in this case a look-through company. A look-through company has a special tax code so that the tax implications are the responsibility of its shareholders. For example, if the company has tax to pay and the company can't afford it, the shareholders will have to pay it.

But most importantly, if the company is due a tax refund, this will pass through the company out to the shareholders. The new entity borrowed the money to pay my client for the purchase of the property, and in doing so mirrored or transfered the debt against the investment property.

To begin with, my client was burdened with an additional personal loan and the corresponding interest payments, but in this new structure the rental property has taken over her debt as part payment for the property it now owns. The rental property is now making the loss, and the big difference is that she now gets tax back on the loss the company is making, which saves her $9000.

How to get a great deal

When buying a property, try to buy below market value. This way, you make a gain up front. And, if you can pull it off, it can be the single fastest way to make money on property.

You might scoff as you read this, but you need to appreciate that the property market isn't a perfect market in the truest sense of the word, where the price you pay for something indicates its worth. *What houses sell for is not necessarily what they are worth.* Houses can sell for below their value when the vendor is not aware of their value, for instance if they are poorly presented, or if the vendor is going through a divorce or relationship break-up. Estate sales, mortgagee sales or the vendor having purchased another property can all play a part in driving the sale price down.

Private sales tend to present the most obvious opportunity to negotiate a lower price, as vendors do not necessarily know where the market is at and don't possess the same level of negotiation skills a weathered real estate agent might. The vendors are also not paying real estate agent fees, so this should be reflected in a lower price.

CASHFLOW VERSUS CAPITAL GROWTH

When considering a property, you need to look at both what income it will generate (rent less expenses), or its *cashflow*, and what *capital gain* it is likely to make. You combine these amounts together to get a feel for how well the property will perform over time.

Some properties don't quite earn enough rent to pay for all the costs associated with owning them. This means that you will have to top up the difference weekly; you will have to physically pay the difference.

Property advocates are quick to point out that for every dollar you put back into your property, you get a tax refund of 33 cents. This means that, if the property was running at a cash loss of $10,000 per annum, you could receive up to $3300 back from the government—making the net cost to you $6700. So, yes, any loss, if structured correctly, is tax deductible, but that doesn't detract from the fact that you are still carrying the can in terms of making the initial payout.

This begs the question: why would you be prepared to top up a property? Well, because you believe that over time the value of the top-up will be superseded by a capital gain when you eventually decide to sell the property. Conceptually this makes sense, but it is not always the case (see page 216).

While all investment properties will have some cashflow attached to them in the form of rent received, not all properties are cashflow positive. High capital growth areas usually mean low cashflow, and high cashflow normally means low capital growth. To be a cashflow property, the property needs to have enough income coming in to pay the mortgage and all the other property-related expenses (insurance, rates, maintenance, etc.). These types of properties tend to be in lower socio-economic parts of town, mid to outer suburbs and in smaller towns outside of the big cities.

Let's illustrate the difference between property prices and returns. In a low socio-economic suburb such as Otara in South Auckland, properties don't cost nearly as much as they do a few suburbs down the road in, say, Mangere. But rents are not proportionately lower. A three-bedroom property in Otara might cost $250,000, whereas the same size property in Mangere might cost $550,000. The rental income is $450 per week in Otara, compared to $500 per week in Mangere.

If you used debt to buy the Otara property, your interest payments would be $15,000 per annum, and $33,000 in Mangere (based on a 6% interest rate). This means that it costs $18,000 less per annum to own a property in Otara, even factoring in the lower rent ($2600 less per annum). From a cashflow perspective, you are $15,400 better off per annum buying in Otara over Mangere. But what tends to happen with cashflow properties is they don't go up in value as quickly, or even at all. So you compromise cashflow for capital gain, and this is an issue in the longer term.

If you want a cashflow property, it usually means that you won't have to top up the property to cover costs, because it stands on its own two feet. This is great if your cashflow is tight, but it is usually at the expense of long-term capital gain. Cashflow and capital gain tend to be mutually exclusive.

This is where it gets a bit confusing. When real estate agents and even financial advisors look to the cashflow of a property, they use a term called *yield*. This is the gross income that a property earns. But it doesn't take into account the property-related expenses (excluding interest), which can be anywhere from $5000 to $10,000, depending on the property (including repairs and maintenance, property-management costs, insurance, rates and body corporate charges). So the often quoted gross yield is a waste of time. You need to understand what the *net yield* is, to determine if it will in fact be a cashflow-positive property.

Looking back at the Otara property, it has a 9% gross yield (the income divided by the price paid for it) or rental income of $23,400 per annum, but it incurs costs of $5000 each year for rates, insurance, accounting, etc. If you factor in these costs, it is actually giving you a return or yield of 7%. If you had no mortgage, then this return is still OK. But if you have a mortgage against this property, fixed at 6%, then it will only be giving you a 1% return. A 1% return hardly seems worth the effort.

> **Tip:** If you are buying a cashflow-positive property, it needs to give you a yield exceeding 10%, otherwise the other property costs will eat into all profits.

So, if cashflow properties don't go up in value as much as those in better areas, why do people buy them? Some people buy them because they think they will make money from them eventually. This is a dumb approach.

In New Zealand, unless you are a full-time property investor with a huge portfolio or have really low gearing, the income you make from an investment property is usually offset by the costs of owning the property. But, if you can hold onto it indefinitely, you can make some pretty awesome capital gains (provided you buy in the right area), and it is these capital gains that create the juicy return. In the last five years, property values have doubled in some suburbs in Auckland. I am not saying this will continue, but if you happened to own a property in one of these suburbs,

Investment Property Costings Calculator

Purchase price	250,000	550,000
	450	500
Rent	23,400	26,000
Less interest (-6%)	- 15,000	- 33,000
Less other costs eg rates, insurance, accounting, repairs	- 5000	- 5000
	3400	-12,000
Tax (.33)	-1122	3960
Net annual return	2278	- 8040
Top Up (-) / Income (+)	43.81	- 154.62
Weekly net surplus (positive) or weekly top up (negative)		

your equity may have increased by $300,000 or more in the past five years, just because you held onto it.

Now some would argue that it doesn't matter, because if you sell your home you have to buy in the same market, so you are no better off. This is true. But what if you had an investment property *and* a home. You keep your home, but you sell your investment property. You have just pocketed $300,000. Crazy . . . but true.

Here is the hook, though. Rent doesn't always keep pace with increases in property values, as evidenced by comparing properties in Otara and Mangere. In our example, the property in Mangere cost $300,000 more, or was 120% more costly than the one in Otara, but the rent was only 14% higher. To own a property in Otara would mean you made $43 per week. To own the same property in Mangere, though, you would lose $154 per week.

Some people would be able to afford the top-up of $154 per week, so for them it would make sense to avoid the hassle of owning a property in a low socio-economic area and head straight to where the capital gains are likely to be made. You just have to accept that you will have to top it up until interest rates reduce, rent increases or you pay off enough debt to lower your mortgage cost.

Let's say it takes 15 years for the property to go up in value, and let's assume that instead of doubling in value, which is what a property cycle suggests, it only increases by 75%. This means that you would have paid $154 × 52 weeks × 15 years of payments, or $97,000 in total. So, at the very least, the property would need to increase in value by $97,000 over that 15 years for you to have not gone backwards (for the purposes of this illustration I am ignoring inflation). This is an increase in value of just over 1% per annum, or 4% per annum if you want to factor in inflation at 3%. This seems like a fair assumption (provided you have purchased in an area with population growth).

But not everyone can afford the top-up, and some people commit to buying the property anyway, usually with devastating consequences. Or they buy a cashflow property, thinking that at least they are on the property ladder. But I would disagree. Buying a dud property will not do anyone any good. A dud is a dud and will always be a dud.

For some reason, these people think that they will be able to live off the property in retirement. But a miserly $2200 per year in net income will do jack-all. The only way you could turn this type of property into a suitable investment for retirement would be by paying off the mortgage before you retire. This would then save you $15,000 in interest costs, and allow the property to give you a real return of 7%—around $18,000 before tax each year. But this outcome is fairly unlikely. Even if you channelled the $2200 surplus annual cash from the property into mortgage repayments, and added another $500 per year of your own money, it would still take you 30 years to repay. So, unless you have 30 years until you retire, it's not going to do much for you.

Tip: Not all properties in a low socio-economic area are cashflow properties. Make sure you do your numbers first.

The exception

There is one reason why you would buy this type of property, and that is to use it as a stepping stone to getting the capital-gain property you really need.

I had one client who owned four properties in low socio-economic suburbs in the Bay of Plenty. She had invested some of her own money and used the bank's money (leverage; see Chapter 18) to buy the properties. Her property portfolio was worth $500,000, but most of this was owed to the bank. She wasn't paying off the mortgages; they were on interest only.

When she came to see me, she was quite proud of herself, because her income was low in comparison to some of my clients yet she owned four properties. I asked her what the purpose of her investments was, and she said to make money in the property market. I told her (politely) that she was going about it the wrong way. She needed to use the cashflow from her investment properties to buy a property in a strong capital-gain area. This capital-gain property would likely require a top-up, because the rent wouldn't cover all the property costs. Based on the cashflow from other properties, however, she could afford to top-up a property by $150 per week.

When you use cashflow properties to facilitate buying a capital-gain property you build what business coach Brad Sugars has called the 'Property Wealth Wheel', pictured opposite. The wheel includes at least one property that is going to go up in value and is negatively geared. But, instead of simply topping up the negatively geared property with your own money (which

Property Wealth Wheel

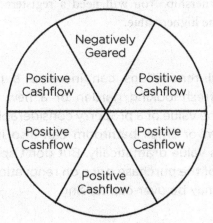

Source: *The Real Estate Coach*, Bradley Sugars

can still be an option), Sugars endorses having four cashflow properties to produce enough income to cover the shortfall of the negatively geared property—this means you do not need to use any of your own money to make it work.

The problem with cashflow properties is that they don't tend to go up in value particularly fast, if at all. That means it is easy for me to say, 'Buy a negatively geared property to make money', but the question remains: how will you actually be able to do this when there is no equity for the deposit for the next property? This is where your cash income needs to be saved. Once again, you might need to go on a 'nil by mouth' spending regime, where you tighten your belt to build your cash surplus as fast as possible.

Alternatively, think about how you can increase the value of your portfolio so you generate some equity. As I said earlier, the easiest way to quickly increase the value of your property is to buy under its value. From the bank's perspective, what you buy the property for sets its value, but if you know the property is undervalued the bank will recognise the difference after six months of ownership. You will need a registered valuation to substantiate the higher value.

> **Tip:** Small renovations can increase a property's value. A fresh-looking garden or a new deck can increase the value of a property considerably. Adding a bedroom or small bathroom can also increase a property's value dramatically. But don't spend more than 10% of the purchase price on renovations, otherwise you may be over-capitalising.

MANAGING MORTGAGES ON INVESTMENT PROPERTIES

As a rule, you want to leverage as much as possible—borrow from the bank as much as you can, provided you can afford to repay it and you are buying a productive asset. But if you buy the wrong property or fail to balance your property portfolio you will run out of money to invest or, worse, have insufficient funds to pay the top-up on the mortgage.

When you take out a mortgage, whether it is for a home or an investment property, you will have the option of paying back both principal and interest, or interest only. Many people will advise you to pay interest only. I disagree with this. *Pay interest only if you have a mortgage on your home, not on your investment property.* This approach will free up cash to allow you to fast-track the payment of your private debt, which has no tax benefits. But, once you have paid off your mortgage on your home, what do you do with the surplus funds? You could invest them, or you could pay off your investment-property mortgages faster.

Some might ask why you would bother to pay off your investment-property debt, since it is tax deductible. This is a fair question, I suppose. The interest you pay on an investment property is tax deductible, sure, but *this deductibility means only that it costs you less, not that it is free.* If you have a $300,000 mortgage at 6%, you are going to pay $18,000 in interest every year. If this property was a rental, you could claim back that cost and receive a tax refund of $5940 (based on a 33% tax rate). This means that the property's interest cost was $12,060, or the tax-effective interest rate was 4%. So while the interest cost might be lower on an investment property by virtue of the tax benefits, it is still not free.

Basic financial management suggests you should pay off all debt, paying the most expensive debt first. If you had a mortgage on your home at 6% and a mortgage on an investment property at 4% (or 6% before the tax benefit), then you would pay off your home first. With the surplus funds that would start to accumulate once you have paid off your home mortgage, then you could channel $1 against your investment property and this would give you a 4 cent saving in interest. This is a guaranteed 4% net return, or a 8% gross return (before tax and inflation). If you could find an alternative investment that was going to give you a guaranteed return of around 8% before tax and inflation, then you might opt to invest in the alternate investment. But in the absence of such a return, then you would normally be better off paying off investment debt, despite the debt being tax deductible.

It is also important to note that, while investment property can stack up as an investment option, the property market has booms and dips. If you can ride out these fluctuations, you should be OK. It is easy to ride out a property cycle if a property isn't costing you anything to hold, or if you are not having to top it up. The easiest way to balance a property's cashflow is to reduce the debt or mortgage to a level where the rent covers all costs.

TAX STRUCTURES

Kiwis continually fall prey to the tax incentives attached to property investment. It's true: for every dollar you use to top up an investment property's shortfall, you will get one-third back from the IRD, provided the property is owned in the correct tax structure.

But here is one simple rule: *don't spend money you didn't need to spend just to get a tax refund.* It is stupid. Spending a dollar on something you could have avoided buying just to get a 33-cent tax refund is false economy. You have three general ownership options for an investment property.

1. Personally (or in partnership).
2. In a trust.
3. In a company (including a look-through company or LTC; see page 214).

Each option has different advantages and disadvantages.

Owning the property in your own name tends to be the easiest option. It doesn't cost anything to set up, because 'you' already exist. If you own the property jointly with your spouse or partner, then it may be deemed a partnership, but this in itself is nothing of real consequence.

The problem with personal ownership is that, if something goes wrong with the property, you are personally accountable, and any personal assets you own could be exposed to the risks of the property.

Owning a property in a trust is another option. This is a little more cumbersome to set up and could cost from $3000 to $5000. Trust ownership makes sense if your property portfolio is profitable. If the properties are making a loss (negatively geared), then the tax refund you would otherwise be entitled to is locked into the trust to be offset against the future profits of the property. This could be problematic if you are relying on the tax benefits to help offset your top-up.

If your property is profitable, then a trust may be an appropriate ownership structure, although I would limit the assets owned by the trust to the investment property only. I would encourage you to hold your family home in a separate trust. This way if something goes wrong with the investment property your personal wealth will not be exposed.

The third option of ownership is via a company. This company can have a special tax exemption whereby the losses can pass out to the shareholders, giving them (that is, you) the tax benefit. This kind of company, where the losses pass to shareholders what is known as a look-through company (LTC).

One of the key benefits of look-through company ownership is the allocation of losses between shareholders. Unlike a partnership, where the tax loss would be split 50/50, an LTC allows the losses to pass to the shareholders at the same proportion as their shareholding. This way, if one spouse earns significantly more than the other, you could assign more shares to the higher-earning spouse to gain them a greater tax benefit.

As with all structures, there are little hooks that catch out the novice investor time and time again. Speak to an accountant who specialises in tax structures so they can help you to determine which structure will work best for you and your situation.

HOW TO AVOID THE MOST COMMON MISTAKES

Buying a good investment property is based on finding a property that fits set financial criteria. People who get burnt either buy the wrong property, pay too much, over-capitalise or have a top-up that is too high to be sustainable. Their due diligence tends to assume that the property will increase in value before their cashflow runs out, but this is often not the case.

The most common mistakes property purchasers make are:
- paying too much for a property
- assuming that all properties make good investments

- spending too much on renovations
- managing the rental property themselves
- not considering the long-term repair costs
- investing in overseas markets
- buying in areas that are unlikely to have capital gain.

The biggest problem with property investment is the lack of diversification. This could be hedged by investing in a property portfolio via a managed fund (see page 248).

To avoid the pitfalls listed above, follow these rules when choosing a property.

- Unless you are in the business of trading properties, assume you will own the property for at least 15 years.
- Use an interest rate of 8% to calculate repayments.
- Don't top up more than $200 per week unless your budget can sustain this.
- Determine what repairs and maintenance will be required over the next 15 years. Factor these projections into the plan.
- Buy in an area that is poised for capital growth.
- Assume a three week vacancy every year and therefore no rent in that time.
- Have someone manage the property for you.
- Ideally, look for a property with someone who is experienced in what constitutes a good investment.
- Buy in an area that will have council investment.
- Buy properties built with permanent materials (brick, tile, concrete, wood).
- Single storey (if possible).
- Near public transport and schools.

WHAT IF I END UP WITH A LEMON?

If you are moving forward, it is fairly common even if you have a financial plan, to occasionally take a wrong turn or make a misstep and end up buying something that you shouldn't be. It might make sense at the time but, before you know it, you have a lemon. The lemon could be anything from a property to a business.

It happens to many of us, and what may start off as a great investment can still deteriorate into a dud due to a change of circumstances, market conditions or just plain bad luck. Twenty years ago, many sensible citizens purchased properties made of plaster. The council approved these buildings, they seemed like a good buy, but when the rain came the building started to leak. This is an example of a lemon. The people who bought those properties could have taken all the precautions in the world and they still would have ended up with a lemon.

Some say it is possible to turn a lemon into lemonade. In many instances, though, the best thing to do is to cut your losses and focus on making up ground with an alternate strategy, rather than wasting your time trying to recoup your losses. I have seen too many people who have a dud investment that has cost them a lot of money holding onto it—I am not sure whether this is out of spite or pride, but they're not willing to get rid of the property until it has recouped the money that has been spent on it.

I had a couple of clients who bought a lifestyle block and rented it out. It made a $30,000 loss annually, which they were funding from their cashflow. They continued to top up this property for five years. They were prepared to do this because they eventually wanted to move onto the lifestyle block. They believed that it would go up in value and that, over time, the capital gain would be greater than their holding costs. But, most importantly, they could easily afford the top-up as their disposable income was very high.

This was all fine and dandy until the Global Financial Crisis hit. In response to the GFC, their income took a dive and one spouse was made redundant. The idea of having a lifestyle block, which had been a considered purchase holding so much promise, had become a noose round their neck and quickly turned into a lemon. They wanted to sell it, but the property had actually decreased in value by $50,000 from when they had first bought it. If they decided to sell it, they would be out of pocket by a total of $200,000 (five years of $30,000 top-ups plus the $50,000 decrease in value). It was at this point that they came to me to determine the best way forward.

As I saw it, they had three options: hold onto the lifestyle block, do something to it, or sell it. The idea of holding onto it was not financially viable and there was no equity to develop it, which meant they had to sell it. But how do you swallow that bitter pill? The only way was to demonstrate to them the financial difference between doing nothing and selling the property. Perhaps most importantly, they needed to determine how they were then going to make up the ground they had lost. *It's OK to take a financial hit, but you then need to have a strategy to get ahead faster.* Kenny Rogers could have been talking about property when he said you need to know when to hold 'em, and know when to run.

Whether your properties are sucking you dry or your business is on the brink, before you take any drastic action you need to be open to ideas of how the situation could be improved, including walking away from the investment. It is best to engage an expert to help you understand your options. Money will likely need to be spent whether you are developing the property or selling it. Don't throw good money after bad; if you have spent a lot of money on something over the years, don't conclude it needs to repay you before you get rid of it.

Chapter 20

Owning your own business

Owning your own business is a great way of creating wealth. In fact, it is one of the most popular wealth-creation assets for Kiwis (ahead of shares, managed funds and property). Perhaps because New Zealand is considered the easiest place in the world to start a business and is in the top three countries in the world to do business, people are drawn to start new businesses here despite high levels of failure [*Doing Business 2014*, The World Bank and the International Finance Corporation].

It is comparatively easy to get started. What many newbies fail to realise is that it can take longer than they think to get started, it is likely to cost more than they expected, will most likely be harder than they imagined and often will not make the money they projected. That said, starting a business and, more importantly, *building* a business remains one of the most common ways of growing wealth for Kiwis.

Approximately 15% of the New Zealand workforce is self-employed. Interestingly, almost 60% of those who are self-employed are aged 45 or older. As the need increases for people

Motivations for starting a business in NZ

Main reason for starting a new business

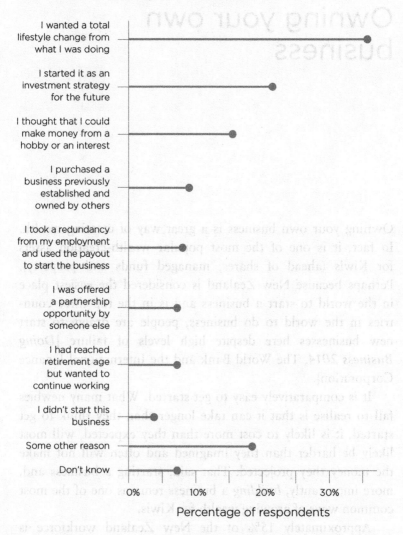

Percentage of respondents

Source: *MYOB Business Monitor*, 2013

Main reason for starting a new business by major city

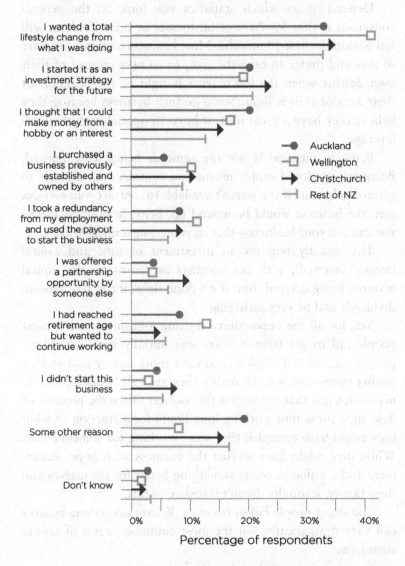

Source: *MYOB Business Monitor*, 2013

to work for longer, businesses are expected to become a more popular medium of facilitating this later working life.

Depending on which statistics you look at, the general consensus is that 50–70% of businesses in New Zealand will fail within the first 18 months. Most business owners are aware of this and prefer to take the risk, or to take control of their own destiny when the job market is tight or the demand for their area of skill is light. Some go into business because they believe they have a great idea or have an opportunity they can leverage.

Being in business is not the same as being self-employed. Being self-employed simply means you contract your services to someone else, and if you weren't available to contract your services then the business would be wound up. Being in business means you can *sell* your business—that is, you create a saleable asset.

This usually requires an investment of time and capital (money invested), with the earnings or return on the capital invested being delayed. But, if it's done right, it can pay massive dividends and be very satisfying.

Yet, for all the opportunity starting a business offers, most people fail to get from it what was initially intended. Many people become self-employed to earn more money and end up paying themselves less. In reality they are still 'working for the man'—it's just that the man is themselves! Often the promise of flexi-time turns into working long hours for a fraction of what they could have earned if they were working for someone else. While they might have started the business with hope, excitement and a vision to create something better for themselves and their family, it usually doesn't translate to this.

Too many people fail in business. What causes these failures can vary dramatically, but the most common causes of failure stem from:

- paying too much to buy the business
- not knowing the cash position of the business

- not knowing what you need to do to break even and be profitable
- burdening the business with personal costs
- having no clear strategy to grow profit.

It is OK to fail in business, but it is not OK to fail simply because you didn't work hard enough.

When you are in business, you need to be aware of your industry's life cycle and your business's life cycle. Only when you understand where your industry is can you determine the best strategy for your business. It is only when you are clear about where your business is at in its life cycle that you can determine which of the many suggestions for improving your business are actually relevant. For example, many books tell you the key to success in business is for you to work *on* the business not *in* the business. At a conceptual level this is correct, but if your business is in its infancy, with a lack of systems and an 'all hands to the pump' mentality, delegation to others so you can work on growing the business is both premature and impossible.

Tip: A business is five times more likely to fail if its growth is less than annual GDP growth. To be successful you need to sustain performance over a long period of time.

I have had many clients over the years with their hearts set on owning a business. Many have little to no financial literacy, but dream of being their own boss. Anyone who owns their own successful business knows that being your own boss can be completely overrated (much like pregnancy, in my opinion), yet, if done right, owning a business can have huge financial benefits.

Depending on whether you are buying a business or starting one, the strategies for growth, profit and success will differ. I will address each separately in the following chapters.

Chapter 21

Buying a business

A new client of mine had bought into a business and paid what I thought was a lot of money for a dead duck. They were now struggling to make the business work. In short, they had paid too much for the business and that cost was now causing them a financial haemorrhage because the business wasn't performing as it was supposed to.

I asked my client if she got any advice before buying the business and her answer was 'No, not really'. She pretty much let the seller jot a few notes down on the back of an envelope and she took that as gospel. She checked out the business in operation and then put an offer on it based on her gut. If she had been my client at that point I wouldn't have let her buy it, but all too often people only ask for help once they are already in trouble. As I said in the previous chapter, New Zealanders like to be their own boss. We like buying franchises or buying businesses and 'having a go'. We tend to trust other people too much, and too often don't understand the numbers of a business. We take the seller at face value. Too many people do buy a business without getting a second opinion from someone who is qualified to give them an unbiased view. We are a DIY nation and this usually extends to financial advice as well.

HOW MUCH SHOULD YOU PAY?

The biggest setback to business success is paying too much for the business in the first place. Much like with an overvalued house, just because you paid more than it was worth doesn't mean that the person who you eventually sell to will do the same. If they are sensible, do their due diligence and have a smart accountant, they will only pay the market value, meaning the person who overcapitalised is the one who suffers—you.

I have found that the main reason people pay too much for a business is that they don't know how to value it—and, to be perfectly honest, most accountants don't know how to do this either. An accountant can apply some methodology to it, but you as the buyer need to understand what you are buying, what it is really costing you and what you are likely to get out the other end when you sell. *Always buy a business assuming you will sell it at some point.* Like negotiating to buy real estate, it is not what someone is prepared to sell the property for that is the issue. The issue is how much are you prepared to pay for it.

People also pay too much because it is easy to manipulate a business's financial statements to show what the vendor wants to, not what the purchaser needs to see. If I have a client looking to buy a business I run through a list of questions with them to help them with their due diligence. (Due diligence is the process of testing whether what the seller is saying is in fact correct; see page 231.) Not surprisingly, none of the following questions take into account what your gut is telling you, which disturbingly seems to be the most commonly used reason for going ahead with a purchase! Ask yourself the following questions.

1. How much are you investing (roughly)? What will this cost you in interest, or in interest you are not earning

on money that could have been invested elsewhere? This needs to be deducted from the profit.

2. If you weren't working in the business yourself, what would you need to pay someone to do your job? This needs to be deducted from the profit.
3. Does the salary/wages cost in the profit and loss include money paid to the owner?
4. Do you think you can grow the business?

Before you buy a business, the vendor will give you a copy of their profit-and-loss statement and the business's balance sheet (what the business owns, usually stock). They will have set a purchase price. Anything above the value of the tangible assets and liabilities of the business you are buying is considered goodwill. *Goodwill is an intangible asset which might reflect the true value of the business, because not all assets are tangible.* For example, if a business has an effective way of generating leads, this is an internal process that won't have a value on the balance sheet but is still an asset. If it has a database, operating manuals, internal systems or trademarks, these are all intellectual assets, but are not reflected in the financial records. The amount you pay for goodwill reflects the value of these intangible assets. So the real question is: what value are you prepared to put on the goodwill, over and above the tangible assets?

Another way to work out how much to pay for a business is looking at how many years you are prepared to take to pay off your initial investment. This involves ascertaining what *profit multiple* are you prepared to use to value the business.

If the vendor has used a profit multiple of three, it means they have multiplied the current annual profit of the business by three to arrive at a value which they are comfortable to sell the business for. This means it will take the purchaser the profit multiple in years to pay off the amount they spent buying the business (using all the profit). A profit multiple of three means it will take three years' profit (before tax, or four years' after-tax profit) to pay off the business, so it will be three years (assuming the business remains profitable to the same level) before you will able to access the profits for your own use. In the meantime you can pay yourself a salary if you are working in the business, but this cost would have had to have been included in the expenses.

This is where so many purchasers go wrong. They base their calculations on the profit that the seller is showing and do not factor in other specific costs to determine a more accurate profit as it relates to them.

It is important to realise that when the vendor is showing the profit they are likely to have made it seem higher than what it really is. Typically they would be working in the business, so they won't be paying themselves a salary, or will be paying themselves a lower-than-market salary, so the wages costs are artificially low. Secondly, they will show the *profit before tax*. And, thirdly, they won't have factored in the interest that you need to pay to invest in the business.

Paring this down to the essentials, if you are investing in a business you are using your own money (or the bank's) to buy it. This money has a cost. By that I mean the business has to give you a return greater than what you could have earned on this money if you had put it in the bank, or if you are borrowing the funds the business needs to give you a return greater than the interest rate you are paying on the loan (the cost of funds).

Next, if you are going to work in the business, it needs to give you a salary to reflect the time you are investing in it or, more accurately, to reflect that, because you are working in the business, you are not able to work for someone else, which is costing you a salary/income. (Personally, I believe that if you are buying a business you need to be prepared to work in it full time. You need to be at the coalface to understand the intricacies of a business, especially when it is your own money involved.) The business needs to pay you what it would pay someone else to do the same job (the market value of the role).

On top of all this, the business is also going to occupy your mind. You will be eating and breathing it for the foreseeable future. This means that you are not going to be free to live the balanced life you want (not in the short term, anyway). If the business grows, it is probably your money that will make this happen. If the business doesn't have enough money to pay wages, it will be you who is staying up at night worrying about it. If someone is unable to do their job, it will be you who steps in or finds the solution. What price do you put on this? What is a fair payment to recognise the risk you are taking on as the business owner?

Before you involve an accountant and start the due diligence process, you need to determine at a core level whether what the vendor is asking is something you are prepared to pay. If the two should never meet, then you are better to save yourself the time, effort and cost of doing due diligence and back out now.

You will need to get a good handle on the numbers early on. You do not need to be an accountant, but you need to be able to understand some basic arithmetic. As an example, let's say you are considering buying a small business which is selling for $200,000, inclusive of stock. It is showing a profit of $50,000 after tax ($69,000 before tax). The owner of the business has been working part time in it but has not been taking a salary. There is $50,000 of stock.

At face value, you are buying stock of $50,000 and paying $150,000 for the business. This is a profit multiple of three—it will take you three years to pay off your initial investment. At face value, this is correct. However, if you use this as your starting point, let's say you need to borrow $200,000 at 6% to buy the business. That results in $12,000 in interest costs per annum. What's more, if you were to pay someone to work in the business to replace the owner, let's say this would cost you $15,000 per annum. This means you need to factor in a further $27,000 of costs (before tax), or deduct $19,000 off the after-tax profit. This means the profit will reduce to $31,000 after tax (when you apply it to your situation). This increases the profit multiple to five, meaning that it will take you five years to pay off the business, or it will be five years before you can take the profits of the business as your own. This also assumes that the business will be able to keep running at its current level for five years, as a minimum. Is that a realistic proposition for your situation?

Let's assume the numbers do work for you, even though the profit is lower than what the vendor is advertising (when applied to your situation). The next thing you need to understand is the cashflow. People new to business think that the profit and cashflow of the business are interchangeable. They are not. This crucial distinction is ignored by the majority. The *profit* of the business is what your tax liability is calculated on. This can have little correlation to the cashflow of the business, which is *how much money you have in the bank at any one time*. Cashflow is king. Cashflow is what pays your salary, and it is how you pay your staff and tax obligations.

When you know how, manipulating the profit of a business is fairly easy. As an owner, you are interested in the cashflow of the business. Cashflow is the best indicator of business performance. It is a window to the business's soul.

Tip: If you are new to business, pay more attention to the cashflow of the business and let your accountant worry about the profit.

Tip: If you are going through a high growth period or phase, the cashflow improvement will lag by about 12 months. This evidences itself with a high profit on paper, but no money in the bank to pay a physical dividend.

Next, and again before you involve an accountant, you need to be thinking about how you might improve the profit position of the company. Realistically, is there an opportunity to increase sales or decrease expenses? What opportunities are at your disposal to grow the profit? If you planned to sell the business in five years, what could you do to make it worth more to the next buyer so you can receive a higher price?

For the income to increase, one or both of the following two things need to happen.

1. You get more customers.
2. You increase the price of your product or service.

Your profit forecast needs to detail how you are going to achieve either of the things above, otherwise it is a target, not a budget.

It is only when you have worked through the preliminary steps listed in the previous pages, and in doing so are happy in principle that it could work, that you can conclude that, based on the information provided, you are comfortable that the business be a good investment. It is at that point that you start testing whether the numbers provided are actually true or not. This is when you start the due diligence process.

DUE DILIGENCE

The due diligence process is a formal process you go through to verify that what the vendor is saying is actually true. Sure, they have provided you with a profit-and-loss statement, but is this sourced from their actual business performance or are they fabricating a spreadsheet and plucking numbers from thin air to make the business look better than it is? Always assume the latter and work through the data to prove yourself wrong.

Due diligence takes a three-pronged approach, incorporating the following elements:

1. financial—verifying the profit and loss
2. legal—verifying the balance sheet (does the business have legal title to the assets it purports to own?)
3. business—determining what liabilities the business could face and the viability of opportunities.

Financial due diligence

- Take whatever the vendor tells you they withdraw from the business with a grain of salt.
- The best way verify the profit and loss is by looking at the business's GST returns for the last two years. Add up the sales. Add up the expenses. Do these amounts match the sales and expenses in the profit and loss? If they don't, how much are they out by? Could this be explained by the fixed assets purchased in the balance sheet? If there is no logical explanation for discrepancies then this should set off warning bells.
- The GST returns will also show you if the business is receiving GST refunds. If so, it means that it is cashflow negative, or running at a cash loss.
- If the number of debtors is high, this means there are a lot of people who owe money to the business, which isn't a particularly good sign. Find out how long an average customer will take to pay.
- What is the shareholders' current account balance? This is money that they have put into the business. If the number keeps going up then it means the business is actually going backwards. If the shareholders' current account is in the red, it means the shareholders are sucking the business dry. This is a bad sign. Check it against the previous year's balance to see how the situation has changed.

- Make sure the profit is real (projections in an Excel spreadsheet do not mean anything unless they can be tied back to a tax return).
- Always get a second opinion on the business from your accountant and solicitor. Make sure your accountant understands business, though. Too many accountants pigeon-hole themselves as bean counters and cannot add much value to someone wanting to grow their business.

Legal due diligence

It is important that your solicitor completes a legal due diligence of the business to determine that:

- the assets of the business are legally owned by the vendors
- there are no pending legal disputes
- the terms of trade, employment contracts and client contracts are in order
- key supplier arrangements are tied down.

A solicitor will also review the terms of the lease you will likely be taking over.

They also need to review the sale and purchase agreement once it has been presented. This could come prior to the due diligence or after.

Business due diligence

Talk to someone who is in business and understands it to get a better idea of the growth opportunities and potential risks you face. Understand where the business is at in its life cycle and where its industry is at. How long before you need to sell it? Do you have enough energy and resource to grow the business to where it needs to be? What is an achievable business forecast?

If you were accountable to someone else, what key performance indicators would you set?

The best business owners run their businesses as if they are working for someone else. They don't think of the business as their own, instead they have a higher expectation of themself than what they would have as an employee.

TERMS OF THE CONTRACT

So you have completed your due diligence and have been made aware of the risks and opportunities. The financials have been verified and you are comfortable with how long it will take you to make your money back (or pay off the investment), despite it being longer that what the vendor suggested. Now it is time to document the terms of the sale in an agreement for sale and purchase of a business. This agreement will record the purchase price and settlement date, the entity buying the business, whether the purchase is subject to finance, and often a restraint of trade on the vendor (as you don't want them starting up in competition the next day). It will include vendor warranties around the turnover of the business and the level of assistance the vendor will provide.

You can then start on the next part of the equation of taking over the business:

- make a profit
- grow
- pay back investments
- grow more
- sell!

Tip: I coach many businesses and I have a business coach. Working with a coach can be a great way to fast track growth. Accountability is the key to success.

Chapter 22
Starting a business

I have seen many businesses through working with my clients. Some people have strived to become self-employed, while others have fallen into or inherited a business.

Some of the businesses I see are a complete waste of time, paying the owner less than the minimum wage. You have to ask why they keep at it; I do ask my clients this, because my fundamental belief is that, if you are going to work harder than before, put in your own money, take on more risk than an employee as well as putting relationships under strain, then it has to be worth it, both financially and emotionally. Personally, I don't buy into the idea that being passionate about your business in isolation is justification for continuing it. I stress to clients that passion is irrelevant if you are not making money. *You need to make money.* You need to make more money than you could earn elsewhere, otherwise the hidden cost (or opportunity cost) of being in business, is too high.

For the right person, however, being self-employed and building a business is their calling, a way to build a strong income and create something of value that can be sold at a later point.

To start a business from scratch, you need to understand how to run a business and you need to know that your business idea can be taken to the market. Having a good idea does not a business make, but it is definitely a good start.

Starting a business is always trickier than you realise. If you are ready for hard work, some long days and weeks, and initially making little money but you are inspired by your idea or concept then starting a business could be just what the doctor ordered.

A lot of people think when they start a business that they will fast forward to business success. While this is possible, few end up here as quickly as they thought they could. Most have to systematically build a business from an idea (which, on its own, isn't really a business), to its infancy (when you have to invest money in it), to its childhood years, right through to its maturity, and this can take years. But if you have it in you, and you do it right, a lot of money can be made, tax efficiencies can be created and you are in the driver's seat of building an asset that can pay you a salary *and* eventually be sold. For those with the stomach for it, it's an exhilarating ride.

To avoid being a statistic, you need to know the top causes of failure—so you can to avoid them:

- lack of due diligence (no market for the product)
- not understanding what your life costs so as to make sure the business can cover this
- no real business plan
- insufficient capital (due to the first three points above)
- personal use of business funds
- poor management of stock
- over-investment in fixed assets
- poor debtor arrangements
- growing too fast
- competition
- low sales

- lack of experience
- poor location.

DEALING WITH TAX

Tax is a necessity of living in the western world. Despite its familiarity, tax can single-handedly wipe out a small business if you don't manage the business's finances well.

Keeping it simple, you pay tax on your business profit. The problem is that, all too often, the money is not sitting in the bank account when you need to pay the tax. There are two main causes of this.

1. Tax is calculated on the business profit, but business profit doesn't recognise if you are yet to be paid for your sales, nor does it take into account when you buy assets that are not expensed through the business. Many small-business owners tend to intermingle personal costs with the business— and so deplete business resources to fund their lifestyle.

2. Tax is paid in instalments that do not align with when you actually receive payment for goods.

There may also be poor cashflow in the business. That is, just because the business has made a profit does not mean that the money is physically sitting in the bank. It could already be spent (not good) or it might still be waiting to come in (payment from clients). In this second situation you need to collect your debtors. Push hard in the next month to reduce the amount of money that customers owe you. This is because you will have to pay tax on the money, even if you have not received it yet.

Also, leading up to year-end:

- try to keep stock levels low (purchase after year-end)
- delay sales
- write off bad debts in your accounts
- write back income that has not yet been earned.

237

In order to minimise your tax going forward:

- push private debt into the company up to the value of your shareholder current account
- use legitimate structures to better manage and minimize your tax
- ensure you have maximised your home-office claim and claimed mileage for your travel
- form an independent opinion of what tax you would expect to pay and use this as a mental measure against what your accountant has prepared, then get them to explain (in plain English) any discrepancies
- run your personal affairs separately from your business. Mixing the two will mean you will have less of an awareness as to how well you are really doing and usually results in missed tax write-offs because your accountant would always prefer to take a more conservative view.

If you have tax arrears, you need a plan to pay these off. Don't bury your head in the sand—it is costing you more than you realise in terms of money, stress and a sense of hopelessness.

THINGS TO WATCH OUT FOR

Just because you have paid for a cost through the business doesn't mean that your accountant is deducting it. I had a client who had paid $30,000 of legitimate costs through their business and presumed that their accountant had deducted them. The accountant made a call that they weren't deductible—and the client was left with a cost. This meant that she had to pay $10,000 more tax than she expected, or should have paid.

Most accountants tell you what you have done for the year—not what you need to do—so I would encourage you to get separate advice on how to take your business forward and how to reduce your tax.

You are in business because you are good at what you do. However, being good at what you do does not mean that you can necessarily run your business the best way, minimise your tax or make as much money as you should. It makes sense to get professional help.

HOW DO I MOVE FROM BEING SELF-EMPLOYED TO RUNNING A BUSINESS?

The answer to this is simple: you have to make your business profitable. You need to separate out your personal spending and drawings and give your business a shot at shining.

For some reason, the average Kiwi business struggles with this notion. You can be good at something, but that does not mean that you will be good in business. The two points are unrelated.

To make money in business, you need to be good at business. There is no formal training for this, and your accountant, despite being your natural first port of call, is probably the worst person you could speak to about the practicalities of growing a business.

There are two main steps.

1. Know what your business needs to do to break even—what are your expenses?
2. What does it need to do to be profitable—how much do you need to sell to cover your costs?

You can then work backwards to get a better understanding of the components that make up profit.

Profit is the output. If you want to change an output, you need to understand how the inputs work together to affect the end game.

In business, you have opportunities to sell your product or service. These opportunities can be called *leads*. You must

Increasing profit formula

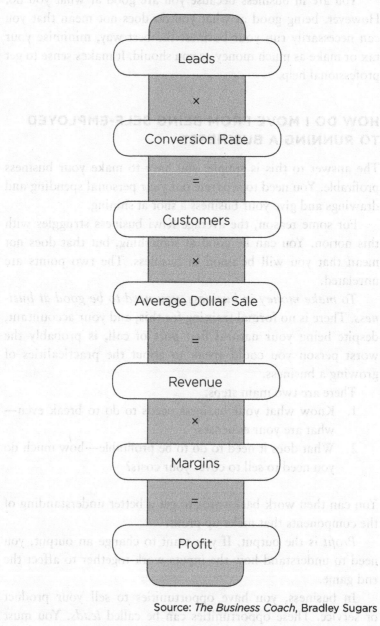

Source: *The Business Coach*, Bradley Sugars

convert these leads into customers. The ratio of success from lead to customer is your *conversion rate*.

Each *customer* will spend an average amount with you per transaction, or over a period of time, depending on the type of product or service you sell. The *average sale* multiplied by the number of customers translates to your income or *revenue*. Depending on your *profit margin* (profit as a percentage of sales), the profit is derived from this.

When working with my clients, I break down each component to determine what can be improved and how. The 'how' is often the toughest part. Many people assume that to increase profit you need to sell more or get more customers. But, as you can see from the diagram on the previous page, you have seven broad opportunities to increase your profit, ranging from more effective advertising, to better training or incentives for sales staff, to cutting the overhead costs of the business. By the time I have finished with a client's business we have sliced and diced and strategised ways to change its landscape.

No matter what you do, you have to measure your performance. You cannot tweak or tune unless you measure. This is where a lot of small businesses come unstuck: they lack the basics of reporting tools or management accounts that illustrate results. The financial statements they get from their accountant tell them what they have done the year before, not what they need to do going forward.

Chapter 23
Other investments

While property and businesses are the most popular forms of investment for Kiwis, there are other valid options to understand, as they too have benefits. The key distinction between property and business and the other, more traditional types of investments is that one usually has to be mortgage free in order to justify other forms of investment. Because the lion's share of Kiwis are not in this position, these investments are not on many people's radars. However, after you have killed your mortgage, you will have an opportunity to consider a wider pool of investment options.

KIWISAVER

KiwiSaver is a voluntary, work-based savings scheme set up by the government in July 2007 to encourage New Zealanders to save for their retirement. If you're employed, living in New Zealand and under the age of 65, you can choose to contribute 3%, 4% or 8% of your gross (before-tax) wage or salary to your KiwiSaver account. Your employer has to contribute as well—at least 3% of your gross salary. If you are self-employed you can make voluntary contributions.

There are many benefits to being in KiwiSaver.

- If you're employed, your employer has to contribute at least 3% of your gross wage or salary to your KiwiSaver account. That's on top of your own contributions.
- Your funds are locked away until you are 65, which means you can't inadvertently fritter away this money.
- It is a forced savings regime, with the money deducted from your pay before you even see it.
- The government pays into your KiwiSaver account as well—paying an annual 'member tax credit' (if you are a contributing member aged 18 or over) of up to $521.
- As well as saving for retirement, you can also use KiwiSaver to help you save for your first home through a HomeStart grant and home-purchase withdrawal system.

Choosing a KiwiSaver fund

You can choose the KiwiSaver scheme in which your savings are invested or let your employer or the government choose one for you. KiwiSaver schemes are run by providers such as banks and investment companies.

Most KiwiSaver schemes have several different investment funds into which you can put your money. Each fund has a different mix of things it invests in—such as bank deposits, bonds, shares and property. *KiwiSaver schemes and their invest-ment funds are not guaranteed by the government.* Each fund has a different risk rating (conservative, balance, growth, etc.) and slightly different fee structures.

KiwiSaver is a great opportunity to jump ahead with your savings. If you can afford to be in it, you should be. However, if you are going backwards, then you might consider opting for a holiday from KiwiSaver in order to channel more income towards clearing debt.

I do not encourage clients to opt out of KiwiSaver lightly, however, as increasing their take-home pay (by not being in KiwiSaver) means their employer is not contributing to the scheme either. Stopping comes at a cost. However, it is sometimes the right thing to do in order to free up funds and tidy up your financial situation. There is no point have money squirrelled away until you are 65 if you are going to go bankrupt tomorrow!

> **Tip:** If you are self-employed, contribute to your KiwiSaver fund up to the level required to qualify for the maximum 'member tax credit'. This works out at around $20 per week for an annual tax credit of $521.

TERM DEPOSITS

A term deposit is money deposited at a bank that cannot be withdrawn for a fixed period of time or 'term' (unless a penalty is paid or interest is forfeited). When the term is over the money can be withdrawn or it can be held for another term. Generally speaking, the longer you leave the money in the bank, the better the interest rate (yield) offered.

The rate of return is higher for a term deposit than a standard savings account because the bank is not obliged to return the money to you on demand. Instead, the bank can take the money and invest it elsewhere for a period of time (within the initial term), to gain higher returns than if the money was on call.

Term deposits are typically provided by mainstream banks. They are usually low risk, as the major banks are unlikely to go bust and the government would step in if something went wrong.

Term deposits are simple to set up and have very few conditions attached. That said, you should understand that for the bank to pay you a return on the money held in a term deposit, the bank needs to lend the money out to another party or parties, investing it with the intention of earning a higher interest rate than it is obliged to pay you. The bank lends the money under general lending guidelines; for example, if the bank lends to a developer, it is normal for the bank to take the first mortgage over the developer as a form of security for the investment. If the entity you have lent the money to is a finance company, they tend to offer higher returns than a mainstream bank. This is usually because the investments they make (with the money you have given them) are riskier because they can't take as much security in the investment as a mainstream bank. This risk is recognised and they will therefore pay you a higher interest rate. In the case of a financial crisis, as happened in 2007, if the developer goes under and the finance company ranks second behind a mainstream bank in getting their investment back, it's your invested funds that are lost. Many of us are happy to get a higher return on our investments but are slow to connect the dots that the higher return means higher risk, and when the deck of cards falls as we saw in the Global Financial Crisis, you tend to lose a lot.

The return on a term deposit is generally lower than that of investments in riskier products like stocks or bonds.

DEBENTURES

Debentures are similar in concept to a term deposit in the sense that you are paid interest over a fixed period and you are supposed to receive your money back at the end of the term. However, unlike a term deposit, debentures can vary in risk. Higher-risk debentures should pay a higher rate of return, although this is not always the case, especially when the finance company wants to downplay the real risk of the investment.

The finance company is free to on-lend the funds, much like a bank, and typically they lend the funds to higher-risk activities. They have terms and conditions that highlight where you rank if the finance company goes under, which means you might not get all your money back if the finance company backs a dodgy investment. Be aware that finance companies are usually smaller outfits than banks and have limited resources if a development they have invested in goes under.

The paperwork will always say if a debenture is secured or unsecured. An unsecured debenture is riskier than a secured debenture, but being secured is a bit misleading because if the finance company goes under the 'security' can count for little.

BONDS

Bonds are a fixed-interest product. You hand over your deposit and collect a payment (in the form of interest or a coupon, which is a certificate giving you the right to receive a payment). Governments, local bodies, state-owned corporations and corporates can all issue bonds. When you buy a bond you are, in effect, lending money to the organisation issuing the bond. In New Zealand, bonds are traded on the New Zealand Debt Market (NZDX).

Governments issue bonds to borrow from the market and fund their day-to-day operations from within their own country or a foreign source. Foreign-currency government debt is also known as sovereign debt.

If you invest in foreign-government bonds, you need to understand what is happening in the country you are investing in, because the quality of the bond you are buying is only as good as the country issuing it (i.e. taking your money). *You should never lend to anyone who cannot afford to pay you back.* The same rule applies whether the borrower is a friend, a company or a government.

Until recently it was assumed that governments of large, stable countries were a relatively low-risk proposition because, like mainstream banks, they have significant resources to call on to honour their debts. The GFC has highlighted several countries which are less stable than first thought.

Bonds issued by councils, local bodies and state-owned utilities are considered slightly higher risk than a government bond, as they are one stage removed from the government's obligations.

Similarly, bonds issued by corporations can be safe or risky depending on who is issuing them. For example, Whitcoulls is an example of a corporation that issued bonds during the GFC. When the bonds matured, they returned the investment to the bond-holders, but two months later the company went into receivership. If this had happened before the bonds had matured, they would not have paid out.

In theory, corporate bonds are considered riskier than most bonds, but this blanket assumption is misleading. Like any investment, the risk is relative. The risk with corporate bonds depends on who the corporation is, where it is and the timing of the bond issue. For example, bonds issued by New Zealand finance companies were great for a long period of time, but in the space of 18 months between 2008 and 2010 most of them stopped trading and defaulted on their obligations. On the other hand if Apple was to issue bonds they would be one of the safest investments in the world. Also, if it is a good investment, you are first in line to be paid out should the company go under.

Some bonds have an expiry or maturity date which indicates when you will be paid out. Perpetual bonds do not have a maturity date, so you pay once and receive coupons/interest at a set rate, but the issuer is not obliged to return your money at any set point. The coupon rate can be reset periodically and this is the main weakness of a perpetual bond—it may be reset at an unfavourable rate. Then, if you tried to sell it, you might lose money.

Like shares, bonds can be complicated and require detailed and impartial analysis and comparisons of performance and projections. If you do not have the understanding or time to do this, but you still wish to invest in bonds, you should probably have someone manage your bond portfolio for you.

SHARES

When you buy a share, you become a shareholder of the company. You are buying an equity participation in the company and, in most instances, the company will pay you an annual dividend based on the number of shares you own. This dividend is your share of the company's profit.

Shares are bought and sold on exchanges. To buy and sell shares in New Zealand you have to go through a stockbroker (who must be an authorised financial advisor) and New Zealand shares are listed on the New Zealand Exchange Limited (NZX).

Interestingly, shares in New Zealand and Australia pay higher dividend yields than anywhere else in the world. However, there is an inherent risk with shares because there is no guaranteed dividend and there is no guarantee that the shares will go up in value. With fixed-interest investments you have a promise. With shares you hand the money over and hope.

In theory the money you invest in shares is worth something, but only while someone else values the shares—they are only as good as the selling price when you come to sell them. The problem with this is that the value of your investment is dependent on other people's perception of its value, because that is what markets are based on, people's perceptions.

Shares go up and down in value. The potential for gain is enormous. In 2010, Xero shares were $6 each. They increased to $40 per share by March 2014. I had a client who made $350,000 on this investment. The lucky thing, though, is that my client cashed out before the share price dropped—and drop it did.

On the other hand, the risk for loss is also enormous. This risk though (much like any potential gain) is limited to the investment made.

MANAGED FUNDS

When you invest in a managed fund your money is pooled with other investors' money and spread across different kinds of investments. A manager chooses the investments the fund invests in and each investor owns a proportion of the total fund. The fund is managed by an agent, typically an insurance company fund manager.

Managed funds is an investment vehicle that encompasses KiwiSaver investments, unit trusts, Portfolio Investment Entity (PIE) investments, mutual funds and managed funds as well as superannuation policies. They have a general focus towards growth and risk management, and can be described as defensive, conservative, balanced, growth or aggressive funds. Alternatively, they can be focused on a particular type of investment or market, such as shares, property, commodities or emerging markets. Funds are purchased in units.

You pay someone to administer the fund and choose the investments for you, subject to the type of market you have selected or general growth focus. You can earn income from managed funds as well as getting capital gains. To get an accurate snapshot of how well your money is working for you, it is important to measure the income after the management fee has been deducted. I have seen some amazing results with managed funds, as well as some amazing fees charged, which counteract a large portion of the gain otherwise made. Fees vary greatly between fund managers and different types of funds.

One of the benefits of a managed fund is that your money is spread across more investments than if you purchased shares or property directly. This means your investment is more diversified than direct investment. This diversification is supposed to give you some comfort, by reducing the volatility of your investment.

Like shares, managed funds are not guaranteed to go up in value all the time. In fact, there is a risk that the value of a fund can drop below what you paid for it. However, the risk of this happening is less than with direct shares, because your risk is spread across more than one company or investment.

SUPERANNUATION FUNDS AND LIFE INSURANCE POLICIES

You can also invest in private superannuation funds. Much like KiwiSaver, you pay into a fund that is ring-fenced for your retirement. This means that you cannot access the money invested until a certain age—maybe 50, 55, 60 or 65, depending on the specific policy.

Like any investment you need to ask yourself two questions about a superannuation fund.

1. If I am contributing $1 to this investment every month, am I better to keep paying into the fund, or should I invest my dollar elsewhere?
2. If possible, should I cash in my policy and apply the capital to another investment, for example, reducing my mortgage?

The answers to these questions will depend on how well the fund is currently performing and if your employer is making contributions to your fund. Unfortunately, it is likely that the regular statements sent to you will not clearly show fund performance. Often they simply indicate how much you will receive if you withdraw your funds at an attractive and imagined rate of return—without showing the actual rate of return. When I have investigated for my clients I have found that the return has been less than 1% for years! If it is unlikely that the return is going to increase it might pay to cut your losses and withdraw the funds to invest elsewhere.

Do your homework and always read your investment statements carefully. Has the investment increased in value? If so, what is the rate of increase? What is expected to happen in the next year? How does it rate as an overall investment (what ranking does it have)?

If you are not sure, call the fund manager and keep talking until you understand exactly what is happening to your investment. If the statement omits key performance data, you can usually bet the fund is not performing well.

WHICH INVESTMENT IS BEST FOR YOU?

In deciding which investment is best for you, you need to ask yourself two questions.

1. How much of my wealth do I want to put at risk?
2. How much risk do I want to take?

You will not be able to answer these questions until you can establish what return you need from the money invested to achieve your financial goals.

To determine what risk to take, you need to clarify whether you are on track to achieve your financial goals with savings alone, whether you want to buy a first home or whether you plan for retirement. If there is a shortfall, this will help you calculate the level of return you need in order to grow your wealth to a sufficient level to meet your goal.

It is important that you distinguish between your *tolerance* for risk and your *capacity* for risk. For example, many retired couples had money invested in finance companies before the GFC. They were getting a good return (interest rate) on the money invested but, unfortunately, a great number of those people who had invested their money in high-interest, high-risk investments could not afford to lose the capital they had invested. They have since been left shaking their heads and asking why they exposed their hard-earned money to such risky investments.

> **Tip:** Sometimes the best investments are the ones you *don't* make. Follow Donald Trump's advice and invest only in products you understand and people you know you can trust.

It's important to note here that whether you trust the celebrity who is endorsing a product or not has no relevance. (Personally, I think it is unethical to have any celebrity endorse an investment or finance company unless they started it themselves.) Famous face or not, there's no good reason for investing your hard-earned money in something you do not understand.

I've heard of so many people who have invested in finance companies because of the face of the company's advertising campaign, then lost their money. It's sad, but these people took no precautions. They simply wrote out a cheque to someone they didn't know for a product they didn't understand. In all likelihood the famous face probably didn't understand what they were representing either. I've said it before and I'll say it again: the only person who will ever truly care about your money is you. Don't be stupid or reckless, and do not cry foul play when you yourself took no precautions. Stand up and take some responsibility for your investments. Invest on sound principles, knowing the merits of each investment and how it will affect your longer-term goals.

> **Tip:** Always check the investment rating to understand the level of risk you are taking and how the company's investment stacks up against market comparisons.

WHOSE ADVICE SHOULD YOU SEEK?

A lot of advisors specialise in one field. They can give you good advice in that area, but it is given in isolation. For example, they may give good investment advice, but not good financial advice as it relates to the nuances of your personal situation.

For example, to buy and sell shares in New Zealand you have to go through a stockbroker—either a bank or a financial advisor. Stockbrokers clip the ticket on both sides of the transaction.

A financial planner will take a look at your wider circumstances, and may do a good job of managing your money to retirement, but may not know much about specific investments. They get around this by handing your investment over to a fund manager, who will manage it on your behalf. The fund manager, like the stockbroker, will clip the ticket on the funds invested, irrespective of the results. If your financial behaviour is a problem, neither the financial planner or a fund manager will have the system to fix it—because changing behaviour requires a degree of accountability and regular check-ins, which is not the core business of someone who wants to invest your money.

An insurance advisor gives advice on insurance policies, but, unless they are qualified to comment beyond that, it is best not to rely on further advice.

Accountants often say they are business advisors, but in a lot of instances they simply complete your tax return and add little value to the day-to-day running of your business.

Tip: Getting advice from the right people is critical to getting ahead, so work out what you need to know and who best can answer your questions.

Part Four

RETIREMENT

Chapter 24

Retirement planning

If you can't fly, run; if you can't run, walk;
if you can't walk, crawl. But, by all means,
keep moving.
—Martin Luther King Jr

In order to have enough money to fund an enjoyable retirement, while you are still working you need to have a cash surplus, own a property and adopt a strategy to kill your mortgage. In conjunction with these foundation principles, you must have a savings or investment strategy to ensure you are going to end up with the money you need by the time you need it. This is the scary, confronting part.

Quite simply, *most people do not have enough money to pay for the sort of retirement they want.* You pay your taxes, so you believe this should entitle you to a pension? Maybe it should. But that's immaterial if, by the time you retire, the government does not have enough money to pay pensions. Whining will not change this fact. However, with good planning for financial success, you should be able to avoid a feeling of panic.

Most people start thinking about retirement after they have purchased their home but while they are struggling to pay off the mortgage. Many people are unlikely to pay off their mortgage much before they retire, leaving them little time to save for retirement. As discussed earlier, the key to changing this is channelling your cash surplus into repaying your debt faster, killing your mortgage (see Chapter 16).

Retirement planning is about taking your savings—the 10% you have at the end of each week, month or year—and making more money with it. Successful retirement planning will enable you to make enough money to fund a lifestyle you will enjoy well after you stop working.

A lot of Kiwis—too many—expect retirement to sort itself out. I am all for positive thinking—that 'she'll be right', attitude we identify as our positive national characteristic. When it comes to money and retirement planning, though, you can dress things up however you want to, but if you are going backwards you are going backwards. If this is the case for you, the sooner you realise it the sooner you have a shot at bridging the gap between where you are now and where you need to be by the time you retire.

HOW MUCH WILL I NEED?

The problem with retirement planning is that everyone's lifestyle differs in style and cost. There is no universal amount that needs to be saved by the time you hit retirement to ensure you have saved 'enough'. What you need to work out is your 'number' (see Chapter 26). Then you need to determine if you are going to achieve that number or whether there is going to be a shortfall. If there is a shortfall, you need to decide what you are going to do about it.

You can borrow for many things in life—homes, cars, children's educations or university fees—but you cannot borrow to pay for your retirement. To fund your retirement, you need to have saved enough money or be able to earn enough equity to live the lifestyle you enjoy.

How much this is will depend on the lifestyle you want. Let's keep it simple. Ask yourself the following questions.

- How much do I need each year to be happy with my lifestyle?
- Do I want to be able to travel when I retire? If so, how often, how far and how much will it cost?
- What one-off costs will I have after I retire? Eg. car replacements, holidays, big dentist bills.
- Do I intend to be mortgage free when I retire?
- Do I plan to downsize my house around the time I retire (to minimise my mortgage outgoings)?
- Do I have a superannuation policy? If so, how much am I likely to receive when I retire?
- Am I likely to get an inheritance?

Downsizing your home and receiving an inheritance both provide one-off income, but it can be tricky to rely on these strategies to save you, because you do not have control over either the amount provided or the timing.

Challenge your assumptions about the things you need now and what you think you will need in the future, and squeeze out frittered expenses to minimise the day-to-day costs of your lifestyle. Understand your annual deficit in retirement to calculate what your retirement will cost and what your shortfall might be. Do it now! Remember, financial success is not about how much money you make, but how much you keep.

Once you have put some numbers to your expected expenses, you can work out what your retirement is going to cost in today's dollars. If the mere thought of doing this is too hard for you, or you don't have time to work it out, enlist the help of an expert. This may be your accountant, your financial planner or your Financial Personal Trainer.

Multiply this cost by the number of years you might reasonably expect to live after you retire. Add any expected major one-off costs, and subtract any expected one-off cash injections and KiwiSaver payments. This will tell you how much you need to have saved before you reach retirement. Subtract what you have now (excluding your house), and the difference is what you need to save between now and retirement.

Retirement cost — Existing wealth (excl. home) = Savings needed

The usual goal is to be able to fund your retirement until the age at which you are likely to die, based on general statistics and family history. This can be anything from 65 to 100! I aim for my clients to have sufficient savings to fund their retirement until the age of 90. In order to do this, some people need to buy and hold an investment property, because the funds they have invested in the bank are not giving them the return they need to achieve their retirement goals; they might also invest in other assets that will provide a higher return. Others, where their financial landscape has no tolerance for the risk that accompanies higher returns, must instead alter their lifestyle. The important thing, no matter what their individual circumstances, that my clients all have clarity around what they are facing and the options available to them.

Money is about choice. Retirement planning is about making the right financial choices.

The gap between where you are now and where you want to be has to be quantified, with a clear plan of attack put in place, otherwise you are not going to successfully sustain your lifestyle after you retire.

Whether you have money to invest, equity to leverage, or both will refine the investment options available to you.

Case study

I have a couple of clients, both aged 45. They have a combined income of approximately $160,000, a daughter, a home worth $500,000 and a mortgage of $300,000, payable over 25 years. Their daughter is planning to go to university, but will take out a student loan to pay for her course. They both contribute 3% of their income to KiwiSaver. They want to retire at 65 and they want to keep living their current lifestyle in retirement. They want to know if this is a realistic goal, or whether they need to get used to the idea of working for longer or spending less in retirement.

Before working with me they were spending all the money they earned. Now, they have a cash surplus of $25,000 per annum. They intend to replace their car every 10 years, spending $10,000 to do so. They also intend to spend $15,000 on a holiday to Europe.

As long as they continued to spend everything they earned, funding their retirement was not possible. However, after we worked to create a cash surplus of $25,000 per annum and channelled that money into their mortgage, they were in a position to pay off their mortgage faster. Even with car replacements and the trip to Europe, you can see from the graph on the following page that they should be mortgage free in 10 years. This will save them $215,000 of interest, which will be a much needed injection for retirement.

The outside line on the graph shows their current mortgage of $300,000 and the number of years before they would be mortgage free if they stuck to their current arrangement with the bank. However, by working to a plan and using their cash

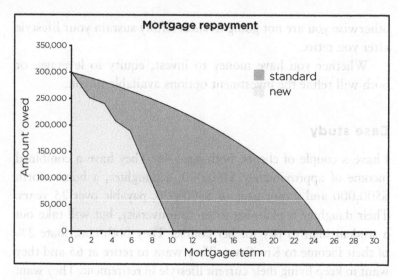

surplus they can repay the mortgage faster, as shown by the green line.

While it is preferable to channel all funds into repaying your mortgage as fast as you can, one-off costs such as car replacements and overseas holidays need to be funded from your cash surplus, which means that, in the years these larger one-off events occur, the mortgage will not reduce at the same rate. Thus the graph above has a few bumps, which indicate when money is being spent on other areas. Overall though, factoring in the things they want to do, they are still in a position to be mortgage free in 10 years, which is a fantastic result.

After 10 years, or once they are mortgage free—whichever is sooner—the money that was going to repay the mortgage can be saved. Their fixed mortgage payments previously cost them $25,000 per annum, so their savings will increase by at least that amount. In 10 years' time, their cash surplus will double to $50,000 once they are not making mortgage payments—and that's excluding pay rises and bonuses.

If this surplus goes into a savings account, even earning just 1% interest after tax and inflation, they will be able to save approximately $480,000 before retirement. They will then be able to access these savings, along with their KiwiSaver, on retirement. These, coupled with the current pension, would allow them to maintain their current lifestyle until age 80, at which point they would need to downsize their home to free up some funds, unless they have received a one-off windfall, such as an inheritance. (It's also worth noting here that most people reduce their discretionary spending after they retire by as much as 30%.)

Chapter 25

Will the government help me?

Consistent with other Organisation for Economic Cooperation and Development (OECD) countries, New Zealand has an ageing population. Although it is exacerbated by the numbers of post-war baby boomers (born between 1946 and 1965), an ageing population is considered a permanent change in our population demographic, caused by people living for longer and having fewer children.

In 2012, approximately 600,000 people (one in eight New Zealanders) were aged 65 or older. This is expected to double in the next 50 years, with people over 65 making up more than one-quarter of New Zealand residents. The number of people living beyond 85 is expected to quadruple.

The fact that people are living longer means they are likely to spend more time in retirement, which creates a rapidly growing pension cost for the government. In 1970, people were expected to live on average another 13 (male) or 17 (female) years after age 65. Now, life expectancy has increased to 20 years beyond 65 (male) and 23 years (female), with the next generation of kids likely to live a further five years.

While on one level this is an achievement, fiscally it is a problem, with the New Zealand Superannuation Fund (NZ Super Fund) having to support people for far longer than was originally intended. Internationally, more than half of the OECD countries have responded to this by increasing the age at which people are entitled to pensions to 67.

Retirement commissioner Diane Maxwell, in her report to the government in December 2013, suggested increasing the pension age to 67 by 2017, with a 10-year notice period before it came into effect. This would effectively mean that, by 2027, the retirement age would have increased to 67, with an ongoing 'schedule and review' of the pension age and fore-casted life expectancy. Amongst other things, the objective is to give transparency and adequate notice of age of eligibility changes. The core principle is to ensure that each resident enjoys the same proportion of their life receiving government superannuation.

In her report, Maxwell also suggests a longer-term schedule for eligibility increases and the year in which they would take effect. Personally, I think the government should just raise it in one go and get it sorted out so people can better plan for their financial future.

Eligibility age	66	67	68
Proposed year for new age to be in place	2036	2046	2056

Other suggested changes include changing the index to calculate the pension entitlement (that is, if 32% of a person's life after the age of 20 should be funded by a pension, the age at which this entitlement starts would rise as life expectancies rise), changing the entitlement depending on when a citizen chooses to use their super (meaning they would receive less when they first retire, then an increasing amount as their ability to work decreases) and means testing. It is unlikely means testing will be used, as it can be seen as punishing savings behaviour and might discourage people from working longer or act as an incentive for them to hide their wealth.

HELPING OURSELVES

New Zealanders are not currently saving enough for retirement, with our level of savings much lower than other countries within the OECD.

Lack of data has meant it is difficult to determine to what level we need to be saving, and whether the government should introduce policies to force people to save. While the amount of money needed for retirement varies from person to person, it is widely accepted that the amount of money the New Zealand Superannuation Fund will provide in the future will be insufficient to fund the lifestyle many want to live. There will be a gap, a shortfall. While the size of the estimated shortfall varies, attempts have been made to establish a general savings target, with a wide range of conclusions.

Based on a 25-year retirement, the Retirement Commission estimates that $205,000 in savings per person (in today's dollars) would be needed on top of NZ Super to fund a comfortable retirement. The Financial Services Council has estimated a higher figure of $300–450,000 per person. This is assuming you are mortgage free going into retirement.

An ANZ study has found that more than 53% of superannuants would like up to $300 per week more than the current NZ Super payout in order to live their definition of a basic lifestyle.

The hardest thing about determining how much you need for retirement is understanding what you need to be happy now and balancing that with what you need to be happy in the future. This is subjective and differs for each person. But let's assume

Will the government help me?

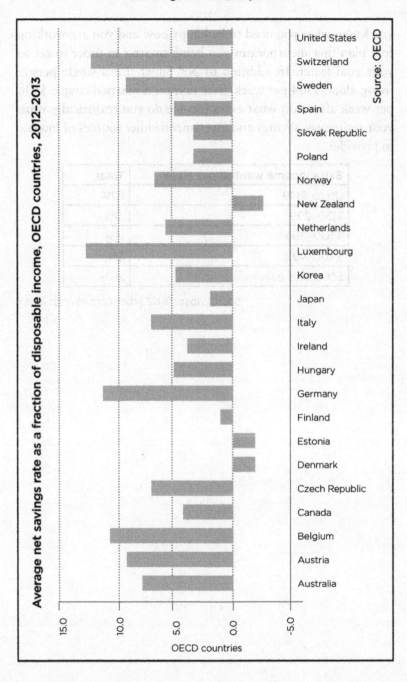

you know what you need to be happy now and you are working to a plan that incorporates you being smarter in order to get to your goal faster. In addition to NZ Super (for a single person living alone $364 per week after tax; for a married couple $536 per week after tax) what extra income do you realistically want your retirement savings and investments/other sources of income to provide?

Extra income wanted per week	Total
Up to $149	22%
$150–299	31%
$300–399	15%
$400-499	6%
$500 and over	26%

Source: Ipsos/ANZ retirement savings index

Chapter 26

What's your number?

To determine how much money you will need for retirement, you need to work through this chapter, which I have divided into four parts. If you work through these points you can determine what your retirement number is—or what you need in the bank by retirement to fund your retirement.

CASH SURPLUS AND MORTGAGE

- What is your cash surplus now?
- Do you have a mortgage?
- How long before you pay off this mortgage?

TIMING

- How many years are you away from being mortgage free?
- What will your annual cash surplus be after you have paid off your mortgage (up until retirement)?
- How many years of working life will you have left after becoming mortgage free?

- How much will you accumulate until retirement through this surplus?

ONE-OFF EVENTS

- When do you plan on taking a big holiday or replacing cars (and how much do you plan to spend)?
- Do you plan to downsize your home when you retire?
- How much do you want to leave to your kids?
- What size inheritance, if any, do you expect to receive?
- What will your KiwiSaver balance be at retirement?

NEEDS IN RETIREMENT

- What will your annual costs be in retirement?
- Determine your annual cash deficit—the difference between New Zealand Superannuation and your annual costs.

Work this out on a giant worksheet—see Appendix III. Forget about inflation, forget about exact numbers—the purpose of this exercise is to get the gist of where you will end up.

When trying to calculate this number for my clients, I run three different budgets concurrently. The first budget looks at what they are doing now. The second budget determines what I think we could achieve if they were prepared to get serious, capture the fritter factor, put a framework in place and be accountable to an outcome. The second budget is my projection of their capability, which is initially untested. The third budget is what their lifestyle will look like in retirement.

CALCULATING YOUR LIFETIME CASHFLOW

If you are trying to gauge where you might end up, then first you need to calculate how long it will be before you are mortgage free.

Then you can multiply your annual cash surplus at the point of being mortgage free by the number of years you will have left until retirement. This becomes your *lifetime cashflow.*

To this amount, add in the amount you might free up by downsizing your home at retirement, plus your likely KiwiSaver balance.

Now subtract your one-off costs between becoming mortgage free and death. How many big holidays do you plan to take? Car replacements? Repairs to the house?

The result is your total cash inflow or *accumulated savings.* At 65 or 70 (or whenever you are planning on retiring), your savings should be at their maximum, as this is what will fund you until retirement.

Now you need to work out when this money will run out. Work out a budget for your retirement. When I am working with clients, I assume their discretionary costs will drop by 20% (because they have to) and some of their fixed costs might also reduce (e.g. life insurance, which usually becomes prohibitively expensive due to its high premiums as you age). This is for you to decide. What income, if any, will you receive in retirement? At a push you could include the pension (if you plan on retiring in the next 10–15 years).

Calculate your annual cash deficit when you retire (the shortfall in income less expenses). Multiply this amount by the number of years you will spend in retirement (up to age 90). This is how much you need. Subtract what you have from what you need. The difference is your buffer—or your *shortfall.*

This exercise is a huge reality check for my clients. Too many go into it with no idea of their financial situation. They are expecting that the laissez-faire attitude they have taken during their working life will flow over into retirement. I assure you it cannot.

Once you know the size of your shortfall, the question becomes: how can I bridge the gap between what I will need, and what I will have? The good news is there are five key options.

1. Earn more.
2. Spend less.
3. Reduce your one-off costs.
4. Invest to get a higher return.
5. Use leverage to buy a capital-gain asset (provided you have at least 15 years until you will need the funds).

Tip: Spending less is probably the easiest option. If you reduce your costs by $5000 per annum for the next 10 years, then that is $50,000 of ground made towards bridging the gap of your shortfall.

Case study: couple in their 30s

My clients were a couple in their late 30s with two young children and a mortgage of $510,000. Initially they were not saving—in fact, they were trying to find enough money to cover their ballooning daycare costs and this became their excuse for their lack of progress. When I started to work with them they were frittering in excess of $20,000 per annum, in spite of their daycare bill.

Our first job was to find this money and redirect it to debt repayment. We also needed to restructure their mortgage to repay their debt faster. Working to this plan they are now on track to be mortgage free in just over 10 years, when they will be in their late 40s.

Barring any major curveballs, we can then assume that the money that was going into repaying their mortgage will then go into a savings account (for later investment). This will continue to grow until they retire, at which point their KiwiSaver will be paid out. Assuming this is added to their savings, they would have accumulated approximately $1,300,000 (in today's dollars).

Once retired, they would start to eat into their savings balance, until the funds are exhausted when they are in their late 80s.

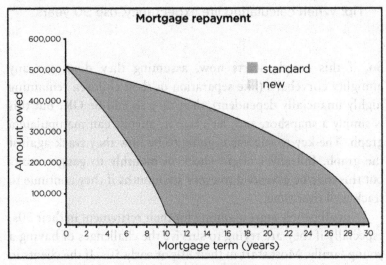

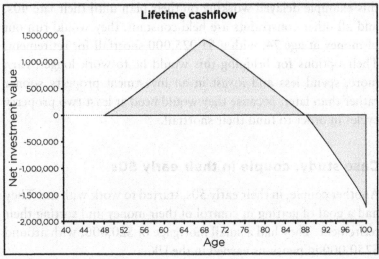

Their cashflow projections do not factor in downsizing their home or any inheritances received. The trick for them is to continue to find the money that is being lost and start to more aggressively pay off their mortgage.

Tip: When calculating life expectancy, use 90 years.

So, if this couple starts now, assuming they don't get any almighty curveballs (like separation or their children remaining highly financially dependent), then they should be OK. But this is simply a snapshot, and, let's face it, anyone can manipulate a graph. The key to success is going to be how they track against the graph. Initially I might check in monthly to gauge results but this may be extended to every six months if they continue to track well over time.

Not all people start planning for their retirement in their 30s, especially if they are trying to survive the challenges of having a young family. Most start in their 40s or early 50s. If the clients in this example delayed working on their plan until their late 40s, and all other constraints are held constant, they would run out of money at age 74, with a $1,025,000 shortfall for retirement. Their options for bridging this would be to work longer, earn more, spend less and invest in an investment property sooner rather than later, because they would need at least two property cycles in order to fund their shortfall.

Case study: couple in their early 50s

Another couple, in their early 50s, started to work with me. They had a goal of getting in control of their money and sorting their retirement. They had a small mortgage of $20,000, with around $250,000 in pensions earned in the UK.

They felt they had left their run late. Initially they were going backwards financially, using their revolving-credit facility to absorb their overspending. I was able to stop them going backwards but could only create a small cash surplus on a week-by-week basis, as their fixed costs were disproportionately high. This was an annual improvement of $25,000, although it created only a moderate cash surplus of $19,000 as a chunk of this money was needed to stop them going backwards. However, it was enough to pay off their overdraft in a little over 12 months.

Based on their improved situation, if they were mortgage free in 12 months, then their cash surplus of $19,000 plus their mortgage repayments of $1500 per annum could be combined and saved for the next 13 years. They would have saved in excess of $300,000 by the time they hit retirement, at which point their pension of $250,000 would be paid out and added to their savings.

If we assumed their discretionary spending was cut back by $10,000 when they retired, then their funds would last until they were aged 76.

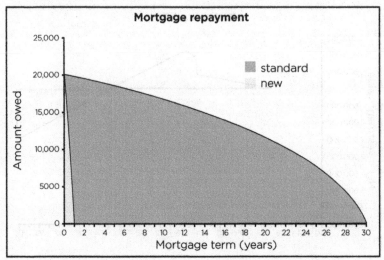

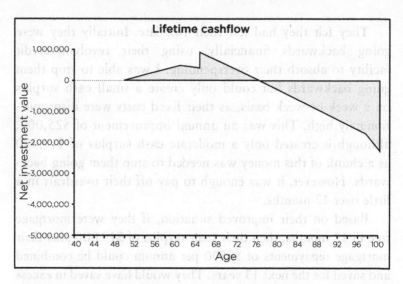

If these clients were prepared to work until the age of 68, however, saving at the same rate they could fund their retirement until they were aged 82. While it is easy to suggest they should work until 68, they would need to be prepared to do this and to be working in an industry where work would be available for older staff.

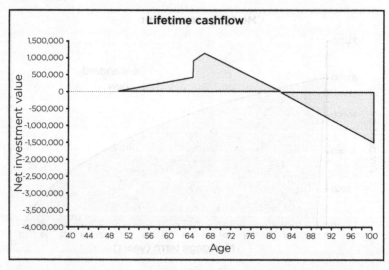

Based on this scenario, we estimated that their shortfall in retirement (up to the age of 90) would be $465,228. They had four options for bridging the gap.

1. Earn more money, either through pay increases beyond inflation, or by working for longer.
2. Spend less—before and during retirement.
3. Downsize their home.
4. Use the equity in their home to buy another property.

Through a combination of higher income and cost reductions they could increase their annual cash surplus before retirement by approximately $27,400 per annum. However, this may come at the cost of not enjoying their lifestyle or, worse, deterioration in health due to overwork.

Using the equity in their property to borrow money to invest in something that will create a return exceeding the cost of borrowings would also be a good option. Because their capital (excluding their home) will run out in 30 years' time (when they are in their early 80s), this suggests they have close to 30 years to realise a capital gain, provided the holding costs are not prohibitive.

Tip: If increasing your cash surplus is an option, then go for it. If downsizing your home is an option, then do it. But if in exhausting these options you realise there is still little room to move, you need to consider leveraging your equity to grow your savings faster, or else lower your expectations for retirement.

Case study: couple in their early 50s with a large mortgage

Kim and Tom, a couple in their early 50s, had a mortgage of $300,000, which was on a 25-year term. They did not have a cash surplus, but were able to meet their mortgage payments each month. Based on this, they would be on track to repay their mortgage by the time they were in their mid-70s, assuming they could earn at the same level until that age. However, they planned to stop working at 65.

Keeping their mortgage payments static, and making no changes to their finances, in order to be mortgage free by the age of 65, they would have to downsize their home by $300,000. They did not want to do this, which meant they had to get serious about their situation and develop a plan to improve it.

They frittered away $30,000 per annum. We found this and put them on a plan to kill their mortgage in seven years. This goal factored in a $10,000 annual holiday and car replacements.

We then had to work on a strategy to prepare for retirement. They had eight years to save for retirement once they were

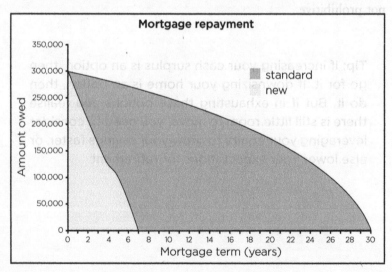

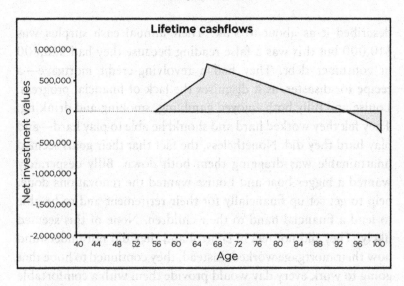

Lifetime cashflows

mortgage free. Based on the assumption they would channel their cash surplus, including what was being put on the mortgage, into savings, they would have saved $415,000 for retirement. These savings, combined with their KiwiSaver balances, meant that they would have a total of $590,000 to live off. From the graph above, you can see that this will fund their lifestyle until they are aged 92, without having to downsize their home.

Case study: couple in their early 50s on an average income

Louise and Billy were aged 50 and 52 respectively, with a combined after-tax income of $98,000 when they first came to me. They were contributing to their employers' superannuation schemes at 4% and these contributions were being matched by their employers. Their home was worth $330,000 and they were partway through a renovation, with a further $20,000 to spend. They had a $224,000 mortgage. They also had other debts, including for the purchase of $20,000 boat.

They said their situation was stagnant, but I would have

described it as about to sink. Their annual cash surplus was $10,000 but this was a false reading because they had $20,000 in consumer debt. They had a revolving-credit mortgage—a recipe for disaster, as it disguises the lack of financial progress. Louise and Billy both enjoyed gambling, smoking and drinking. They felt they worked hard and should be able to play hard—and play hard they did. Nonetheless, the fact that their goals seemed unattainable was dragging them both down. Billy desperately wanted a bigger boat and Louise wanted the renovations done, help to get set up financially for their retirement and to be able to lend a financial hand to their children. None of this seemed likely. They did not feel in control and they did not understand how their mortgage worked. Instead, they continued to hope that going to work every day would provide them with a comfortable retirement.

After our first meeting, my assessment showed their mortgage would not be repaid by retirement age, nor would there be any additional money to fund their retirement. A bigger boat was certainly not possible. They had no inclination to change their lifestyle, so any plan would need to factor in gambling, smoking and drinking. The best plans make allowances for natural tendencies!

Their mortgage rate was high given the type of property they owned and because of how their bank had structured it. We were able to refinance with another bank that viewed their property more favourably, reducing the interest rate and allowing a much-needed top-up to clear their debts and fund the last of the renovations. You could say they went backwards to get ahead, but time was not on their side—their retirement was less than 15 years away.

If Louise and Billy kept doing what they had been doing they would have been mortgage free in 20 years, but would still be feeling weighed down by their finances and not making any additional progress towards helping their family. After factoring in their goals and working backwards to establish what needed to be adjusted, we were able to build a plan that not only had their mortgage repaid in seven years but also allowed for the bigger boat and opened the door for them to have the choice of retiring at 62 (and they didn't have to give up their vices).

Three years later they have completed their renovations and bought the bigger boat. They are $3300 ahead of schedule, and projecting forward at that rate of progress they will be mortgage free in less than three years, which is much better than what was initially projected. After that point, the mortgage-repayment money can be saved too, putting them even further ahead of their plan.

If they continue to stick to this plan until they are aged 62, they will be able to fund their retirement until they are 81— assuming they receive a government pension at age 65. If they get a pay rise above inflation during this period, they could extend the time over which they could fund their lifestyle in retirement or even decide to retire sooner.

As a further step, Louise and Billy have decided to acquire an investment property for their children to live in. The children will pay market rent and this will be sufficient to cover the mortgage, so Louise and Billy are not topping up the property. However, the main objective of this purchase is to make a capital gain on the property, from which the entire family will benefit in the long term. This is a great example of using family resources to everyone's advantage.

Case study: single woman turning 60 with a mortgage

Doris had just turned 60 and was single (having been widowed three years earlier) with two adult children when she first came to me. She worked as a human resources advisor and had a before-tax salary of $70,000 per annum. She had just started contributing to KiwiSaver at a rate of 3%. She had had a stroke approximately 12 months before coming to see me.

She owned a property worth $700,000 that was next door to her daughter's property. She had a $250,000 mortgage. There was a large home and a minor dwelling on her property, and Doris lived in the minor dwelling and rented out the main house for $600 per week.

The mortgage on her property had 17 years to run. She thought she was operating her finances to break even. However, if she had factored in the biennial trips overseas she enjoyed, she would have seen that she was going backwards. Because of the support she got from her daughter living next door she did not want to move, nor did she want to give up her overseas travel. She was happy to work for another eight years.

She got a reality check when she had the stroke. Immediately afterwards her primary focus was on being able to return to work at full capacity. After that her concerns focused on her financial future, particularly looking forward to her retirement. Having no partner and not wanting to burden or involve her children in her finances, her resources were limited. As a single person, she knew it was up to her to make sure she was on track.

Doris realised that, although she had equity in her property, her cashflow was tight. If she continued paying her mortgage as it was currently structured it was going to take her 17 years to pay off, assuming she was able to keep up her mortgage repayments after her retirement in eight years' time.

Living in the minor dwelling was a good idea and suited her fine, but it wasn't enough to solve the problem of having to work until the mortgage was paid off, by which time Doris would have been celebrating her seventy-eighth birthday!

Doris had made some good decisions, but these decisions in isolation were still not enough to give her a good retirement fund. She needed to make a number of tweaks across the board to have the retirement she wanted. A plan would give her clarity about what she needed to spend to maintain her current lifestyle, and to reassure her she would still have a cash surplus. This meant restructuring her mortgage to allow her to build up a surplus and reduce her debt faster, and to save on interest. She also needed to maximise her tax deductions. Executed correctly, these simple changes were enough to achieve her goals, including her overseas travel.

When we started working together, we projected she would be mortgage free in eight years. After three years she is on track to achieve this. She has also enjoyed a lovely trip to Spain and is planning a trip to Alaska next year. If Doris can continue this plan until she is 68 she will have paid off her entire mortgage and be able to retire 10 years before she would have originally been able to. The rental income she receives from her former home will sustain her lifestyle indefinitely.

Chapter 27

It's time for action

Winston Churchill said that continuous effort, not strength or intelligence, is the key to unlocking our potential. I agree. But for effort to be continuous you need to see results, and you will not get results unless you have a plan and clarity about what you need to do to get there. Clarity, or a framework and structured process, builds confidence, which builds competence, which gains momentum to see results.

Before you can develop a plan of attack you need to understand where you are starting from. What is your financial BMI? And, more importantly, if you keep doing what you are doing, will you achieve the results you need for a prosperous life and enjoyable retirement?

This is where most people fall short, because they misdiagnose their starting point and are uninformed about the speed at which they can get ahead. Some set their goals too low, underselling themselves, while others are lofty in their financial ambitions, setting themselves up for failure. If you don't see the expected results within the agreed timeframe, you will lose heart and fall off the wagon—I get it. But this is avoidable. You want to know that you are on track, or what you need to do to get on track. Knowledge is power, and power is control. You need to be in control of your finances, and the easiest way to do this is to see results fast. The beauty of managing your finances without emotion is that the outcome is a mathematical certainty.

Once you get started, you will build some momentum by initially moving in the right direction. But you need to build this up as fast as possible if you want to get results quickly.

In my opinion, being accountable to someone outside of your relationship is key to getting an accurate diagnosis of your starting point and determining what you are capable of, but most importantly to keep you honest and working to your plan. *Do not let your genetics determine your financial potential.* Understand your money personality and the role money plays (or doesn't play) in your relationship to increase your chances of success.

Follow these steps to ensure you make progress fast:
1. understand your psychology of spending
2. create a cash surplus
3. make a plan
4. stick to your plan
5. buy a property
6. pay off the mortgage
7. save
8. retire!

Remember, money is not bigger than you, and retirement is not unachievable. It does not matter if you are starting on the back foot—everyone is capable of doing better. Take control of your money and take control of your life.

It is one thing to start a journey, and it's another thing to finish it. It's yet another thing altogether to finish it in the shortest possible time. Perseverance is key—and getting the right results time and time again is what creates the best outcomes. There are no shortcuts.

Calvin Coolidge, the thirtieth president of the United States, said it best when he said:

Nothing in the world can take the place of persistence. Talent will not; nothing is more common than unsuccessful men with talent. Genius will not; unrewarded genius is almost a proverb. Education will not; the world is full of educated derelicts. Persistence and determination alone are omnipotent.

KEEPING MOTIVATED

The most effective motivator is getting results, fast. Anyone would be prepared to make a concession on a day-to-day basis if they could see the benefits immediately. Likewise, there is nothing more demoralising than trying hard but not seeing a result.

The beauty about managing your money without emotion and following a plan exactly as it is set out is that the results become a mathematical certainty—you simply can't stop yourself getting ahead faster. The plan must be the perfect balance of stretching you to your capability without compromising your ability to achieve.

To do this you need to optimise all aspects of your financial life—that means every aspect of your finances, including your mortgage, bill payments, any investments you may have and your discretionary spending—to make sure they are working together to get the best possible results for you.

It is my experience that, when all the elements of a plan are working together well, your past behaviour will not dictate your capability. Don't leave anything to chance. Tweak everything a little bit and you won't notice much change in the things you need to be doing, but you will notice a different outcome. For something to be sustainable, the change has to be minute, but the impact huge.

THE CERTAINTY OF RESULTS

It is comforting to be able to rely wholly on an outcome, leaving nothing to chance. Looking forward to a promised result brings comfort and builds confidence. Equally, the surprise of an unexpected outcome, especially a negative one, creates confusion and despondency.

Nothing demonstrates this better than trying to lose weight. I know when I go on a strict diet and follow it to the letter—drinking eight glasses of water and exercising—but hop on the scales at the end of the week to find that I haven't lost any weight, the despair is overwhelming. This is the same feeling many people get when they make a concession in one area of their spending or receive a pay rise only to find their circumstances don't improve.

That said, positive outcomes can also cause confusion and, if you do not make adjustments to the change in your circumstances, all too often the positive is not exploited to its full potential. (What really is the best thing to do with Great-aunt Maud's unexpected legacy?)

There are other parallels between trying to lose weight and trying to get ahead financially. This is one of the reasons I call myself a Financial Personal Trainer! As I said above, if you have tried to lose weight one week and not achieved anything—or even worse, put on weight—this can be a trigger to fall off the wagon well and truly. Instead of hitting the gym with more force many simply feel demoralised, and open and finish a packet of Tim Tams. It's emotional and illogical, but it still happens.

Similar emotions affect people who've experienced a setback with money. If they feel like they have tried to stick to a budget but their circumstances do not seem any better or they are not seeing their debt reduce, then they get frustrated and demoralised. Instead of trying to save more, they hit the shops and splurge in frustration. This reaction, while emotional, is fairly common.

The key to combating this is to ensure you get the results you expect and for those results to be sustainable.

GAINING MOMENTUM

To gain momentum you need to be on the move. With a good plan in place you will start to move in the right direction and that is when you want to gain momentum—not when you are going backwards! Remember these three steps for gaining and building momentum to achieve your goals.

1. A good plan creates forward movement.
2. Movement builds momentum.
3. Momentum gets you to your goals.

In the beginning, moving in the right direction is the goal. After that, you can begin to gain momentum towards your financial goals and look to build speed. The first 12 weeks of any plan are the most critical. You have to get some runs on the board during this first quarter, otherwise you will lose interest and likely splurge on some unnecessary spending as a way of numbing the disappointment of your poor performance.

In building momentum, it is important you create an environment that empowers you and encourages you to behave the way you know you should. If you need to be accountable to someone in order to reach your potential, find a reliable advisor that you trust and get on with it.

Personally, I check in with my financial coach every 12 weeks, as I have a way of rationalising anything and everything to myself, and I still sometimes lose sight of my longer-term goals.

HOW DO I STICK TO A PLAN?

To stick to a long-term financial plan, you need four things to be operating in unison.

- You must not be feeling deprived.
- You need regular, independent assessment of your potential as your circumstances change.
- You need to get results.
- You need to be accountable for the results you get.

BEING ACCOUNTABLE

Fact: being accountable to someone qualified and impartial increases the chances that you will reach your goals faster. Many people happily use personal trainers and sports coaches to improve performance on the sports field, or in their day-to-day lives to help them keep their weight under control. Whether you are morbidly obese or an elite athlete, it is accepted that the support and guidance of a coach or personal trainer can help you do things better and faster. They help remove imaginary limitations and overcome real obstacles. They motivate you and keep emotion out of the equation. For the same reasons, you should seek assistance with managing your finances to get further ahead faster. Good financial coaches can dance between the dynamics of different money personalities and different financial goals to get the best results for you.

A Financial Personal Trainer is there to quantify your potential, down to the last dollar. If you are time-poor, their expertise can fast-track your progress. Not only will you get ahead faster, but you will also have a sounding board for all your financial decisions—having someone impartial to discuss your finances with allows you to mitigate the effects of the money dynamic in your relationships and helps you suppress any irrational behaviour you may have around money. A Financial Personal Trainer will also help you master any negative natural tendencies by cutting to the chase without emotion. They'll keep you on track to achieve your goals as quickly as your circumstances allow.

Getting ahead faster is not reserved for the financially successful; it is an entitlement for all.

If you do not want to work with a Financial Personal Trainer, you have to have the ability to be honest and open about your finances. You could sit down with friends and set goals and check in with each other to make sure you are on track to achieve them. Have a budget party! Just remember that if you are struggling it can often pay to speak to someone who is qualified and independent. You need to know your capability and often self-diagnosis sets the bar too low.

Even though I have written a comprehensive and effective programme to help people get ahead faster, I still apply the same principles to myself. We have paid off one mortgage. I still check in with my coach to make sure that we are living to our potential. Some of the stuff he tells me I already know, and some of it I know but am not doing. Someone emotionally disconnected from my situation can see things that I can't because I'm too close to see the wood for the trees—even though I'm the financial equivalent of an arborist.

Tip: It is important that your coach does not have anything to gain if you increase your debt or invest in a particular asset field. If this is the case they must, at the very least, disclose their conflict of interest. Conflicts of interest are rife in the world of finance, so be sure to ask any advisor directly if they know of any conflict of interest they may have.

Part Five

OTHER FACTORS

Chapter 28

Helping your children— a hand up, not a hand out

As you get older, the two most common and costly risks to your retirement goals are your adult children and relationship break-down (see Chapter 29).

It's natural to want to help your children. Many people enjoy seeing their children benefiting from their generosity, and living to see this is a joy. But remember, some gifts, no matter how well intentioned, may be something that will hurt your children in the long run—especially if the gifts encourage a lifestyle your child cannot afford. You want your gifts to encourage independence, not maintain a dependency.

So, how can you support your kids to achieve their financial potential without undermining the necessary life skill of money management?

To raise a financially responsible kid is to raise a socially responsible one. Whatever you teach them about the environment, you should be teaching them in equal part about managing money well. Do you want your children to inherit your work ethic or the bludger ethic? I have seen parents scrimp and save to better their position and give themselves a chance for a comfortable retirement, only for one of their useless children to suck them dry while their parents are unable to stop it. It is a parent's job to train their kids in the competencies they need to grow and keep wealth.

I am not suggesting that you shouldn't be generous with your children. If you are going to be generous, though—and even if you aren't—bear in mind that as a parent you play a huge part in the financial makeup and ongoing success of your children. A hand up is always better than a hand out.

The first step is to be a good example. Get your finances in order and start living within your means with a strategy to own a house, kill the mortgage and sort your retirement, or at the very least be getting ahead financially. Then you need to teach your children. This is where most people fall short. They are their children's worst enemy when it comes to financial fitness.

Being generous with your kids can be just what they need to reach their potential. But, in most instances, it will become the very thing that derails their financial growth. I am seeing more and more children enabled by their parents to under-achieve financially, whether the parents have wealth to spare or not.

Research and common sense confirms that children given too much too soon tend to develop a distorted sense of entitlement, which makes it difficult to cope with the roller coaster of life.

The financial environment you provide for your child while they are growing up will be one of the most important influences in their financial fate. This is a huge responsibility for parents who also lack the necessary life skills of successful money management.

The behaviour you instil in your children will stay with them long after they leave home. This makes it doubly onerous as, on an emotional level, you don't want them to go without, especially if you can afford to be generous.

As a parent, you need to make sure your children know how to:
- save
- spend wisely
- earn money
- talk about money.

The parents of daughters need to take greater care to discharge this responsibility, as too many adult women are still dependent on their partner to create financial success. Women might start to care more about gender inequality if we showed them how to develop plans without relying on someone else!

Reality check: Over-indulging your child with material possessions will almost certainly seal their fate as shoppers and make it very difficult for them to cope with instances of delayed gratification. Kids often come home and cite things others have or advertising they have seen as justification for their wants. If your kids do this—and mine are just starting—then simply say, 'We can afford it, but that is not how we choose to spend our money in this family.'

Children tend to be disconnected from the reality of their family's financial situation, usually because parents enable this—often because the parents are also disconnected. For all the families I work with, I encourage age-appropriate honesty with the kids. If the money is running out, explain this and explain what you as a family need to do to fix it, the reasons why and the rewards at the end. *Don't devalue this critical learning experience.*

We teach our children to try their very best at everything they do. But what if they lose? What if they are aiming to be top and they fail? Learning to work through failure constructively is just as important as learning to be a humble winner. Financial failings are some of the best learning experiences for everyone, including your children.

Some parents don't want to share their financial situation with their kids because they are embarrassed. Yet, because of that, you should. We are accountable to our children. They are trusting us to do the right thing by them—socially, physically and financially. If things are tight, demonstrate this to your kids. Show them that when the money runs out it is gone. Teach them that credit is not their friend. Get your house in order. The happy side effect of teaching your kids good money habits is that you, as their parent, will need to lift your game to lead by example. Everyone wins!

TEACHING YOUR KIDS ABOUT MONEY

First things first: teach your children that income less expenses equals surplus or deficit. Surplus equals choices or options. Deficit equals problems.

A tangible example is the most effective way of showing this. Gather the family round the kitchen table and show them, using real money, what is coming in and what is going out.

- Withdraw your entire monthly income after tax in cash (in $50, $20, $10 and $5 notes).
- Print out your bills (utilities, mortgage, etc.). Show receipts of your car bills, groceries, school costs, hobbies, etc.
- Put all the money you make into the middle of the table. Tell your kids that this is what you earn every month. They can touch it, count it, hold it, but the point is that there is a fixed amount of money coming into the household every month. It can seem like a lot initially.
- Next, ask your kids what the costs are for running the household. Get them to yell out the things they think of,

such as mortgage or rent, electricity, phone, food and
school costs. Get them to write these things in a list.

- Check off their list against your list, getting them to add
  the expenses they missed to their list.
- Beside each expense, get them to write down the monthly
  cost. Show them the bill so they can see how much it is.
  After they have written the amount down, have someone
  remove that money from the middle of the table.
- Continue writing down expenses and removing money
  from the table until you are left with an amount which
  represents how much money you have left over to spend
  on discretionary items.

This exercise is a very effective way of engaging the family with
the reality of your financial position. When working with my
clients, I encourage them to bring their children to our meetings
so they start to understand how financial discussions should be
handled, and what obstacles Mum and Dad are facing and how
they are choosing to navigate them. It is a powerful learning
exercise that can make the parents a little uncomfortable, but is
enlightening for their kids.

POCKET MONEY AND ALLOWANCES

Sound financial parenting begins with pocket money. It is fixed
and regular, and is the most effective tool for teaching your
children about money management.

The amount you should pay varies according to your
children's ages. I advise $1 for every year of age up to the teenage
years, when you need to take a different approach to paying
allowances. You need to increase the child's responsibility as
they get older, increasing the allowance and stretching out the
frequency of payment from weekly to monthly once they hit high
school. Too many adults struggle to budget if they are not paid

weekly or if their pay cycle is out of alignment with when bills are paid. Adjusting the frequency of your child's allowance helps them to develop this skill.

People often ask me what is an appropriate time to start paying your child an allowance. Realistically, an allowance needs to be introduced when the child is asking to buy things like clothes, travel and technology.

From the age of around five or six, the general principle of an allowance should be introduced. Discuss with your children what the allowance can be used for—and what it can't. An allowance should be used to cover specific costs such as clothing, mobile phones and entertainment—things that children can control and choose to spend money on.

By the age of seven or eight, children should be required to do basic chores, such as making their bed each morning, setting the table and tidying their rooms every night. A child should be made to do chores to earn 'pocket money'. Pocket money is different to an allowance. An allowance is a set figure attributed to specific costs that the child is made responsible for managing. For example: as a parent you may chose to give your child $600 per annum to spend on clothes. This is the budget for clothes and the child is responsible for managing this budget/allowance. The allowance stands apart from pocket money, which is an incentive to earn more money.

By the age of 10 or 11 kids will have developed maths skills that you can put to work. Give them a list of everything they need for school and an allocated budget. Give them the money to pay for it, and let them keep the change.

Between the ages of 12 and 13 you should be adding money to their allowance for clothes purchases. Excluding big-ticket items (coats, shoes, etc.), let your child choose where the money goes and make their own mistakes.

Tip: Do not top up your child's allowance if they run out of cash before their next allowance is due. Give them the option of trying to sell some of their stuff (preferably not to you) or doing more jobs (refer them to the list of special jobs on the fridge).

INTRODUCING EFTPOS

- Give your kids an EFTPOS card, but encourage them to check their balance and to withdraw cash for purchases instead of using EFTPOS.
- Do not give your child access to your EFTPOS card.
- *Do not give them your credit card.*
- If your child wants something expensive (like going on a school trip), ask what they are going to do to contribute to it, what they will give up and why this thing is important (what are they going to get from it).

Allowance guidelines
- Give $1 for every year of the child's age (e.g. a six-year-old should be given $6 a week).
- Give the money to them in cash. Encourage them to physically bank the money or to put it into a money jar.
- You are trying to teach your children that the money received is not simply for them to spend on their wants. It is to teach them to plan for the future, to enjoy their purchases, to give and, most importantly, to save.

299

- For the first two years of pocket money (from the age of six or seven) give your child three piggy banks. Label them:
  - Fun money (45%)—for something they want to buy
  - Giving (10%)—for charity
  - Saving (45%)—for something that lasts, an asset or something you need.
- So, of the $6 given to a six-year-old, for example, allocate $2.50 to fun, $1 to giving and $2.50 to saving.
- Let your children research the charity they want to give money to and take them to visit the charity with their donation, so they can make a physical payment and see first-hand what they are supporting.
- Start bringing their financial decisions to life. Show them how their financial actions have consequences. Let them experience the joy of giving and the excitement of saving for something.

The great thing about allowances or pocket money is that you can teach your children in a safe environment the difference between want and need.

Fun money is to be spent on doing things they want and love—things like buying an ice cream, going to the movies or buying a kids' magazine or book.

Savings are a way for them to get what they want or need. Naturally, items that need to be saved for tend to be more costly and are supposed to have a lasting benefit. Things kids might put their savings towards could include buying sports equipment or more expensive books or games. When it comes to savings, encourage your children to think about what they want to buy. They might not know initially, and in the absence of a specific goal encourage them to keep growing their little nest-egg.

Sit down and help them with the maths so they have an idea of what they could afford if they saved for a longer period of time. Based on the numbers above, my five-year-old would save $2 per week, so over the course of a year he would build up $100. He could grow it faster by doing extra jobs.

Show them that they could grow their savings even faster if they saved some of their fun money as well. They will determine something they want to save for once they have some financial boundaries.

Once they select their savings goal, get them to cut or print out a picture of their goal and glue it to the savings jar. A bit of positive visualisation is never a bad thing.

More tips
- Encourage your teenager to get a part-time or holiday job—the more mundane and boring the better! It teaches them to suit up and show up every day, to get on with others and to realise that if they don't want to work in this type of job for the rest of their lives then they need to apply themselves.
- Teach your children the value of a purchase. When buying something, get them to go through the process of determining if they need it right now, or if it can wait a week, or what could be substituted for it.
- Teach your children to always turn the lights off when they leave the room. Assign someone the task of being the household 'energy saver'.

- Talk to your children about money. It shows you respect them.

IMPROVING YOUR CHILDREN'S FINANCIAL LITERACY

Developing your child's financial literacy requires consistent effort. You must assume responsibility for this. Help your child to build age-appropriate financial skills beyond budgeting and delayed gratification.

The following table, which is based on my work with families and draws from books such as *Bratproofing Your Children: How to Raise Socially and Financially Responsible Kids* by Janet and Lewis Solomon, shows a suggested programme of financial development.

Age	Suggested implementation
5–6	Pay pocket money in coins Have clear jars, so they can see the stack of coins growing Start playing Monopoly and teach the concepts behind it
7–8	Open a savings account at the bank Explain the principles of interest Encourage them to save 40% of their allowance Encourage 'birthday cash' to be deposited in the bank
9–10	Help them understand the household budget—show them the income coming in (using real cash) and the standard household expenses (see page 296)
11–12	Explain different wealth-creation options Introduce stock-market basics Chose a stock and follow it for the year—get them to pay you for a share, and if it makes money or pays a dividend pay this to your child

12–13	Encourage them to get a job and earn some extra cash on a regular basis Give them an EFTPOS card Entrepreneurship starts to develop at this time Encourage this by helping them with business plans, including how to market the venture and the profit it will make. If they want to set up a business, encourage them; this is a teachable moment
14–16	Introduce them to the concept of bonds Talk to your children about your own situation, including what you have done right and your failures Help them to work out their own budget and what income levels they will need to enjoy their current lifestyle—this can help them to narrow down suitable jobs based on the quality of life they want
16–18	Start saving for university—for every $1 they save you need to try to match it Involve your children in the discussions around significant financial family decisions
18 and over	Introduce your child to your family's financial plans Introduce them to your financial advisor, to develop a more sophisticated understanding of money matters

LOANS

If you loan your adult child money, be sure to document this as a loan that has to be repaid on demand. If your child is in a relationship with someone, make sure you lend the money to both of them (with a loan agreement) because, in the event of their relationship ending, you want to make sure that the money owed to you is part of the relationship settlement. Obviously you could forgive your child's portion (post-settlement) or reimburse this to them once you have been repaid. I have seen two instances where parents loaned money to their child to buy a home with their partner only for the relationship to end and the ex-partner to take no responsibility for repaying the loan back to the parents.

This could have been avoided if things were better documented (see Chapter 29).

Using the equity in your home can be a way to help out your kids, as well as being a great opportunity to leverage to buy a second property for yourself. Obviously this comes with some risk and losing is an unacceptable outcome when your home is exposed.

To limit risk, borrow 20% of the value of the investment property against your home from your existing bank. For the mortgage for the investment property, go to another bank, and use your 20% deposit to obtain funding for the remaining 80%. This way, you have limited the exposure against your home to 20% of the investment-property value.

> **Tip:** Your bank will always try and cross secure your properties, but often they don't have to, and you don't need to in order to get the finance.

Chapter 29

Relationship property

With relationships breaking down in record numbers, many people are having to start again both financially and emotionally later in life. While, on the one hand, this can be seen as an opportunity for a new start in both life and love, if you do start a new relationship, you could be exposing yourself to the risk of further diluting your wealth should that relationship fail too.

Few people can afford to lose their assets, so you need to protect them and understand that you could lose key components of your wealth unless you take time to protect yourself—from both your partner and yourself.

Generally all property acquired after a relationship begins is relationship property pursuant to the terms of the Property (Relationships) Act 1976. However, there are exceptions to this, one of which being the ability to acquire separate property during the course of a relationship even though that relationship may have existed for several years. This is particularly relevant to inheritances received.

WHAT IS RELATIONSHIP PROPERTY AND SEPARATE PROPERTY?

Under the Property (Relationships) Act, relationship property is usually shared equally and includes:
- the family home
- cars
- household furniture
- all property acquired while you are together, irrespective of who is on the title to those assets.

All property that is not relationship property is called 'separate property'. Most property owned by one person before the start of the marriage, civil union or de facto relationship is separate property, excluding the relationship property described above.

The Act provides that some limited forms of property acquired from third parties during the course of a relationship can be held as separate property. In particular, the following, if acquired from a third party (i.e. not the other spouse/partner) are separate property:
- property acquired by inheritance or gift, or
- property acquired because the person receiving the property is a beneficiary under a trust (which has been settled by a third person).

The Act also provides that property acquired as above will remain separate property unless:
- with the express or implied consent of the spouse/partner who received it, it becomes relationship property, or
- that property (or the proceeds from the sale of that property) has been so intermingled with other relationship property that it becomes unreasonable or impracticable to regard that property (or the proceeds) as separate property.

A common example is where one spouse/partner receives an inheritance. If that inheritance is then banked into a joint bank account (for example, by transfer from a solicitor's trust account) then, depending on what happens with the funds in that account, an intermingling argument could arise.

It is possible to protect an inheritance from intermingling by banking it into an account in the sole name of the person receiving the inheritance. However, this then prevents free use of those funds, as the receiving spouse/partner will always need to be aware of not using the funds in such a way as to suggest they have been intermingled. For example, it may prevent them from using those funds to reduce the mortgage on the family home. If the inheritance is property or personal chattels, and that property becomes the family home or family chattels, then it is deemed relationship property, unless both parties enter into a contracting-out agreement (see page 308).

To get around this, the spouse/partner receiving the inheritance could:

- transfer the funds into an inheritance trust, or
- enter into a contracting-out agreement to protect that asset from an intermingling argument.

If the relationship ends, assets are divided. They are either divided as agreed between the parties, or in line with a contracting-out agreement. Where no contracting-out agreement is in place, and no agreement can be reached, the assets are split under the rules of the Property (Relationships) Act.

DEBTS

Debts are also separated into personal debts and relationship debts. Relationship debts are taken into account when dividing the joint assets. Personal debts usually remain the responsibility of the person who incurred them.

RULE NO. 1: PROTECT WHAT YOU HAVE

If there is an uneven split of wealth between spouses when entering a relationship (either getting married or becoming de facto), then you need to protect yourself. (In NZ a relationship becomes de facto for relationship property matters after three years of living together as a couple.) It's not particularly romantic, but you need to ensure that if the relationship goes south you walk away with what you brought to the table. Whether you draw up a contracting-out agreement or put your property into a trust, take precautions.

When advising clients, I tend to take a simple view: what you bring to the relationship should remain separate property and what you amass in the relationship can become joint property. This is particularly relevant if you have children from a previous relationship. You need to make sure you are all protected.

> **Tip:** No reasonable person should take offence to you wanting to ring-fence your wealth built up before the relationship started. If they take offence this may be a 'red flag'.

Contracting-out agreements

If you agree to divide your property differently to how the Property (Relationships) Act splits it, you can contract out of the Act by entering into a contracting-out agreement. It acts in a similar way to how a pre-nuptial agreement (pre-nup) might, but it can be entered into before, during or after you split up.

For the agreement to be legally binding, you must ensure:
- the agreement is in writing and signed by both partners
- each partner gets independent legal advice before signing

- each partner's signature is witnessed by his or her lawyer, who must also certify that the lawyer has explained the effect and implications to that partner.

The High Court can cancel a contracting-out agreement if the agreement was so one-sided it could be considered a 'serious injustice'.

Receiving inheritances

If you receive an inheritance from a family member or friend, *please do not intermingle it with relationship property*, because if you separate from your partner at a later date you could lose half of it. I have seen this happen too often.

I recently had a female client who had inherited $200,000 and wanted to use this money towards home renovations. She was in a relationship which was a bit rocky. She did want to protect her inheritance, but she did not take any precautions and spent the money on the family home, which she owned jointly with her then-husband. The money spent increased the value of the house. They later split. Her husband got access to half the value of the house, which was inflated by her inheritance. Sad. Dumb. *Avoidable.*

Inheritances are supposed to be sacred, in the sense that if you were to separate from your spouse or de facto partner tomorrow, and had received a lump of money, they should have no claim to it. The problem, though, is that ignorant spouses can inadvertently jeopardise everything.

You need to understand what triggers an inheritance becoming relationship property so you can ensure you do not fall prey to this. If you use the inheritance for general living costs, then it could be said that you have intermingled it, therefore making it joint. If you share it with your spouse or apply it to joint assets, this could inadvertently taint it too.

To avoid this, you need to transfer the inheritance into a separate trust before it is used for any purpose. *Do not spend a dollar of it before doing this.* Ideally you would have the trust formed prior to receiving the inheritance, so that the inheritance bypasses any personal bank account altogether, but this is not always possible, especially when an inheritance is unexpected. At the very least, make sure the bank account the inheritance is being paid into is at a separate bank from your joint banking and is an account in your name only.

Transferring the money into a trust means that you no longer hold the inheritance; the trust does. This is a pertinent point in the case of a relationship break-up. If you do not own the property/wealth, then it cannot form part of the relationship property pool of assets for joint splitting.

If you want to use the inheritance to improve the joint family home, or within your relationship generally, then be sure to document the transfer as a loan to be repaid back to your trust on separation. If you want to use the inheritance for personal enjoyment, like a family holiday, you will need to advance the funds to you as a beneficiary of the trust, as opposed to linking the trust to your joint finances.

Take steps to protect the wealth your family has amassed and gifted to you. All too often it is the spouse of the beneficiary who has the most to say about the inheritance they are not entitled to. I have seen families torn apart by the spouse who has too much to say about something not directly related to them.

Do not think your relationship is sacred and therefore you don't need to take measures to protect your inheritance. It's not, and you do.

Chapter 30
Trusts

Trusts are becoming an increasingly popular way of protecting property and managing assets in New Zealand. You transfer the legal ownership of your assets to the trust, meaning you no longer personally own the property.

A trust is created when a person (usually you), called the *settlor*, transfers property to people known as *trustees* (usually you and an independent trustee such as a lawyer or accountant). Trustees are obliged by law to protect the assets of the trust for the *beneficiaries*, the people who have been set up to benefit from the trust (usually you and your family).

The way the trust property is to be dealt with and the parties involved are usually set out in a legal document known as the *trust deed*. Trusts can also be created by wills. Trusts can be set up for charitable purposes such as education, or they can be established specifically for the benefit of the members of a particular family.

The terms of trusts can differ markedly depending on the purpose for which a trust has been established. The type of trusts I most often work with are family trusts.

If you have wealth, I would encourage you to consider protecting it in a trust. The benefits of a trust can include:

- protection against claims from creditors—for example, to protect your family home from the potential failure of a business or general risk
- protection against relationship-property claims
- setting aside money for special reasons such as your children's education, or to ensure your children's partners or your future partners cannot access your wealth in the event of a relationship split
- managing the assets of someone who is unable to manage their own affairs, for example a child under 18 or a person with a disability
- avoiding unwanted claims on your estate when you die
- changing your tax liability.

The trust deed should be prepared by an accountant or lawyer who is experienced with trusts. Once the trust is established, assets can be sold to the trust at their market value. The trust does not have money to pay you for the assets, so it owes you the money and this is documented as a loan back to you (deed of debt). You do not want to be paid this money, as you have simply transferred one asset (the family home) for another asset (a loan back to you), which hasn't achieved any form of protection. On paper it is showing that, while you may have divested yourself of your home, the trust is recording a loan to you which it is obliged to repay unless you forgive the debt. To this end you go through a process of gifting or forgiving the debt to remove the trust's obligation to repay.

Before October 2011 there was a limit of $27,000 you could gift each year without incurring government gift duty. However, now that gift duty has been abolished so there is no limit to what you can gift each year. This means that a home worth $300,000, which prior to 2011 could have taken you over 11 years to transfer fully into the trust, can now be transferred immediately.

It is important to note that trust ownership is now unlikely to be used as a way to avoid rest-home fees, unless you have chosen to gift the debt back at a rate of $12,000 per annum per couple, over time. This is an arbitrary amount set by the government. For many people, the cost of prolonged gifting outweighs the benefit.

A family trust can last for no longer than 80 years, although the trustees can usually wind it up before then. The settlor (usually you) can add and remove beneficiaries as you need, as well as change the trustees.

The structure of a trust will depend on what the settlor specifically wants the trust to do. It is important to note that trustees, once appointed, cannot go ahead and just do anything they want with the trust property. They have powers that allow them to do certain things and duties that must be observed. These restrictions are based on:

- the trust deed—what does the deed expressly allow the trustees to do?
- legislation—what does the printed law allow or stop the trustees from doing?
- case law—what do cases that have already been decided prohibit or allow the trustees to do?

Depending on the complexity of your situation and the assets to be transferred into a trust, it may cost a few thousand dollars to get the trust set up correctly. Ongoing costs may include paying a professional trustee and completing financial statements for the trust.

Where most trusts come undone is in their ongoing management. I see too many clients who have gone to the expense and sometimes inconvenience of forming a trust only to not execute it correctly, or to not complete their gifting. In conjunction with this, they tend to run their personal spending through their trust bank account or revolving credit, potentially undermining the integrity of the trust and running the risk of the trust becoming a sham, which means that you could lose the advantages you were hoping to gain from a trust because the assets are not really the trust's but are in fact still yours.

> **Tip:** Forming a trust is a big decision, but usually a prudent choice if you have wealth you cannot afford to lose. Talk to your accountant or solicitor to understand more about family trusts.

> **Tip:** When you set up a trust, insert a clause to preclude future spouses from benefiting from the trust. This will protect your kids' inheritances from their partners. Also insert a clause that prevents new beneficiaries being added to the trust after you die.

Chapter 31

Death—what happens when you die?

When first working with my clients, I always ask them if their wills are up to date. In more than 80% of cases, they are not. In fact, many do not even have a will. What is more disturbing is that a lot of people without wills have children.

Everyone plans to get around to it eventually, so it is never in the urgent pile of things to do—but it should be, as a messy estate is awful to work through and places unnecessary stress on an already grieving family. Even a strong and close family can be destroyed through a lack of estate planning or a poorly executed will.

They say that weddings bring out the worst in people, but I would disagree: death brings out the worst in people. It brings out grief and greed. What astonishes me most is that the greed isn't usually from the direct family, but their spouses and wider family. The easiest way to remedy this is to have an up-to-date will (and trust, where appropriate—see Chapter 30).

WILLS

You can form, revoke or change a will at any time during your lifetime as long as you have the mental capacity (i.e. you are of sound mind) to do this. You should review your will annually and make changes as laws or circumstances change. If you have separated, married, have had more children or grandchildren, or someone named in your will has died, then your will needs to be adjusted to reflect this.

What some people do not realise is that your will is automatically cancelled when you marry or enter into a civil union. The only exception to this is if you specifically state in the will that the will is written in contemplation of your marriage. Similarly, if your marriage is ended by a dissolution order, any benefits given to your ex-spouse under the will are cancelled. But be careful—if there is no dissolution order (you don't formally separate), then unless you change your will to say differently your ex-spouse will continue to inherit.

WHAT IF YOU DON'T HAVE A WILL?

If you die without a will, or your will is invalid, you are said to be intestate. If you die intestate (without a will), your property is distributed according to the Administration Act 1969, where an order of priority of distribution is in place. The basic order is:

- your spouse, civil-union partner or de facto partner (of more than three years)
- your children
- your parents
- your siblings
- your grandparents
- your uncles and aunts.

Under the rules of intestacy the estate is totalled and divided as follows:

- your spouse takes all personal chattels, $155,000 and one-third of the balance of the estate, and
- your children take the other two-thirds, divided evenly.

If there is no spouse, the children take the entire estate, split equally. If there is no spouse or children, the parents take everything. If there is no spouse, children or parents, the siblings take everything in equal shares, and so forth.

Money is contentious at the best of times, and even more so at death. Sort out your affairs while you are living to avoid a nightmare for those who are left behind.

Conclusion

What do I want you to take away from this book?

- Financial success favours the brave and those who have a well thought-out plan.
- For a financial plan to work, you must understand your psychology of spending, and learn how to budget effectively, how to save for a property and how to navigate the many financial curveballs life will throw at you.
- If you have a mortgage, you must learn how to attack it, to kill it.
- Do not be naïve enough to think the bank is your friend.
- Do not be silly enough to think that a celebrity endorsing an investment makes it a good investment.
- Paying your mortgage off is a strategic step towards financial progress, but this in isolation will not achieve a comfortable retirement. If you can't afford to buy in the area you want to live, then buy an investment property and rent in your preferred area.
- Learn what you need for your retirement and work out your options for achieving it.

- Understand how much time you have before retirement and the investment constraints you must work within.
- Being the underdog simply means you have to take a less traditional route to get to the end.
- Don't buckle under the pressure and don't give up. There are more opportunities than obstacles, but you need to get serious about your finances.
- Retirement is not bigger than you, and financial success need not be an elusive goal.

Anyone approaching retirement has a financial place to be and a deadline to get there by. Some of you will be ready to push forward and take more purposeful steps on an already long-planned journey, but many of you will be starting off on the back foot.

Irrespective of where you sit on the financial spectrum, to achieve financial success you need 80% clarity, 10% confidence and 10% competence. If you are serious about arriving at your financial destination within an allocated timeframe, then you need a plan to get you there, with executable steps and measurable progress.

Best of luck on your journey!

Special offer

I would like to offer a special discounted first meeting with an enableMe Financial Personal Trainer to anyone who would like help to get ahead faster after reading this book. In that meeting, we will work together to ascertain where you are at financially, where you want to be and whether it is possible to reach your goals faster. It will then be up to you whether you decide to work with us from that point. Either way, the outcome of your first meeting will be that you will know your capability and your next step will be to unlock it.

Visit www.enableme.co.nz to request a consultation, and make sure to mention this book.

Acknowledgements

This book is the result of so much effort and support from so many people. Firstly I must mention the Allen & Unwin team. It has been a pleasure to work with such a passionate and competent group of people. Specifically, I would like to make special mention of Jenny, Michelle and Abba, whose support and feedback has been invaluable.

Sarah Ell is a rock star, enough said!

John Schell of Sure Plan. You provided valuable feedback and information. I appreciate you being an impartial sounding board and am in your debt. Thank you.

At enableMe, I work with an amazing group of people who share my vision of improving the financial future of Kiwis by providing practical advice and support using a proven (and patented) methodology to create positive change in our clients' lives. The enableMe team are fighting to create a better future for us all. I am flattered I can lead such an inspiring group of people, and I consider you my 'comrades in arms'.

To the working mums everywhere—you all deserve a hug. No-one understands the balls you juggle, apart from other working mums—I salute you all.

To Mum, Dad and Nanny Diana, thank you for your continual support. Being able to call for a chat or rely on your help with the children is invaluable to myself, and my family.

And lastly, my husband Billy, Cameron and Madison—I do it all for you.

Appendix I—The 10-step programme

Becoming financially successful is as simple as following these steps.

1. Understand your psychology of spending.
2. Become financially literate.
3. Make a plan.
4. Stick to your plan.
5. Buy a house.
6. Kill your mortgage!
7. Save or leverage.
8. Invest.
9. Retire.
10. Enjoy your retirement!

UNDERSTAND YOUR PSYCHOLOGY OF SPENDING

Don't let your genetics determine your financial potential. Understand your money personality (see Chapter 2) and figure out how to work with it to increase your chances of success. If you are in a relationship and you understand your partner's spending and your partner understands yours, and you work together to mitigate any conflict around money issues, it should be impossible for you to fail.

BECOME FINANCIALLY LITERATE

Learn the rules of money and apply them to your unique circumstances to get ahead faster. Sadly, New Zealand has one of the lowest levels of financial literacy in the developed world. Even many of our successful businesspeople don't know how to manage their personal money.

MAKE A PLAN

Develop a plan to make sure you are doing things smarter—as smartly as you possibly can. I believe that if I cannot radically improve the financial position of a client from when I first meet them, then either you have missed something or you are not trying hard enough.

I aim to optimise people's positions and empower them to stretch themselves to reach for and achieve goals that would have seemed impossible before we began working together.

The key to every successful financial plan is spending less than you earn so that you can repay any debt you have as quickly as possible.

STICK TO YOUR PLAN

It's important to continually review your circumstances. If you do not have time to do this—and it does take time—get someone impartial to do it for you. Small slippages can add up to big numbers over time if left unchecked.

Once you have a written plan, be accountable to it. Make it fluid enough that curveballs can be absorbed and the numbers can change as circumstances change, for example, if you get a pay rise. Be accountable to someone, somewhere, who is qualified to comment and will challenge you and your assumptions.

BUY A HOUSE

You need to be on the property ladder, as this has historically been one of the better performing asset classes. Psychologically it is easier to pay off debt than to save. Be sure to buy in an area where capital gain is expected. Rent and own an investment property over home ownership if you have the choice (see Chapter 9).

KILL YOUR MORTGAGE!

Once you have your property, you need to attack the mortgage, as the total cost of having a mortgage for 30 years can be up to three times what you initially borrowed. Channel all surplus funds into the mortgage.

SAVE OR LEVERAGE

Once you have paid off your mortgage, focus on saving for retirement. If it is unlikely that you will save enough, you need to think about what you are investing your funds in, and whether a better return can be achieved without exposing yourself to unnecessary risk. Alternatively, use the equity in your home to borrow money and invest in another property.

INVEST

If you are able to leverage off your equity, buy an investment property in an area that is going to have high demand and therefore strong capital-gain prospects. This property needs to be as close to cash-neutral as possible. The capital gain less the holding costs is what is going to help cover your retirement shortfall.

If you have saved enough funds these can be invested in myriad investments. Remember that your appetite for risk needs to be curtailed by your situation. If you are approaching retirement, don't invest big, because you will probably not be able to afford to lose big.

RETIRE/ENJOY YOUR RETIREMENT!

Once you have retired, you will need a new plan to follow as your capital will likely reduce over the next 25 years. This decrease in capital is needed to fund your lifestyle but, unless it is built into a clear plan, you will not feel you have permission to enjoy the money you are spending. Get a plan, get perspective and stay in control.

Enjoy your retirement—you've earned it!

Appendix II—Financial compatibility questionnaire

Money is one of the most common sources of tension in relationships. If this is true for you and your relationship, the first thing you need to do is talk to your partner. To see where the greatest problems lie, complete this financial compatibility questionnaire.

For each question below, grade your answer from 1–5.

5 = strongly agree
4 = agree
3 = don't feel strongly either way
2 = disagree
1 = strongly disagree

	Question	You	Partner
1.	I think it is important to make compulsory savings every month, even if the amount saved is small.		
2.	Life is short. If you work hard, you should be able to spend what you earn when you want to.		

327

	Question	You	Partner
3.	Couples should keep their finances separate, and only share finances for costs that are equally split (such as rent, power, phone).		
4.	Couples should have a budget that they stick to every week.		
5.	I prefer to save up for things, rather than use credit cards or hire purchase.		
6.	I always pay off my credit card in full at the end of the month.		
7.	If I get a build-up of debt on my credit cards I consolidate it all into one low-interest credit card or loan.		
8.	I spend more on holidays each year than I did the previous year.		
9.	Having the latest gadgets is important to me and part of the image I want to project.		
10.	If we can't afford it I would rather not go on holiday, however much I need a break.		
11.	I plan to retire early by making as much money as possible and living to a financial plan.		
12.	If one of us brings in more money, then the other should compensate by taking over more of the household chores.		
13.	When my parents die I am expecting an inheritance. I believe that this is my property and will not be intermingled with my relationship finances in any way.		

	Question	You	Partner
14.	I am a feel-good spender and get a kick from buying things, even if they are small and inexpensive. I have also been known to buy things when I can't necessarily afford them.		
15.	I expect my partner to contribute equally to the costs of our living expenses.		
16.	If I earn more than my partner, I should be able to spend more on myself as I have worked harder for it.		
17.	I think that whatever money comes into the partnership, regardless of where it comes from, should be shared equally. We are a team, after all.		
18.	I prefer to spend spare money on property or investments, rather than stuff, like cars, holidays, clothes or shoes.		
19.	If we were to split up I think the person who has earned most should be entitled to most of the possessions.		
20.	I sometimes hide the fact that I have spent money, by hiding purchases or saying things cost less than they did.		
21.	I think my partner wastes money on some things and can be too generous with family and friends.		
22.	I think my partner is over-careful with money and I am sometimes embarrassed by their stinginess, especially if it means someone else is forced to pay due to their meanness.		

	Question	You	Partner
23.	I am afraid to discuss money issues with my partner, as it tends to get personal and usually ends in a disagreement.		
24.	I would like to know more about what is happening to our money but my partner controls the day-to-day finances.		
25.	We often disagree on what we should spend our money on.		
26.	I don't understand finance in general; it intimidates me, so I choose to ignore it and bury my head in the sand.		
27.	I think it is OK if one partner wants to handle all the money affairs, provided they are actually in control of the money.		

INTERPRETING YOUR RESULT

It is important to interpret your scores in two ways: first focus on your overall compatibility by looking at your overall score difference, then concentrate on the results of the questions where you have the highest points of difference.

An overall score difference of 0 means that you are perfectly compatible on every aspect of money management and are unlikely to have conflict around money. Be aware though that compatibility does not immediately translate to increased capability.

An overall score difference of 1–24 means that you are compatible on most things but may have one or two areas to discuss and work through.

An overall score difference of 25–49 indicates that you have different attitudes regarding money management in a number of areas, and this is likely to be creating some tensions in your relationship. While you should sit down and discuss these issues, the discussion could become heated and personal. You might need to engage an impartial third party if you are committed to working towards a better end-game and do not want emotional baggage and conflict to interfere with it.

An overall score difference of 50–74 clearly highlights that you have significant differences in your attitudes to money which will inevitably put a strain on your relationship and carry over to other parts of your lives. Remember, money is indirectly linked to most areas of life, so if you do not have a healthy synergy the impact will be far-reaching. Money is important and you must set aside some specific time to work through these issues. You may also wish to consider getting some relationship coaching to help you through this. While you may be coming at the issues from different perspectives, it usually pays to focus on your common goals. Once you agree what you are working towards and your individual requirements, a good financial coach can help you to tailor a plan so that everyone gets what they need individually and less emphasis is placed on each other's behaviour.

An overall score difference of 75+ means that you have totally different attitudes and behaviour in relation to money and you are likely to need to really focus on this area in order to resolve conflict in your relationship. Consider whether you tackle this together, for the sake of the relationship. If that is not the best approach, you may need some professional help. I have worked with many couples, some of whom were polar opposites. Their coping mechanisms were either serious conflict or disengaging themselves from reality. Neither option will work in the long term. If you are committed to the relationship, keep working on these issues, otherwise they might tear your relationship apart.

Appendix III—Financial assessment template

Part 1—Your income   **333**

Part 2—Your financial position   **334**

Part 3—Your outgoings   **338**

Use this template to figure out where you are financially at the present time. Part 1 will help you understand the money you have coming in; Part 2 breaks down your current assets and liabilities; and Part 3 is a spending analysis that you can use to figure out where your money's going, and where you can make changes to start getting ahead.

PART 1—YOUR INCOME

INCOME

Net per annum

Name

Annual $
(after tax)

Source of income

Type of income

Total

Name

Type of income

Total

Income totals

Net per annum

Person 1

Person 2

Joint TOTAL

© enable Me Ltd

PART 2—YOUR FINANCIAL POSITION

Assets—Property

Property address	Owned by	Purchased when	For how much	Current value
Total property assets				Current value total: $

© enable Me Ltd

Current mortgage structure

Which bank	Fixed or floating/for how long	Comes off fixed rate when	At what interest rate	Monthly repayment	Current balance
Total mortgage debt				Current debt total:	$

Net property assets (Current value total LESS current debt total) $

© enable Me Ltd

Other assets

	Value
Car (1)	
Car (2)	
Motorbike	
Caravan	
Boat	
Savings	
Superannuation	
KiwiSaver	
Shares	
Bonus bonds	
Investments	
Term deposits	
TOTAL OTHER ASSETS	$

Other liabilities

Details (e.g. credit cards, hire-puchase car loan)	Interest rate	Card limit	Monthly payment	Amount owing
TOTAL AMOUNT OWING				$

© enable Me Ltd

Total other assets from p. 336	$
Total amount owing	– $
Total net other assets (other assets less amount owing)	= $
Total net property assets (from p. 335)	$
Total net other assets (from above)	+ $
Sum = total wealth	= $

PART 3—YOUR OUTGOINGS

	Monthly amount	Current annual
Accommodation		
Cleaner	x12	
Furniture and homewares	x12	
Gardening (lawns, garden bin)	x12	
House maintenance	x12	
Landscaping	x12	
Mortgage	x12	
Rates (water, land, regional)	x12	
Rent	x12	
Whitegoods and electrical	x12	
Other (e.g. body corporate fees)	x12	
	Subtotal 1	$
Basic living costs		
Clothes, shoes (including dry-cleaning)	x12	
Electricity/gas	x12	
Food and household shopping	x12	
Internet	x12	
Mobile phones	x12	
Alarm	x12	
Firewood	x12	
	Subtotal 2	

	Monthly amount	Current annual
Children, education, family costs		
Day care	x12	
Babysitting	x12	
Children's clothes	x12	
School extras (trips, etc.)	x12	
School fees	x12	
School uniforms	x12	
Tertiary education fees	x12	
Text books, stationery	x12	
Tuition/activities	x12	
Contributions to other family	x12	
	Subtotal 3	
Car, vehicle expenses		
Boat/campervan	x12	
Boat/campervan insurance	x12	
Boat/campervan maintenance	x12	
Maintenance	x12	
Parking	x12	
Petrol	x12	
Registration and WOF	x12	
Taxis, public transport	x12	
Tyre replacement	x12	
AA membership	x12	
	Subtotal 4	

	Monthly amount	Current annual
Financial		
Bank fees	x12	
Car insurance	x12	
Child support payments	x12	
Contents insurance	x12	
Credit card repayments	x12	
House insurance	x12	
Investment/savings	x12	
Life insurance	x12	
Medical insurance	x12	
Other (e.g. professional fees)	x12	
Other (e.g. ongoing support)	x12	
Other (e.g. property top-up)	x12	
	Subtotal 5	
Medical		
Chemist and prescriptions	x12	
Dentist	x12	
Doctor	x12	
Optometrist	x12	
Podiatrist	x12	
Naturopath	x12	
	Subtotal 6	

	Monthly amount	Current annual
Discretionary		
Alcohol	x12	
Annual holidays	x12	
Bars, clubs, pubs	x12	
Birthday presents	x12	
Books and magazines	x12	
Christmas presents	x12	
Church, tithing	x12	
Cigarettes	x12	
Donations	x12	
DVDs	x12	
Easter	x12	
Guy Fawkes	x12	
Hairdresser	x12	
Hobbies	x12	
Make-up, toiletries	x12	
Memberships (e.g. gym)	x12	
Movies	x12	
Music	x12	
Newspapers	x12	
Pet costs	x12	
Restaurants and cafes	x12	
Short breaks/weekends	x12	
Sky TV	x12	
Special events/outings	x12	
Sports	x12	

	Monthly amount	Current annual
TAB, casino, lotto	x12	
Takeaways	x12	
Vet	x12	
Work lunch	x12	
Dog registration	x12	
Coffees	x12	
Other	x12	
	Subtotal 7	

© enable Me Ltd

Total expenses	Add subtotals 1-7	$
Total net income (from page 333)		$
Total expenses (from above)		– $
Initial surplus / deficit	(Total net income LESS total expenses)	= $

If your total net income is greater than your total expenses, you have a surplus.

If your total expenses are greater than your total net income, you have a deficit.

Bibliography

Books

Brodersen, Stig and Pysh, Preston, *Warren Buffet Accounting Book: Reading Financial Statements for Value Investing*, Pylon Publishing Company, Pennsylvania, USA, 2014

David, Jeffrey, Lessons from Rich Dad, Poor Dad, FamilyMint Publishing, 2012 (ebook only)

Duhigg, Charles, *The Power of Habit: Why We Do What We Do in Life and Business*, William Heinemann, London, 2012

Gladwell, Malcolm, *David and Goliath: Underdogs, Misfits and the Art of Battling Giants*, Little, Brown and Company, New York, 2013

Gladwell, Malcolm, *Outliers: The Story of Success*, Little Brown and Company, New York, 2008

Gladwell, Malcolm, *The Tipping Point: How Little Things Can Make a Big Difference*, Little, Brown and Company, New York, 2000

Hazledine, Sam, *Unfair Fight: Give Your Small Business the Winning Advantage*, Penguin Random House NZ, Auckland, 2014

Hawes, Martin, *The New Zealand Retirement Guide*, Penguin Random House NZ, Auckland, 2013 (ebook only)

Hawes, Martin, *Martin Hawes' Investment Guide: 7 Timeless Rules for Investment Success*, Penguin Random House NZ, Auckland, 2012 (ebook only)

Hawes, Martin, *Twenty Good Summers*, Allen & Unwin, Crows Nest, Australia, 2006

Kiyosaki, Robert T., Rich Dad's CASHFLOW Quadrant, Plata Publishing, Scotsdale Arizona, USA, 1998

Kiyosaki, Robert T. and Lechter, Sharon, *Rich Dad Poor Dad: What the Rich Teach Their Kids About Money—That the Poor and the Middle Class Do Not!*, Grand Central Publishing, New York, 2001

Levitt, Steven D. and Dubner, Stephen J., *Freakonomics*, William Morrow Paperbacks, New York, 2009

McQueen, Hannah, *The Perfect Balance*, Allen & Unwin, Crows Nest, Australia, 2012

Orman, Suze, *The Laws of Money, The Lessons of Life*, Free Press, New York, 2003

Orman, Suze, *The 9 Steps to Financial Freedom*, Crown Publishing Group, New York, 1997

Sandberg, Sheryl, *Lean In: Women, Work and the Will to Lead*, Ebury Publishing, London, 2013

Solomon, Lewis D. and Solomon, Janet Stern, *Bratproofing Your Children: How to Raise Socially and Financially Responsible Kids*, Skyhorse Publishing, New York, 2013

Somers, Jan and de Roos, Dolf, *Building Wealth Through Investment Property*, de Roos Associates Ltd, Christchurch, 1996a

Somers, Jan, and de Roos, Dolf, *The New Zealand Investor's Guide to Making Money in Real Estate*, de Roos Associates Ltd, Christchurch, 1996b

Stengel, Jim, *Grow: How Ideals Power Growth and Profit at the World's 50 Greatest Companies*, Virgin Books, Penguin Random House, 2011

Sugars, Bradley J., *The Business Coach*, McGraw-Hill Education, New York, 2006a

Sugars, Bradley J., *The Real Estate Coach*, McGraw-Hill Education, New York, 2006b

Sugars, Bradley, J., *Real Money, Real Estate: Winning the Real Estate Game*, Action International Publishing, Brisbane, Australia, 2003

Trott, Dave, *Predatory Thinking*, Pan Macmillan, London, 2014

Whitburn, David, *Invest and Prosper with Property*, Random House NZ, 2011 (ebook only)

Withers, Mark, *Property Tax: A New Zealand Investors Guide*, Empower Leaders Publishing Ltd, Auckland, 2004

Useful websites

Housing New Zealand Corporation <www.hnzc.co.nz>

interest.co.nz: Helping you make financial decisions <www.interest.co.nz>

KiwiSaver <www.kiwisaver.govt.nz>

Money Instructor <http://content.moneyinstructor.com>

New Zealand Federation of Family Budgeting Services <www.familybudgeting.org.nz>

New Zealand Property Investor magazine <www.landlords.co.nz>

Reserve Bank of New Zealand <www.rbnz.govt.nz>

Sorted: Your independent money guide <www.sorted.co.nz>

Statistics New Zealand <www.stats.govt.nz>

The Treasury <www.treasury.govt.nz>

Welcome Home Loan <www.welcomehomeloan.co.nz>

Vertex42: The guide to excel in everything <www.vertex42.com>

The Guardian, *How to Negotiate a Pay Rise*, <www.theguardian.com/careers/careers-blog/how-to-negotiate-pay-rise>, 30 June 2013

The Huffington Post, *5 Household Budget Templates That Will Help If You Actually Stick With It*, <www.huffingtonpost.com/bob-lotich/5-household-budget-templa_b_5696244.html?ir=Australia>, 21 August 2014

Robert Walters, *How to Negotiate a Pay Rise*, <www.robertwalters.co.nz/career-advice/negotiating-a-payrise.html>